Grow It Cook It

Grow It Cook It

Sally Cameron
Photography by Charlie Smith

Penguin Books

ACKNOWLEDGEMENTS

These projects cannot be completed without the help of very special people who give their time and energy to inspire creativity.

For the hours and hours behind the camera and computer, I thank Charlie Smith. Your guidance and passion have been truly rewarding, uplifting and the guiding light behind this project. And of course, Trudie Smith, for many cups of tea and hours of passionate chat.

For all those hours on a keyboard punching in recipes I thank Dianne Kennedy. All the helpful people at my local plant store for teaching a layperson how to grow things, and providing wonderful plants and pottery.

To the lovely Holly Smith and her great mates Madison, Mikayla, Hannah, Lachlan, Sophia and Taylor; thank you for being our models.

To the team at Penguin Books, Alison Brook for believing in us at the 11th hour, Brigid Adams for pushing the buttons, and the fabulous team of editors, designers and production staff who get these projects onto paper and into print.

Of course, I can't do these things without the help and support of my family – the hours and hours of day care that Margaret and Dianne have given me.

Most importantly to my partner Craig, son Maxwell and daughter Jacqueline, who make the sun shine in my garden every single day. You inspire me to make these things happen.

I would like to dedicate this book to my dad, Allan, for all the years of unconditional mentoring, help and love. You inspire me to be a better person.

PENGUIN BOOKS
Published by the Penguin Group
Penguin Group (NZ), 67 Apollo Drive, Rosedale,
North Shore 0632, New Zealand (a division of Pearson New Zealand Ltd)
Penguin Books Ltd, Registered Offices: 80 Strand, London, WC2R 0RL, England

First published by Penguin Group (NZ), 2009
1 3 5 7 9 10 8 6 4 2

Photography by Charlie Smith

Commissioning Editor Alison Brook
Managing Editor Andrea Coppock

Designed by Seven
Prepress by Image Centre Ltd
Printed by Everbest Printing Co. Ltd, China

ISBN 978 0 14 301096 8

A catalogue record for this book is available from the National Library of New Zealand.

www.penguin.co.nz

Contents

Introduction

It still amazes me every day, all the wondrous things that can happen in a garden. Being a cook, I transpose food into meals, baking, and combinations to please both the eye and the palate. I have the control. In a garden, control is Mother Nature's domain, not mine. Plants grow quickly, with wondrous stems, vines, leaves, roots and flowers. And then, as if by magic, the flowers transform into fruits and pods of edible delight.

The beauty of any garden, big or small, is what you can get from it – its colour, scent, fruit, leaves and food. It isn't hard work to reap the rewards from a small patch of land or even an overhanging balcony. Growing your own food for your own existence is the basis of every culture and civilisation in the world as we know it.

In our modern world, it is just too easy to travel to a shop or supermarket to make all our daily decisions on what to eat. We can buy strawberries in the winter transported by plane, and hydroponically grown tomatoes from all-year-round greenhouses. Fruits and vegetables are freighted in from all over the world to be available whenever. There aren't seasons anymore, just convenience.

How virtuous it is to grow your own vegetables, you might say. I agree that in a perfect world you would have to spend much time in a garden planting, fertilising and harvesting to supply all your vegetable needs, to be completely self-sufficient. And time is what we lack. But consider growing just a few plants here and there to provide a small harvest every season – some supplementary crops. Edible plants are beautiful and colourful and can fill spaces in the smallest of gardens where ornamental flaxes, flowers or textural grasses might have previously grown.

Balconies, patios, decks, verandas, conservatories, side paths, back garden plots, walls, trellises, even the front garden flower box, can all overflow with a bounty of vegetables. Pull down that creeping, hay fever-inducing jasmine and replace it with a crawling fruit-laden passion-fruit vine. Rip away the infesting oxalis that grows in the stones at your back door and replace it with parsley plants in a pot. Remove the attractive but very ornamental Algarve, and replace it with a few strawberry plants that will drape with luscious sweet fruit in the summer.

When a friend of mine moved into her first home, she exclaimed one day: 'I can do whatever I want to this house now I am happily paying a mortgage.' She realised quickly that the plot of land out the back by the deck was hers to mow and tend. 'I will need some plants for the patio,' she said. I suggested that a planter or two, filled with herbs and the odd silver beet and celery plant, would look just as attractive and give her something for her cooking. 'Oh,' she said with furrowed brow, 'I buy my herbs from the supermarket. What I don't use I throw away!' This is a common problem in today's consumer-driven society. I calmly suggested if she had herbs that didn't need throwing away, she could pick what she needed and leave the rest to fill that sunny corner of the deck. She took my advice, and now she enjoys her fresh herbs in every meal.

A small effort can give so much. The buzzwords of today include carbon footprints, recycling, renewable energy sources and global warming. Considering all this, the world as we know it is facing a food crisis. Third world countries can not afford the inflated prices of rice, corn and grains because of increased demand. These countries suffer from drought and therefore famine, because they do not even have the resources to grow their own vegetables. How fortunate we are to have land, space, water and sunshine to provide our own food.

As the world's forests are being cut down for commercial land, the earth's 'lungs' are being lost. We consume a lot in our daily lives and only a small minority of us put anything back into the environment. Planting a tree or growing our own food is a small, but nevertheless worthwhile, step to take in order to give back to the earth. We can support the atmosphere by encouraging plant growth around our houses or apartments. We can support the ecology by creating somewhere for insects to live and therefore feeding the birds and the whole food chain. And we can create environments in which our families want to grow and explore and pass on traditions that were once close to being lost.

Growing your own food isn't just a hobby; it is part of a healthy lifestyle. Children learn where food comes from. They can appreciate nature and the effect that we can have on our environmental horizon. Simple tasks, such as raking leaves, pulling weeds, growing seedlings or peeling a carrot they grew themselves, put them in touch with the world outside the plastic packet in the fridge.

The biggest reward . . .

From your own green-fingered efforts comes the produce at the end. There is no greater taste sensation than the freshest of peas pulled from the tendrils of a summer pea vine. Or the baby spring carrots, straight out of the ground, or plump juicy berries warmed by the energy of the summer sun. Your potted plants may not give the biggest or best-looking lemons that you have ever seen, or passion-fruit as round and perfect as the ones in the shop, but the satisfaction of growing your own food from a small seed is huge – trust me.

There is one drawback to an edible garden – abundance. Ever grown a packet of seeds and not heeded the instructions to plant thinly, then realised the mass of seedlings are all going to be ready at once? Have you ever had a neighbour or grandparent bring you a big bundle of silver beet, complaining that they have too much growing and would you eat it? Ever had a basket full of tomatoes, or too many lemons on your tree, which are just falling to waste? There are many methods of preservation for the months ahead when lemons and tomatoes aren't so plentiful. It doesn't mean days of sterilising jars and bottling fruit: a good freezer, a few choice jam recipes and one or two hours in the weekend, and your winter pantry is prepared. Plus, you have the satisfaction of knowing what actually went into that food and what you are feeding yourself and your family.

Nowadays, we can also buy and supplement seasonal produce from farmers' markets. What is ironic is that farmers' markets aren't new; they have been around for centuries as a way to trade home-grown vegetables, free from commercial pesticides and plant bionics, within the community. Over time, farmers' markets were bought out by larger retail grocers, eventually ending up as the supermarket conglomerates. The big-business mantra is to supply what we want – fruit and vegetables on cue, in convenient packaging, whatever the cost to the quality of the plant.

When I grow something in the garden I like to think of the ratio between time input and quantity of end result. A broccoli for example takes a lot of space to grow, a lot of time to mature and at the end of the harvest leaves you with not very much, even less if the white caterpillar gets it or it quickly goes to seed. I leave these plants to the professional dedicated gardeners and get on with the plants that can give more sustainable gratification.

Plants in this book are selected on ease of growing for someone who is not used to planting and harvesting. If you have never grown a parsley plant in your life no one is suggesting that you should convert your whole back yard or deck to an elaborate pottager garden. Start small – a plant here, a citrus tree in that corner – and evolve from there. Before you know it your outside world becomes an edible garden.

So grow your own food . . .
It is trendy, it is politically correct, it is wholesome, it is good for the environment, it is good for our tight budgets, and it is good for our burgeoning waistlines. And it isn't hard. I like to think of it as a whole process, from ground to chopping board, from pot to plate. The end result is equally dependent on the effort I put in at the beginning when the plant was a mere seedling. We care for our children in a similar way; why should we not have the same issues with the food we give our children and family?

And cook your own food . . .
Gratification from my garden is reproduced in the prizes from my kitchen: the freshest corn, picked that day and on a plate 20–30 minutes later; or an abundant supply of summer tomatoes bottled in a sauce for winter comfort food. My recipes are designed to be simple, accessible flavours, understated and achievable. Cooking is about experimenting and accessing different flavours, so weights and measures give guidelines to complete a dish. But never be nervous to try, or explore. If you use lime instead of lemon, or an extra chilli where it says only one, more power to you.

Most importantly, enjoy the process.
Bring yourself back to earth and the world which we come from. Get your hands dirty and enjoy the soil and the sunshine. Pick and plunder from outside your own windows. Enjoy the process from garden to table and all that is in between. Savour each mouthful and feel your halo shining . . . I grew this and I made this delicious meal. That's pretty neat.

— Sally

Section 1

Gardener's Notes

Where to begin? An edible garden, like everything in nature, is an evolution not a revolution. A little bit of energy every day can give huge results in the end. The key ingredients are care, attention and of course a little bit of enthusiasm. Try not to look just at that you are getting dirty and there are many insects, but that the plants will repay you with luscious edible fruits and stems en masse. The key is to start small – get one or two crops growing successfully first before launching into a full-scale allotment.

PREPARE THE GARDEN

For any size garden, get your basics right first. For a patio garden, no bigger than your living room, you need to organise the space well. Look at the sunny, sheltered spots for the best place to put pots and containers. Make sure there is a nearby supply of water, or invest in a watering can. Beg, borrow or buy pots and containers that are clean, sturdy and have good drainage holes.

With more natural space, an edible garden can be spread around your whole garden. Let berry canes or passion-fruit vines ramble over and down a trellis or balcony railing; strawberry plants can sprawl and crawl under trees and hedges; plant carrots and beetroot in amongst flowering annuals and use the natural textures of rhubarb and silver beet in less sunny parts of the garden.

If you have more space in your natural garden, select a sunny, sheltered spot with good drainage for a built-up garden square. Think about it first – you don't want to start digging up the lawn and then realise that your garden is in the way of the path to the laundry line.

HOW TO BUILD A SMALL VEGETABLE GARDEN

Find a place in your garden that gets the most sun all day, is reasonably sheltered from strong prevailing winds and is close to a water supply. Outline your space – keeping in mind access, longevity, height from ground and handling. For example a 1.5-metre-square patch will give enough length and width to reach all parts of the garden. In larger spaces, rows or blocks of squares can be achieved *(pic 1)*.

Remove any grass or existing plant material. Turn over the soil underneath, leaving to dry out slightly, which allows the soil to break down and aerate.

(2)

(3)

Edge the garden with logs or sleepers, bricks, paving stones or something to stop grass and weeds spreading into the garden *(pic 2)*.

Top the turned-over soil with a good spread of compost, blood and bone and/or organic fertilisers. Spread another layer of garden mix or topsoil, and turn over with a fork. Allow soil to settle for a few days before planting *(pic 3)*.

For ease of access, plant seedlings in rows *(pic 4)*. Rotating plants can help with long-term success. Good leguminous crops like peas and beans help to fix nitrogen into the soil.

Plants have friends – some plants like growing side by side and help each other defend against pests. See tips in each vegetable segment.

Gardener's Tip

For a great organic defence – snails and slugs don't like salt. Protect your garden from slugs and snails by sprinkling sand, salt or seashells around the edges.

GROWING SEEDS

Pots & Trays

Forget about clumsy seed trays unless you're an old hand, and buy or resurrect small plastic flowerpots instead. Old egg cartons, large fruit juice containers or fizzy-drink bottles can be recycled to grow chosen seeds *(pic 5)*.

(4)

Seed Growing Mix

Don't be tempted to use garden soil, as it's full of pests and diseases that will attack your newly hatched seedlings. Instead invest in a bag of good seed-raising mix. Bring it indoors overnight before planting, as cold soil won't encourage your seeds to grow. Fill your pots almost to the top.

Sowing The Seeds

Sprinkle about five to ten seeds on to the surface, depending on how big they are, and space them out evenly. Rub a little soil between your hands over the top until the seeds are just covered. Sprinkle with lukewarm water, or better still, soak the pot from the bottom up in a dish full of warm water. Cover the pots with a loose clear plastic bag (freezer bags are ideal) or the cut-off top from a drink bottle. If the weather is still frosty, keep indoors on a well-lit window sill, away from heaters. Remember to label the pots.

(5)

(6)

Germinating The Seeds

Keep the soil moist, allowing it to dry out a little between watering. As soon as the seedlings emerge, take off the plastic cover. Healthy seedlings are green; yellow spindly seedlings may mean uneven light and need to be thrown out.

Growing Seedlings

If you've sown five seeds to a pot, you should have nicely spaced seedlings, which can grow for a week or so without needing to be moved. If they are too close together they may experience overcrowding. It is best to let them grow until they are large enough to handle before attempting to pot them.

Transplanting Seedlings

Eventually you want one plant in each small pot. After about a week, tip the seedlings out of the pot and gently tease them apart with a fork, taking care to hold by the leaf and not the delicate stem. Add fresh soil to a new pot, place one seedling on top and fill around the roots and the stem with fresh compost. Before planting outdoors, the plants need to be acclimatised. Place them outside, but if there is any threat of frost, bring them indoors into a cool room for the night. Water regularly for best results *(pic 6)*.

FEEDING THE GARDEN

Simply, compost is organic matter, decomposed and rotted down to give nutrients back to the earth. Fertiliser may be organic or manufactured, but is based on the same nutrient structure as rotted compost.

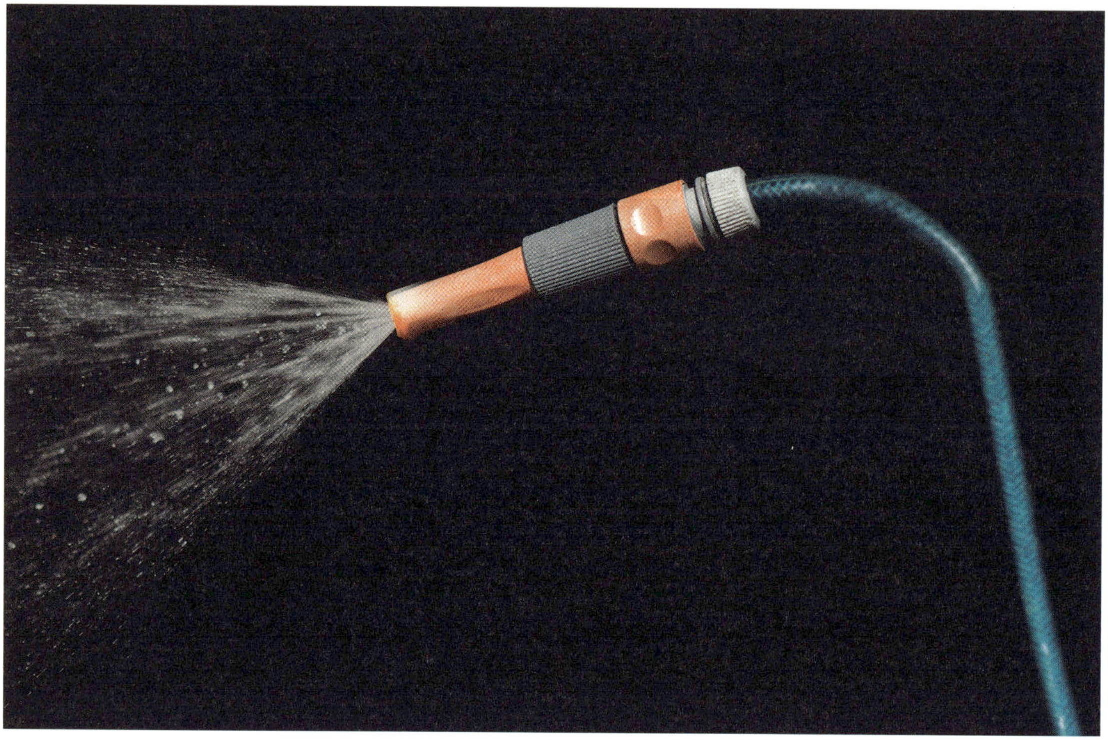

Compost

Compost is nature's own recycling system. In the environment dead plant material breaks down on the forest floors, providing the living plants with rich nutrients and mulching to prevent excess water loss. Composting sets up a similar environment in your own garden. It speeds up the natural process and uses organic waste to make a rich fertiliser.

For your conscience, composting can recycle more than 30 per cent of your domestic rubbish and therefore save landfill space. If you have a vegetable garden it is essential to replace the necessary elements leached from the soil with each crop grown. Compost does this as it is a rich, natural fertiliser to put on your garden, which costs little and is right at your fingertips. It's a win-win situation. Importantly, edible plants grown in pots and containers need added compost and fertiliser regularly, as watering can leach valuable nutrients out of the soil.

Select a compost system that suits your needs. Modern polythene bins work well and are tidy and effective. Or you can build your own, boarded with wooden planks. To start, find a dry yet partly shaded location in your garden. Fork over the soil before you start to allow worms to move up into the heap.

Allow for air entry and drainage by placing a layer of sticks and twigs at the bottom of your heap. Make layers of finished compost with manure or fertiliser, organic material, e.g. leaves, grass clippings and a few handfuls of blood and bone. Continue the above layering method until heap is full.

Kitchen scraps like fruit and vegetable trimmings, and all vegetable matter, can be layered directly onto the heap. Tea leaves, coffee grounds and beer dregs are also good. Any garden matter like leaves and soft weeds can go in, but avoid problem weeds such as oxalis, dock, dandelion or couch. Grass clippings are great.

Speed up the process by chopping material into small pieces before adding to the heap.

Fork over your heap a few times, placing undecomposed lumps into the middle. Apply onto your garden only when material is thoroughly decomposed. It should look dark and even in colour and crumbly to touch.

Air is essential for micro-organisms to act. Plastic compost bins normally have air vents built in. Otherwise ensure air entry – you can place poles vertically into your heap and remove when pile is full, or push a crowbar through the heap. Dampen your heap regularly but do not saturate. Keep about as moist as a squeezed-out sponge.

Never use compost in your soil that has not properly broken down, it borrows nitrogen from the soil which growing plants need. Cover heaps in colder months to keep the rain off and the heat in. If you want to use your bin and the compost is not ready you can remove the bin, mix all matter together and enclose it in a black polythene bag. This will also keep compost that you are not ready to use.

If you don't have room for a compost bin, not to worry, garden centres supply plenty of ready-made bags and fertilisers for all sorts of edible plants.

Gardener's Tip

Do not compost meat scraps or fatty foods, dog or cat droppings. Nitrogen is essential to the process. Include matter that is high in nitrogen, e.g. tea leaves, coffee grounds, beer dregs, seaweed, human hair, feathers, or add a fertiliser containing nitrogen. A sprinkling of lime prevents acidity.

WATER, THE SOURCE OF LIFE

Where would life be without water? If there is one important process that every gardener must understand it is the need to provide water to the plants. Just the same way we drink litres of the stuff every day, a plant needs a source of H_2O. Unfortunately, we can't rely on the weather all year round to provide consistent moisture. Especially in the spring and summer when growth is peaking, rainfall is not.

Water provides the essence in which nutrients are carried around the stems and leaves of each plant. They keep cells turgid, stems straight and flowers budding, which are essential for fruit production. When plants don't have sufficient water they become weak and flaccid. In this state plants not only don't grow properly but also become susceptible to diseases and pests. Every vegetable, fruit and herb section in this book talks about watering the plant and always comes back to how important it is. It is as simple as this – without water your plants will not thrive and will die!

Section 2

Cook's Notes

EQUIPMENT

There are a few essential kitchen gadgets I can't live without. I use them every day and even take them on holiday with me. Most certainly, I spend money on this equipment, making sure that it is the best quality.

Firstly, you need a good set of knives. It doesn't have to be a gilded set of knives with a different blade for every food type, but a few strong, well-crafted blades suitable for any occasion. A cook's knife, a boning knife, a paring knife and serrated blade are a great start. Just make sure they are well cared for, have good balanced handles and are kept sharp!

Secondly, invest in a set of scales. I prefer digital, and again of a good quality. Scales help get exact measurements in cooking, which controls the ingredients and means less chance for the recipe to fail. You will notice that most ingredients in this book are given as a weight rather than a cup size. All cups are not created equal, and so with a little discipline the end product will be more reliable.

Thirdly, a food processor is a must – and a good one at that. It doesn't have to have all the bells and whistles, but it can take the hard work out of most cooking situations, and therefore make the whole process more enjoyable. You can bypass a cake mixer or blender and have a good food processor on the bench achieving all the same tasks.

And finally, a bit of advice. There are many impostors when it comes to kitchen equipment; many gadgets and inventions that are supposed to take the time and effort out of your cooking. However, sometimes all these do is cause more washing up, rust quickly or clutter up the cupboards. When buying equipment for your kitchen, think quality tools. They will outlast most others, they often don't have many sizes and, for the number of times you use them, they will be worth it. Quality will always outlive the cost.

COOKING TECHNIQUES

Blanching

This is a term used to describe the quick cooking of vegetables and fruits. Blanching usually involves bringing a pot of water to the boil and then dropping the vegetable or fruit into the water very quickly. Some ingredients may only need 10–20 seconds; others may need 2–3 minutes. It breaks down the exterior and brings the colour to the surface. The vegetable or fruit is then removed and usually plunged into ice-cold water to immediately stop the cooking process. Other techniques for blanching include: pouring boiling water from a kettle; quick steaming in a microwave or steam basket. The trick is to cool quickly. Blanching is a great technique for getting vegetables ready to freeze, or can be used to peel tomatoes, capsicums or chillies.

Cooking Pasta To Perfection

Al dente is an Italian term, meaning 'to the bite', which describes the way pasta should be when cooked properly. In Italy, the home of pasta, there is no other way to eat pasta, other than al dente. Always read the instructions on the packet of pasta you are cooking. Normally the cooking time ranges from 8 to 12 minutes, in boiling water, depending on the size of the pasta. Use a large saucepan or stock pan and use a lot of water. Most importantly, add plenty of salt to the water once it is boiling. Pasta is bland and can use the salt to flavour. Test it is cooked by scooping out one piece and letting it cool slightly and then eat. The pasta will be soft with a slight firmness in the middle. Drain well and then use in your favourite dish.

Cooking Risotto To Perfection

There are many ways to cook a risotto, but some will say there is only one proper way. The rice at the end of the cooking process should be, as the Italians say, 'all'onda'. This means that it should be cooked through and still firm, but not chalky in the centre, and not mushy. The risotto should have a minimum amount of liquid at the end, or enough to achieve a 'flowing' consistency. Short-grain rices such as arborio and carnaroli are good to use, and should only take between 18–20 minutes to absorb enough liquid to make the risotto taste perfect.

Season To Taste

When a recipe says 'season to taste', it means to use your own taste and judgement for how salty or spicy you like it. Salt and freshly ground black pepper will usually be listed in the ingredients. Use good sea salts, ground or flaked. By freshly grinding the black pepper, the taste will be vibrant and piquant and not stale. It is important to taste food as you are cooking to judge for yourself how the end product will turn out. The best chefs will taste whatever they cook as they go, even in a raw state, to make sure the food that leaves their kitchens is perfect.

Setting Point In Jams & Jellies

Setting point is the required temperature and consistency that a jam, jelly or chutney must be to make it set. This is when enough liquid has evaporated during cooking to make the jam or jelly thick, and it holds its viscosity or thickness when it is spread on toast or spooned out. To test for setting point, pour a tablespoon of the jelly onto a saucer and chill quickly in the freezer or over ice. When it has cooled, push the surface of the jelly gently with a fingertip; if it wrinkles, setting point has been reached. Alternatively, before starting to make the jam or jelly, put two saucers into the freezer and leave to chill. When you put a spoonful of jam onto the plate it will instantly thicken (or not). If the jam or jelly hasn't thickened and no wrinkle appears, the best thing to do is put the pot back onto the stove to keep cooking. Cook again for a few minutes and then test again. Be careful not to over-cook sugar-based jams, jellies or chutneys as they burn easily.

Good Equipment To Use For Jam Making

Preserving pans have been specially designed for making jams and chutneys. Their large surface area allows the liquid to evaporate more quickly. Use a long-handled wooden spoon for stirring so your hands don't get splashed with the hot mixture. A sugar thermometer is an essential tool for making any jam or confectionery.

Sterilising Jars For Preserving

Select jars that are not chipped or cracked. Preferably, find jars that have lids that can be used to reseal the jar. Mason jars are special preserving jars that can be resealed with caps and screw-on lids. These lids can be purchased from most supermarkets. Clip-seal jars have spring-tight lids and are useful for sealing pickles, whole foods and pesto that will be stored in the fridge. These jars are found at any good home store. Look out for any particularly elegant or special looking jam jars in cook shops. Re-using old glass jars and lids is the cheapest way to bottle preserves.

Preparing Jars and Lids — Sort out the jars before you start making preserves. If the jars don't have plastic-lined screw tops, you'll need cellophane covers. Wash and dry jars thoroughly. Preheat the oven to 150 °C/300 °F. Lay the jars upside down in the oven for 15 minutes to sterilise, turn the oven off and leave them in there until ready to use. Most jams require the jars to be hot or warm when ready to fill. Some chutney or sauce recipes may tell you to leave the jars and sauce to cool before sealing. Sterilise the lids by dipping in boiling water.

Filling Jars — Use a sterilised metal cup and funnel. Try not to drip too much sauce down the outside of the jar. Don't put hot product in cold jars or cold product in hot jars. Some recipes require a little headspace between the top of the lid, and others require that all air is gone. Jam, for example, is better if all air is removed to take away the dangerous microbes that can spoil jam. Clean any spillages or sauce away from the lip of the jar, before they are sealed. Use a clean hot cloth to do this.

Sealing and Labelling — If the jars don't have lids you will need cellophane covers or wax lids. Either way you need to cover the jam or jelly with waxed paper discs (to keep air – and mould – away from the jam). Always label the jars with the name and date made. This is important if these jars go into the cupboard and aren't found for some time. Every food product has a shelf life – nothing lasts forever.

Cook's Tip

To help prevent jams and chutneys from catching and sticking to the bottom of the cooking pan, rub the bottom and sides with the paper from a pack of butter, or greaseproof paper with butter. This creates a lining for the pot and, as long as the preserve is being stirred well, should prevent unnecessary catching.

INGREDIENTS

Pectin Or Jam Sugar

Pectin is a substance found in ripe fruits that makes jam set. Even though strawberry is the most popular jam, strawberries themselves are notoriously low in pectin. Pectin or jam sugar contains natural apple pectin to help give a good set. In New Zealand, pectin is sold either mixed into sugar, or in a packet of jam setting agent. Do not confuse jam sugar with preserving sugar, which is pure sugar granulated in a way to make it dissolve quickly. Another way to tackle the pectin problem is to replace some of the strawberries with a high-pectin fruit such as apple or rhubarb.

Chicken Or Vegetable Stock

A good stock can be the difference between good flavour and not. If you have taken the effort to grow your own vegetables, then making your own stock is another easy step. You can use the offcuts from your garden. Carrot stems, herbs, celery leaves, onion skins, tomato skins even, can all go into a pot with the carcass of a chicken or the head of a fish, to create a broth that will light up your food. There are many supermarket alternatives of different quality levels. Choose stock that is fresh, with few additives and preservatives. Watch out for added salt as well.

Pastry – To Make Or To Buy?

Sometimes life needs to be made easier. Ready-made pastry is one thing that is really handy to have in the freezer. Making your own pastry will give different results: sometimes you need a softer, more buttery pastry; other times, you need crispy and more short pastry. Combining a bit of flour, fat and water to create your own dough is an art in itself, and a worthwhile stage in becoming a great cook. But sometimes when life is busy and all you need is to get a meal on the table, a thawed packet will suffice. There is a golden rule with any pastry, keep it cold. It will help the gluten in the dough and give you better results.

Child's Play

Ideas for entertainment and keeping kids interested in an edible garden. Getting kids involved in the garden early in their lives gives them an understanding of where food comes from and how to be self-sufficient. And it can be fun, explorative, rewarding and educational without being boring. Throughout the book the pink flower icon indicates recipes that are easy for kids. Here are some ideas for things kids can do.

HOME-MADE LEMONADE STAND

Make jugfuls of home-made lemonade (see page 148). Keep cold with loads of ice. Set up at the front gate an old picnic table, an ice bucket, plenty of plastic cups, a rubbish bag, chairs and the lemonade. You will need to make a sign to advertise, and a money box to collect the profits. Let kids hustle the neighbours for drinks as long as they use 'please' and 'thank you'.

SPROUTING CARROT TOPS

When you pick out a carrot in a shop, often the leaves have been cut off. However, with your own crop you can keep the leaf on when you slice the top off a carrot. Keep the leaf end and place it on a piece of cotton wool on a window sill. Dampen the cotton wool with water. Eventually the carrot top sprouts leaves again. The promise is there that a new carrot will grow.

GROWING HERB BASKETS

Herb baskets are an ideal way to introduce children to the commitment of caring, long before a pet, and can be set up even in small gardens. They encourage kids to have their own piece of garden. A basket or pot can be painted or covered with ribbons. Make a name tag for the child's basket. Ideal plants are ones that grow easily and can drape over the sides. Mint works well because not only can you take cuttings from other plants, it grows easily and it is a taste and smell that children will respond to. Parsley or basil will work as well, but the flavours aren't as sweet. Teach the child the lesson of regular watering, picking, feeding and caring.

SWAN PLANTS, BUTTERFLIES & BUGS

Although they aren't edible, swan plants can be easily grown in pots in the garden. As they attract the Monarch butterfly to your garden, they teach children the life cycle of insects. The creatures are magnificent as they metamorphose from caterpillar to butterfly. You can teach children about good and bad bugs in a similar way. For the more adventurous child they can catch insects in jars and use the internet or garden books to identify them. It helps you as well – you can determine what pest is invading your patch.

PLANTING SEEDS

The exercise of watching seeds form plants is enthralling for littlies, but they do like instant gratification as boredom sets in quickly. Use rocket or mesclun salad seeds that sprout quickly and grow into life-size plants quickly. It is an excellent way for kids to appreciate salad leaves. If each child has their own pot, they can have a competition for whose grew fastest, biggest and best.

DECORATING POTS

Hand-made presents are always great gifts. New terracotta pots from your garden centre look great painted up. You will need terracotta pots, paintbrushes and test pots of paint from the home decorating section. The pots can be colourful or named – it is up to the child's imagination. Sow seeds of something edible – herbs or chillies are good – and let the child take care of it. When Christmas or a birthday comes around they have a living present to give.

In Eastern Europe basil plants were given as a gift of love. It is said that in Moldova a young man can fall in love with a maiden who offers such a gift. Paint terracotta pots with love hearts and transplant fresh basil plants into them. Start a new tradition and give a potted basil plant on Valentine's Day instead of roses.

PASSION-FRUIT NAMING CEREMONY

When the passion-fruit vine starts to bloom and then fruits appear, the young green fruit has a soft outer coating. Give your child some help to inscribe their name into the green casing by carefully using a pin, needle or even your fingernail. Be careful not to pull the fruit off its delicate stem. Kids can watch the passion-fruit all summer long, waiting for them to change colour and watch as the scratched name becomes permanently scarred into the outer layer. When the fruit is ready they can show their friends that their fruit has their name on it.

TIE-DYEING WITH BEETROOT JUICE

Beetroot juice has been used for many centuries as a colour dye in fabrics and cottons. It is a strong magenta colour that adheres to fabric fibres very easily. Warning: be very careful, the strong colour also adheres to hands, skin, benchtops and nearly everything else. Cut and peel 2–3 large beetroot. In a large pot of boiling water, cook the beetroot until tender, usually about 30 minutes. Sufficient colour will drain from the beetroot into the water. Remove the beets and cool, these can be eaten in salads or roasted in the oven. Keep the remaining juice warm. Using a white t-shirt, tank top or even a piece of white cotton, dip the whole piece in to change the colour completely, or scrunch the material up to make patterns. Tying rubber bands around some pieces of the t-shirt will create the tie-dyed effect that hippies are famous for.

PRESERVED PRESENTS

Harvesting fruits and vegetables from the garden can be just as interesting to a child as sowing the seeds. If your child helps pick the strawberries or collects all the feijoas, they can feel involved in the process of jam making. Teach them to hull a strawberry or scoop the flesh out of a feijoa. Many hands make light work and little hands can be fully utilised for the more tedious part of the preserving process.

PODDING PEAS

Kids love opening the pods of peas, and extracting the little green pebbles inside. Make it a competition. A group of youngsters can make light work of a bowl full of podded peas if there is a bonus at the end of it.

DECORATING PAVLOVAS

Kids like to help if it is fun. Rose pavlovas (see page 128) are a fun dessert, especially with pretty flower petals sprinkled everywhere. First, teach kids which flowers are edible and which aren't, and then let them pick their own topping to decorate their pavlova. Don't be too heavy-handed, some petals can be edible but bitter. Mix them up with sweet berries.

EMBRACE DIRT

Make the exercise of being in the garden fun. Have clothes set aside which are gardening clothes, with gumboots to match. The youngsters should be free to get as dirty as they possibly want to – making mud pies under large trees, or sliding down muddy slopes. Getting outside in the mud is what it is all about as a kid.

Section 4

A Start-Up Garden

Basil

Ocimum basilicum

Fresh basil has been cultivated for over 4000 years, its use dating back to biblical times. In India, basil is considered sacred to the Hindu gods, Krishna and Vishnu – it was once customary to place a sprig of basil on the dead before burial to ensure their safe passage to the next world.

Nowadays, basil is an important culinary herb for adding a flavour like no other. Cooking takes on a new dimension when fresh basil leaves are added. Basil will go with almost anything, but it has a special affinity with tomatoes. What's more, it is really easy to grow in any size garden or window ledge.

Basil is native to India and was brought to Europe in the sixteenth century by savvy traders. Now it is a staple of Mediterranean foods.

The most common basil we use is sweet basil or sweet genovese, which comes from the Labitae family. Other varieties include anise, lemon and cinnamon basil. In past times basil was also called 'cobbler's orange' and 'herb royale'. Dark opal is the purple variety and is ideal for adding to salads. In times gone by basil plants were kept on window sills to keep flies away.

Basil can act as a natural disinfectant, can improve digestion and enhances a feeling of well-being. Basil tea is said to stop vomiting and nausea and is a preventative for travel sickness. It has been used externally for acne and insect stings and bites, and hot basil tea will relieve colds and flu.

HOW TO GROW

Basil grows easily outdoors from seeds sown in spring. Supermarket pots are an instant source of fresh basil and can be easily transplanted into the garden when the weather is warm. You need to protect the plants from frost. Sow indoors from April to August and plant outside in mid-October in a sunny, sheltered position with a light, rich soil and keep well watered. Water basil in the heat of the day to make it really thrive. Harvest outdoor plants before winter sets in. Basil plants are annuals which means they will only be at their best for one year. Growing basil indoors in a pot on a window ledge, or in a greenhouse, means you will have a supply of leaves all year round. If you plant basil among tomato plants or flowering roses it will help keep hungry sucking bugs away and give an added fragrance to your blooms.

Gardener's Tip

After basil flowers, let the stalks dry on the plant. When dried, harvest. Wearing gloves, run your fingers down the stem to release millions of seeds for next spring's crop. Place in a lightly closed plastic bag until planting time.

PICKING AND STORING

In fresh cooking the beauty of having a plant near to the kitchen is the instant fresh flavour in any dish. If you are going to pick the leaves to preserve, always pick them when the sun is shining the most, and the plants have had a full day of sun.

Fresh — Fresh leaves can be kept for a short time in plastic bags in the fridge. Alternatively, preserve the leaves in olive oil or vinegar, or freeze them. Basil leaves will blacken easily, so tear rather than cutting.

Freeze — Wash the leaves well and drain. Leaves should be puréed with a little water and put into ice cube trays. When frozen, the cubes can be stored in the freezer in plastic bags. Beware: frozen basil will turn black, but it does taste better than dried basil leaves.

Dried — Leave on sheets of brown paper or newspaper in a warm, dry place until the moisture has gone. Keep in airtight containers at room temperature away from light and heat. Remember dried leaves lose their flavour with the moisture so you need twice as many when cooking with them.

Preserve — Make pesto (see recipe page 32), or preserve the leaves in oil. Layer basil, a pinch of salt and the best olive oil in a wide-necked sterile jam jar until full. Use within a week of making and strain thoroughly before using.

Cook's Tip

To make basil vinegar. Push some leaves into good quality white wine vinegar, leave to infuse in a sunny spot for two weeks, shaking the bottle occasionally, then strain into a fresh bottle, discarding the old basil and substituting new leaves, if you like. Store in a dark place.

CULINARY USES

Fresh is best, use the leaves liberally in any summer meal. Basil and tomato are made for each other – they grow well with each other and are very complementary in flavour.

This herb is also wonderful in omelettes, soups and stews and is the basis of the soupe au pistou. And, of course, there is pesto. Remember that the flavour of basil intensifies with heat so use it sparingly.

QUICK PICKINGS

Basil Pasta

Place a large pot of water on to boil to cook the desired pasta. When water boils add 1 tsp salt and 200 g orzo or risoni pasta. Cook for 9 minutes. Drain and return to pot. Add 2 tsp extra virgin olive oil, ½ cup torn fresh basil leaves, 2 cloves crushed garlic and season with salt and freshly ground black pepper. Toss through 25 g butter until melted. Mix and serve. **Serves 2.**

Sautéed Basil Prawns

Heat a frying pan with 2 tbsp olive oil. Cook 500 g prawns, shelled, de-veined and washed. Add 2 cloves crushed garlic, 2-cm piece fresh grated ginger, 25 g butter and a handful of torn fresh basil leaves into the pan. Quickly fry until prawns have turned pink. Finally squeeze over juice of ½ lemon and 1 tsp honey. Heat for 1 minute, and then serve. **Serves 4.**

Barbecued Salmon with Basil

Combine 2 tbsp lemon juice with 2 tbsp olive oil and 1 tbsp chopped fresh basil leaves. Brush over both sides of 4 salmon steaks. Grill on a medium hot grill, for about 10 minutes each side, or until fish flakes when tested with a fork. Serve with lemon wedges. **Serves 4.**

Basil Aioli

Combine ¾ cup mayonnaise with ⅓ cup finely chopped fresh basil leaves, 1 tbsp lemon juice, 1 clove crushed garlic and 1½ tsp finely grated lemon zest.

Season with salt and freshly ground black pepper. Cover and refrigerate for at least 1 hour. Can be made two days ahead of time. **Makes 1 cup.**

Basil & Lemon Sorbet

Place 125 ml water and 125 g sugar in a saucepan. Bring to the boil and then simmer for 4 minutes, adding the zest of 3 lemons. Remove from heat and allow to cool for a while. Add the juice of the 3 lemons and about 100 g basil leaves, pounded to a purée. Stir this up and leave to infuse for a while. Pass through a sieve and pour into a plastic tub and place in the freezer. Generally, sorbet takes 2 hours to set. Try to stir it around every 30 minutes, if you remember.

Basil Pesto (pictured)

When the basil is at its most fragrant in the garden, after a long day in the sun, pick the tender leaves and make jars and jars of delicious pesto. This brew will keep, covered in oil in the fridge, for months and months. **Makes 3 x 330-g jars.**

125 g fresh basil leaves, stems removed
15 cloves garlic, peeled
100 g pine nuts
300 g Parmesan or other hard aged cheese, grated
1 tsp sea salt
½ tsp freshly ground black pepper
500 ml extra virgin olive oil

Wash all the basil leaves, and drain well. Place basil and garlic cloves into food processor or blender and blitz until pulpy. Toast pine nuts in a dry pan until just browned. Pine nuts are oily so they will burn easily. Toss them all the time until browned then remove from heat immediately. Add pine nuts and Parmesan to the processor and blend for another minute. Add salt and pepper and finally, while the motor is running, add olive oil slowly, to make a smooth paste.

Put in jars with lids or sealed plastic containers and cover the top with a little olive oil. Remember, when you use some of the pesto, add more olive oil to cover the top and therefore stop it from going off in your fridge.

Variations

Basil and Walnut Pesto — substitute the same weight in walnuts for pine nuts.

Lemon Basil Pesto — use lemon basil and peanuts or cashews, and pecorino cheese.

Purple Basil Pesto — use purple basil and put chilli in it for extra punch.

Basil and Artichokes — blend with 2–3 artichoke hearts.

Pesto Chicken Schnitzels

Prepare these schnitzels ahead of time, and allow to chill before cooking under the grill, in a pan or even on the barbecue. Use any type of pesto for different flavour combinations. **Serves 4.**

- 4 (about 680 g) chicken breast fillets
- $^{1}/_{3}$ cup basil pesto (see page 32)
- 1 cup fresh breadcrumbs
- salt and freshly ground black pepper
- 2 tbsp cooking oil, e.g. rice bran

Remove skin and any sinew or fatty bits from chicken breasts. Lay a piece of plastic wrap on a wooden board or flat surface. Lay a chicken breast on and then place another piece of plastic wrap on top. With a rolling pin, cooking mallet or another heavy object pound the meat until it is about $^{1}/_{2}$ cm thick. Take off the top piece of wrap and smear over a teaspoon of pesto. Sprinkle with breadcrumbs and season with salt and pepper. Cover again with plastic and turn the whole fillet over. Repeat the pesto, breadcrumb and seasoning on the other side and cover again with wrap. Set aside. Repeat with the other three chicken breasts. Leave to chill in the fridge until ready to cook.

Use a frying pan with oil, or a lightly greased grill plate on high. Place each schnitzel onto the pan or grill plate by removing the wrap from one side and placing on the pan. Remove the other side of wrap gently so you don't lose too many of the breadcrumbs. Cook chicken on one side for 3–4 minutes, then turn and cook the other side for another 3–4 minutes until cooked through and browned. Remove, cover and rest for 5 minutes.

Serve with salad greens or wilted silver beet leaves and plenty of crunchy potato wedges.

Bacon & Basil Tarts

The sweet flavour of basil complements bacon so well in these tasty tarts. Great for a picnic or easy lunch, they refrigerate well and will last a few days. **Makes 8 tarts.**

- 750-g packet pre-made short crust savoury pastry sheets
- 8 rashers middle bacon
- 50 g fresh basil leaves, stalks removed
- 8 eggs
- 100 ml cream
- salt and freshly ground black pepper

Preheat oven to 180 °C/350 °F. Cut 8 circles out of the pastry using a saucer as a cutter shape. Use the pastry to line 8 well-greased 10-cm tartlet tins.

Cook bacon until just crispy. Cut roughly into smaller pieces. Roughly chop basil leaves. Scatter basil and bacon pieces together evenly over tart bases. Beat together eggs and cream. Season well with salt and pepper. Pour egg mixture over tarts. Bake in oven for 18–20 minutes until golden brown. Leave to cool before removing from tart tins.

Variation

Spread some basil pesto over the base of the pastry before placing the bacon for extra basil flavour.

Pizza Margarita with Fresh Basil

A good cake mixer with a dough hook makes light work of this pizza dough. Otherwise, knead the dough the old-fashioned way! Working the dough until you get a smooth silky texture will prove the best when the crispy base comes out of the oven. Fresh mozzarella is the best for this simple pizza. It is readily available these days, however, plain grated mozzarella will do. **Serves 4–6.**

20 g dried yeast
2 tbsp honey
650 ml water, warm
1 kg plain flour
1 tbsp salt
1 tbsp extra virgin olive oil

Sauce
2 tbsp olive oil
1 onion, finely diced
4 cloves garlic, crushed
400-g can chopped tomatoes
2 tbsp fresh basil leaves, chopped
salt and freshly ground black pepper

handful fresh basil leaves
fresh mozzarella balls, sliced

Mix together yeast, honey and half the water. Leave to bubble for 5 minutes. Mix flour and salt together, then add honey yeast mixture. Add remaining water and beat with dough hook in a cake mixer for 10–15 minutes. Alternatively, once the water mixture is incorporated into the flour, turn onto a well-floured surface and knead for 10 minutes, until smooth and silky.

Place the dough in a greased bowl, cover with greased plastic wrap and place in a warm area – near an oven or in a hot water cupboard. Leave to rise for 30 minutes. Knock back using your fist in the middle of the dough. Turn onto a well-floured board. Separate mixture into quarters and roll out into thin bases to fit a tin or baking sheet. Brush over the pastry with a little olive oil. Preheat the oven to 220 °C/425 °F.

To make the sauce, heat oil in a saucepan and add onion and garlic. Add tomatoes, chopped basil and season to taste. Leave to boil for 10 minutes. Allow to cool slightly. Spread tomato sauce over top of the pizza and top with fresh basil leaves and slices of mozzarella. Leave with topping on for 5 minutes before putting in oven for 8 minutes. Serve immediately.

Mussels with Basil Cream (pictured)

The basil gives a fantastic sweet flavour to the mussels. Use lemon basil or the stronger-flavoured Thai basil for a difference. Serve this dish as an entrée or as a main with bread or rice to mop up the remaining sauce. **Serves 4–6.**

24 live green-lipped mussels
2 tbsp olive oil
2 cloves garlic, crushed
1 lemon, juice of
¼ cup Sweet Thai Chilli Sauce
30 g fresh basil leaves, roughly chopped
salt and freshly ground black pepper
300 ml cream
to serve, fresh lemon wedges and basil leaves

Clean mussels well, removing the stringy beards and other debris, and rinse whole shells in cold water. Discard any damaged mussels or those that don't close when tapped.

In a large saucepan, with a lid, heat oil and sauté garlic for a few seconds. Add lemon juice and Sweet Thai Chilli Sauce, basil and seasonings and bring to the boil. Add mussels, cover and cook for 4–8 minutes, removing them as they open. Stir in cream and bring to a rapid boil, stirring all the time. Cook for 2 minutes until sauce reduces and begins to thicken. Pile cooked mussels into a serving dish and pour over the sauce. Serve with wedges of lemon and fresh basil leaves.

Beans

Broad, runner, green, butter, French, Thai, haricot

How many beans can you grow? Perfect for a spare pot by a trellis or in a sunny corner of the garden, a bean plant or two can produce enough for a few meals. There are short ones, long ones, butter, yellow, dwarf, broad, speckled, white, the list goes on. The legume family is broad indeed. What is common to most beans is the way they are grown, the seeds, the stakes and the picking. Choose your own beans to make any one of these tasty recipes, or look to the ideas for storing the fine crop that a small number of plants will give you.

A crop of twirling bean plants in a wooden tub can be a great feature of an apartment garden.

Beans are an excellent source of dietary fibre, particularly soluble fibre, which can help reduce high blood cholesterol levels. They also provide useful amounts of vitamin B1 and iron.

HOW TO GROW

Beans are best planted directly into warm soil (read the packet for the best soil temperature). Beans often need warmer weather to germinate, and a good soaking is sometimes necessary too, to break through the hard crust of the legume. Follow the packet instructions for best results. Beans can be trial and error to get the right germination time and quantity.

Fertilise the soil well with organic matter and a good general fertiliser and you won't need to feed so much while growing.

Put stakes or wire netting around the bean seedling to encourage the growing tips to catch on and twirl upwards. Garden stores have crafty tripod frames ready-made for your pot or garden, or be inventive and use interesting sculptured frames. Be careful of over-handling the growing tips as these can break and then won't grow upwards. Water often, as they need plenty of liquid while the bean buds are forming. Make sure the plants are sheltered from dry prevailing winds.

Gardener's Tip

Don't plant your beans in soil that has recently had a crop of tomatoes, potatoes, lettuce, cabbage or beans. They don't like it and probably won't grow.

PICKING AND STORING

The secret to increasing your green bean production is to keep picking them. The more you pick the more will grow.

Beans are at their best when slightly younger. The flesh is sweeter and the seeds within are not too over-developed. Test whether a bean is ready to be picked by snapping one in half. A good snap and sweet texture indicate they will be perfect. Alternatively, feel the flesh in the middle of the bean; if too spongy when lightly squeezed the bean is probably too mature. Keep these to use later for seeds.

Fresh — Broad beans deteriorate faster than any other beans so use them quickly or freeze them. The fresher and younger they are, the sweeter they taste; take care not to over-cook them – they should have a slight crunch. Late-season broad beans can taste stale, and with these the only option is to cook them, then meticulously peel off the outer covering so you are just left with the bean's apple-green kernel.

Freeze — Pick the beans and aim to freeze them the same day. Rinse them in cool water and drain. Cut off the ends, and cut the beans to whatever lengths you prefer. Put them into rapidly boiling water, cover the pot and time them for 3 minutes. Remove using a slotted spoon and immediately plunge them into a bowl of ice water to stop the cooking. Keep them in the ice water for 3 minutes. Drain. Pack into zip-lock bags or freezer bags. Squeeze as much air out as possible to help prevent freezer burn. Fresh beans will keep in the freezer for up to 6 months if done properly.

Preserve — Fresh green beans can be preserved in vinegars and oils and even in relishes. Freezing is the best way to store the flavour, but pickled beans are not uncommon on antipasto platters.

Dried — Dried beans are a staple the world over. Usually removed from the outer pod, a dried bean's longevity helps make the world go round. Dried beans are a great option for keeping until next year and for years to come.

CULINARY USES

Beans go back to the ark and, as a staple of many cuisines for thousands of years, they have been the base of many dishes. Fresh beans in their pods will favour fresh ingredients, like olive oil, cured hams, fresh tomatoes or most other vegetables. The savoury taste of onions and garlic, the sweetness of honey and chilli sauces are great accompaniments.

Green beans are best if the tops and tails are removed. These can be hard and not so palatable to eat. To quickly top and tail green beans, gather them together in one hand and then slice away the top 5 mm, then do the same at the other end. If necessary pull off any stringy bits that come away from the side of the bean.

To blanch beans, plunge beans into rapidly boiling salted water and cook until al dente. When over-cooked, beans have a flabby texture and also lose much of their flavour. Drain and toss in butter or sauce. For salads, cook the beans until just tender and then refresh under cold water. Serve with carrots or other root vegetables to complement the flavours.

QUICK PICKINGS

Beans À La Française

Plunge 600 g French beans that have been topped and tailed into a pan of boiling salted water. Drain well. Heat 75 g butter in a large frying pan and add 2 bunches spring onions that have been trimmed and sliced on the diagonal. Finally add 1 tsp sugar. Cook until the spring onions have wilted, then toss in the blanched beans and cook over a medium heat for 5 minutes more, stirring regularly. Sprinkle with a little chopped parsley and chervil to serve.

French Beans With Almonds

Cook 350 g French green beans in boiling salted water for 7 minutes, then drain. Melt 25 g butter and fry 70 g flaked almonds until just browned. Mix them with the beans, season with salt and freshly ground black pepper and serve immediately.

Green Beans With Pears

Bring 450 ml vegetable stock to the boil, then add 4 hard pears, peeled, cored and sliced and a twist of lemon peel. Simmer for 10 minutes. Add 225 g green beans and simmer for 20 minutes. Add 1 tbsp tarragon vinegar (see page 256) and 2 tbsp demerara sugar. Season to taste with salt and freshly ground black pepper. Continue simmering until the liquid is almost absorbed. Serve immediately.

Oven-Roasted Green Beans

Preheat oven to 225 °C/450 °F. Wash, drain and thoroughly dry 500 g fresh green beans. Snap off the ends. Cover a baking sheet with foil. Scatter dry green beans onto baking sheet in one layer. Drizzle over extra virgin olive oil and sea salt. Toss to make sure all the beans are coated. Put in oven for 10 minutes. Take out of oven and turn the green beans over and around a bit. Put back into the oven for another 10–12 minutes. Serve hot with main meal.

Stir-Fried Green Beans With Sichuan Sauce

Cut 500 g green beans diagonally into 4-cm lengths. Mix 2 tsp soy sauce with 2 cloves crushed garlic, 1 tsp sugar, 1 tsp sesame oil and 2 tsp chilli paste. Heat a wok until very hot. Add 3 tbsp vegetable oil, tilt wok and coat the side. Add the green beans, stir-fry for 1 minute. Add ¼ cup liquid chicken stock, cover and cook for 5 minutes. Add soy sauce mixture and stir-fry until green beans are coated and moisture is evaporated. Stir in 2 tbsp sesame seeds.

Broad Bean Pâté

Try this creamy dip this summer instead of the usual guacamole. Fresh broad beans have a taste all of their own. One strong plant should give enough beans to make this pâté. **Serves 10.**

2 kg broad beans, podded
3–4 cloves garlic, peeled and crushed
6 spring onions, chopped
1 lemon, juice of
4 tbsp fresh flat-leaf parsley, chopped
salt and freshly ground black pepper
to serve, sour cream and corn chips

Plunge beans into a pan of boiling salted water, return to the boil and cook for 4–5 minutes until tender. Drain and, when cool enough to handle, peel off the outer skins of beans and pop into a wide bowl. Mash or pulse beans in a processor to make a chunky mash, then mix in remaining ingredients. Season and serve with sour cream and freshly ground black pepper. Best served with crispy corn chips or toasted bagel crisps.

Shredded Green Beans with Herb & Caper Dressing

Fresh beans pick up strong flavours really well. The strong taste of herbs and salty capers will bring this dish to life. Serve with lamb or beef steaks, or as a side dish to a vegetarian feast. **Serves 4 as a side dish.**

150 ml extra virgin olive oil
4 tbsp fresh mint leaves, finely chopped
4 tbsp fresh flat-leaf parsley, finely chopped
2 tbsp fresh chervil, finely chopped
2 tbsp fresh dill, finely chopped
400 g fresh green beans, sliced
4 tbsp small capers, rinsed and drained
1 lemon juice of, and zest, finely grated
1 tsp Dijon mustard
2 small shallots, peeled and finely chopped
salt and freshly ground black pepper

In a deep frying pan, heat oil gently over a low heat. Remove from heat and stir in finely chopped herbs. Leave until required.

Bring a large pan of water to boil. Add beans and cook for 8–10 minutes until tender. Drain. Meanwhile, add the capers, lemon juice and zest, mustard and shallots to herb mixture. Finally, stir in beans and season to taste. Return to heat to warm through. Serve immediately.

Baby Bean & Tuna Salad

A small piece of fresh tuna will go a long way in this dish. Avoid over-cooking – it is better to sear in the juices and enjoy the fresh flavour. The better and fresher the tuna, the better the dish will be. **Serves 4.**

450 g fresh green beans
4 tbsp extra virgin olive oil
300-g piece fresh tuna
1 red onion, peeled and finely chopped
2 cloves garlic, peeled and sliced
3 tbsp balsamic vinegar
1 tbsp tarragon leaves, finely chopped
4 tbsp flat-leaf parsley, finely chopped
freshly ground black pepper
to serve, extra olive oil and crusty bread

Bring a large pan of water to the boil, add the beans and cook for 8–10 minutes, until tender. Drain and set aside.

Heat 2 tbsp of oil in large frying pan and sear tuna on each side for 1 minute until outside is browned and inside is warmed but still pink. Remove from pan, cover and set aside. In the same pan, reduce heat to low and stir in onion and garlic and cook for 6–7 minutes until soft but not browned. Remove from heat and leave for 5 minutes.

Away from the heat, stir in beans, balsamic vinegar, herbs and remaining oil. Season with freshly ground black pepper.

Leave to cool for 20 minutes for the flavours to infuse. Arrange beans on a platter and lay slices of tuna on top. Drizzle with extra olive oil. Serve with toasted crusty bread.

Green Bean Pasta with Parmesan

This is a simple dish and is equally special with any type of fresh green bean. Longer French beans, haricot or tender Thai beans work well sliced and blanched. **Serves 4.**

500 g pasta, like rigatoni or penne
6 tbsp extra virgin olive oil, plus extra for drizzling
2 cloves garlic, peeled and finely chopped
½ tsp dried crushed chilli flakes
500 g fresh or frozen broad beans, thawed if frozen
3 tbsp water
2 tbsp fresh parsley, finely chopped
1 tbsp grated Parmesan, plus extra for serving

Cook pasta in a large pan of boiling salted water until al dente. Follow the instructions on the packet for perfect pasta. At the same time, heat oil in a large frying pan. Fry garlic and chilli flakes over a medium to high heat for 1 minute. Add beans with 3 tbsp water and cook for 3–5 minutes until beans are tender and water has evaporated.

Drain pasta and tip into the broad beans with parsley and Parmesan. Toss well and season. Serve drizzled with olive oil and grated Parmesan.

Broad Bean & Lemon Risotto (pictured)

The effort taken to remove the shells from broad beans seems laborious, but the results are sublime. The beans are creamy and work perfectly with this saucy risotto. Complement this result with a nice buttery chardonnay – perfection! **Serves 4.**

350 g broad beans, fresh or frozen
salt
25 g butter
1 medium onion, peeled and finely chopped
2 stalks celery, finely chopped
200 g arborio rice
1 litre hot vegetable stock
1 lemon, grated zest and juice of
75 g Parmesan, freshly grated
to serve, grated Parmesan and thin strips lemon zest

Blanch the broad beans in a large pan of boiling salted water for 3–5 minutes or until just tender. Plunge into icy cold water to cool. Drain, peel off outer skin and set aside.

Melt butter in large pan, add the onion and celery and cook over a medium heat for 5 minutes or until they begin to soften. Add rice and continue to cook, stirring for 1–2 minutes. Pour in a ladleful of hot stock and simmer gently, stirring frequently until rice has absorbed most of it. Keep adding stock this way until the rice is all'onda (see page 18). This will take about 18 minutes. The risotto should look creamy and soft.

Add broad beans, lemon zest and juice, and warm through. Stir in the Parmesan and season to taste. Serve the risotto immediately, garnished with grated Parmesan and lemon zest.

Green Beans with Crispy Parma Ham

Parma ham fries to a crisp very quickly and the salty flavour goes well with most green vegetables. Bacon can be used as a substitute in this recipe, but use streaky for the best flavour. **Serves 6.**

450 g green beans, trimmed
1 tbsp olive oil
85 g Parma ham or prosciutto, torn into strips
1 bunch spring onions, sliced diagonally
1 tbsp balsamic vinegar
salt and freshly ground black pepper

Bring a pan of water to boil, blanch the beans for 3–4 minutes. Plunge into cold water to stop the cooking and keep the beans green. Meanwhile, heat oil in a large frying pan or wok and fry ham until crispy. Add spring onions and vinegar and stir for 1 minute. Drain beans and tip them into the pan. Toss to coat beans in oil. Season to taste and serve immediately while hot.

Beetroot

Beta vulgaris

Easy to grow and a delight to eat, beetroot (or sugar beet as it is sometimes called) is one of the best vegetables to have in the garden all year round. They are easily grown from seed or seedlings. A tub full of beetroot can give fresh baby leaves for a crunchy salad, or baby beets to be roasted with lamb. If you hold out for a mature tuber they can be preserved for the all-year-round super beetroot taste.

Beetroot has always been thought to have valuable medicinal functions. Given its bloody colour, it's no wonder that it was associated with disorders of the blood. Beets have been known to correct jaundice, and help with earache and toothache.

Red beet contains about 6 per cent pure sugar and baby beets are the sweetest and can be eaten skin and all. The ability to metabolise the red pigment in beetroot is genetic. For some people, eating beetroot in any quantity will stain their pee bright pink, so don't be too concerned if this happens after eating a bowl of beetroot soup.

HOW TO GROW

Beetroot seedlings are readily available from local plant shops, but when growing from seed go for the cheaper option. Soak the seeds for a couple of hours before sowing to bring on germination. Plant the seed in the warmer weather, starting in early spring. The plants will go to seed very easily if grown too far out of season. In a large wooden planter, make sure the soil is rich and reasonably fine. In the ground, prepare the soil you are sowing them in by spreading an organic fertiliser first. Sow each seed 5 cm apart. The seedlings will need thinning after a couple of weeks to allow for good root growth. The roots will grow slightly above the ground level, and there is no need to cover them with soil.

PICKING & STORING

Beets can be eaten at any stage – they are quite delicious as baby beets, and the leaves can be picked for salads.

Fresh — Beetroot, once harvested, will keep well out of the fridge for 2–3 weeks. Don't cut the roots too close to the stem to avoid losing moisture. In the fridge, the roots will keep for two to three months.

Freeze — Freezing works if the roots are blanched first then packaged. But beware, the 'bleeding' from the ruby red roots will be very messy when thawing.

Preserve — Preserving in vinegar or a relish is the best way to retain the flavour all year round.

CULINARY USES

If cooking raw beetroot whole, do not cut or scrub with a stiff brush – the colour will flood out if the skin is damaged. Twist off the leaves, leaving about 5 cm of stem intact and leave any roots whole.

Beetroot can be boiled, baked or microwaved. Medium-sized beets will cook in 45–75 minutes in boiling water. Baked beetroot has a deeper, earthier flavour than boiled beetroot, which is sightly sweeter, cleaner and less complex. They take about 1½–2 hours to bake at 180 °C/350 °F, wrapped in foil with a couple of tablespoons of water, or about 10–12 minutes in a microwave, wrapped in plastic wrap, turning frequently.

QUICK PICKINGS

Stir-Fried Beetroot

Shred a raw beetroot, and cook in a hot frying pan or wok with a little sesame oil. Cook for 3–4 minutes and then toss in walnut oil, freshly grated ginger, orange juice and lime juice. Serve with wok-fried chicken pieces or fish.

Baked Balsamic Beetroot

Place 4 fresh washed beetroot in a roasting dish. Bake in a 180 °C/350 °F oven for 40 minutes. Peel and remove any stems or roots. Cut into wedges, season with salt and pepper and a good splash of balsamic vinegar. Sprinkle with shredded mint and serve at room temperature on an antipasto platter.

Beetroot & Red Onion Relish

Grate 2 large raw beetroot and cook in a pot for 1 hour with diced red onion, tamarind pulp, fresh chilli and fresh coriander. Sweeten with 2 tbsp muscovado sugar and add the juice of one lime. Best served alongside grilled venison or duck.

Baby Beetroot Leaf Salad

If the leaves of your bunch are young and fresh you can eat them. Stew them with olive oil, garlic and cumin seeds, stir into cooked black-eyed beans or Puy lentils.

Raw Beetroot Salad

Grate raw, peeled beetroot. Place on a serving platter and sprinkle with lemon juice. Just before serving, mix some mayonnaise with a small amount of horseradish, and drizzle over the top. Sprinkle with some mint and coriander leaves. Best served with fillets of smoked fish.

Beetroot & Anchovy Salad

Try dressing a grated beetroot salad with anchovies and make a Thai salad dressing with chilli, lime juice, sugar and fish sauce.

Beetroot & Egg Salad

Hard-boiled eggs are great with beetroot – make a dressing with hard-boiled egg yolks, anchovies, lemon, oil and parsley. Or serve a cooked leek and beetroot salad with a dressing of chopped hard-boiled eggs, parsley, chives, oil and vinegar. A beetroot and egg salad is good served with salsa verde dressing (see page 222).

Sautéed Beetroot

Dice 2 beetroot and 2 dessert apples. Heat 1 tbsp butter and 1 tbsp oil in a frying pan until it foams. Add apple and fry briskly until golden brown. Scoop onto a serving plate and arrange around the edges. Keep warm. Add the beetroot to the pan and quickly sauté until hot. Place in the centre of the plate. Add juice of 1 lemon and ½ tsp horseradish to the pan and stir. Pour over the beetroot. Season well with salt and pepper and serve sprinkled with chopped chives.

Roast Balsamic Beetroot

Roasting root vegetables like beetroot brings out a sweetness and tenderness in them. Serve these hot or cold as a side to any roast meats or on an antipasto platter. **Serves 8 as a side dish**

4 large beetroot, washed
4 tbsp olive oil
4 tbsp balsamic vinegar
4 cloves garlic, peeled and finely chopped
2 tbsp sugar
salt and freshly ground black pepper

Preheat the oven to 200 °C/400 °F. Bring beetroot to the boil in a large saucepan of water and cook for 30 minutes. Remove from the saucepan and refresh under cold water. Rub off the tough skin with your hands, or peel with a vegetable peeler (wear gloves to avoid bright purple skin).

With a sharp knife, remove any remaining roots or skin, then wash beetroots. Cut each beetroot into rough segments, place in a baking dish and mix through the oil, vinegar, garlic and sugar. Season to taste. Roast in the oven for 30 minutes. Serve while hot.

Beetroot Risotto

The smaller the beetroot the more tender and sweet the flavour they will bring to this dish. The roots don't take long to grow in a fertile soil. Pick the tubers when they are the size of a golf ball or just bigger. Reserve the baby beet leaves for an accompanying salad. **Serves 6.**

6–8 small beetroot
1.5 litres chicken stock
125 ml olive oil
1 onion, peeled and finely diced
1 carrot, peeled and finely diced
1 stick celery, peeled and finely diced
2 cloves garlic, peeled and crushed
1 sprig rosemary, stalk removed and leaves very finely chopped
500 g arborio or carnaroli rice
125 ml red wine
salt and freshly ground black pepper
100 g butter
to serve, rosemary sprigs and feta

Wash and trim beetroot of any stems and roots. Cook beetroot in a saucepan with just enough water to cover, for 30 minutes or until easily pierced with a knife. Drain, reserving 1½ cups of the juice, and set aside. Using a vegetable peeler, remove skins from beetroot and cut into wedges.

Bring chicken stock to simmer over a low heat. Heat olive oil in a heavy-based saucepan and sauté onion, carrot, celery, garlic and rosemary over a medium heat for 5 minutes.

Add rice and cook for a few minutes more, stirring to coat rice with oil. Add red wine and bring to a simmer, stirring constantly so rice does not stick to the bottom of frying pan. When the wine has been absorbed, add simmering stock, a ladleful at a time, adding more when the stock has been absorbed. Do not stop stirring and loosening the rice from the sides of the pan.

After 15 minutes add beetroot wedges to risotto with reserved beetroot cooking liquid, and cook until rice is tender but still firm to the bite and most of the liquid is absorbed. Total cooking time should be about 18–20 minutes until the rice is all'onda (see page 18). Remove from heat. Season to taste and stir through the butter. Serve with crumbled feta and garnish with rosemary.

Cook's Tip

A wooden spoon is a risotto's best friend. It easily scrapes any rice grains from the bottom of the pan, and yet delicately keeps the mixture moving while cooking. The grains should be soft but have a bite to them when cooked. A wooden spoon won't make it mushy.

Spiced Vinegar Beetroot

A good tip is to wear rubber gloves in the kitchen sink while peeling the beetroot. The juice can stain easily, so watch for wayward splashes. **Makes 2 x 1-litre clip-seal jars.**

8 medium beetroot
375 ml white wine vinegar
½ cup water
240 g sugar
¼ tsp ground cinnamon
6 whole cloves
6 peppercorns
½ tsp caraway seeds

Wash and trim stems off beetroot. Add to a pan of boiling water, and allow to simmer gently, covered, until just tender, for about 30–40 minutes. Drain, peel beetroot and remove stems. Reserve about 1 cup of the cooking liquid for the dressing. Slice the beetroot thinly. Combine the reserved juice, white wine vinegar, water, sugar, cinnamon, cloves, peppercorns and caraway seeds in a pan, stir over medium heat until sugar is dissolved.

Bring to boil, add beetroot slices, simmer, uncovered, for 2 minutes. Pack into hot, sterilised jars (see page 18), pour hot vinegar mixture over beetroot. Seal jars well. Keep refrigerated.

Beetroot & Ginger Relish

The colour of rich magenta is preserved in this zesty relish. Serve with aged Cheddars and pickled onions on a traditional ploughman's platter or as a side dish to your tasty lamb burgers. **Makes 8 x 300-g jars.**

1 kg beetroot
500 g onions, peeled and finely diced
250 g currants
600 ml malt vinegar
2 tbsp salt
450 g brown sugar
2 tsp mixed spice, ground
1 tsp white pepper
5-cm piece fresh ginger root, peeled and finely chopped
50 g plain flour
125 ml malt vinegar

Wash and trim any leaves from the beetroot without damaging the skins. In a pot of boiling water cook beetroot for 30 minutes. Peel away the skins with a vegetable peeler. Mince, grate or finely chop beetroot. Put the beetroot, onions and currants into a large preserving pan or saucepan with first measure of vinegar. Boil until onion is tender, about 10 minutes.

Add salt, sugar, mixed spice, pepper and ginger. Boil for 25 minutes, stirring occasionally. Mix flour and second measure of vinegar to a smooth paste. Stir into pan and boil for 5 minutes. Pack into sterilised jars (see page 18). Seal well. Keeps for 3–4 months.

Beetroot Soup

Delicious, blood-warming soup. Use gloves to peel the beetroot to avoid the pink hand stains for the rest of the day. **Serves 4.**

- 50 g butter
- 1 large onion, peeled
- 1 clove garlic, peeled and crushed
- 2.5-cm piece fresh ginger, peeled and finely chopped
- handful of mint
- handful of coriander
- 1 kg raw beetroot, diced
- 6 stalks celery, roughly chopped
- 1 medium potato, peeled and diced
- 2 tbsp sugar
- 1.5 litres chicken stock
- salt and freshly ground black pepper
- to serve, sour cream and shredded mint and coriander

Melt butter in a large pan and sauté the onion, garlic, ginger and mint. Add remaining ingredients, season to taste and bring to the boil. Cover and simmer for 1 hour, or until beetroot is completely soft. Purée in batches in a food processor or blender. Return to saucepan and bring back to heat. Serve with sour cream and shredded herbs.

Slow-Roasted Duck with Beetroot

Duck is best cooked either quickly or, like this recipe, very slowly. The meat becomes very tender and falls off the bone. Combined with the beetroot and orange the duck takes on a wonderful flavour. A perfect dish for the weekend gardener to prepare. **Serves 4.**

- 4 duck supremes (bone-in)
- 4 beetroot
- 1 orange, whole
- sea salt
- 450 g red onions, peeled and thinly sliced
- 3 oranges, juice and zest of
- 2–3 rosemary sprigs
- 6–8 bay leaves
- 2–3 sage sprigs
- 2.5-cm piece fresh ginger root, peeled and grated
- 500 ml red wine
- to serve, green vegetables, onion marmalade

Preheat the oven to 150 °C /300 °F. Trim excess fat off duck and score top piece of skin. Peel beetroot using a sharp knife. Slice beetroot and whole orange and set aside.

Sprinkle duck breasts with salt. Cook, skin side down in a hot frying pan until some of the fat has been rendered out of the skin. Place beetroot pieces, duck and onions in a 5-litre casserole dish and cover with orange juice and zest, slices of oranges, rosemary, bay leaves, sage and ginger. Pour over the red wine.

Cover dish with a lid or foil and roast in oven at for 2½–3 hours. Remove from oven and allow to stand for 10 minutes, before serving with green steamed vegetables and a little onion marmalade.

Beetroot & Orange Salad

Be careful not to break the skin as the beetroot may bleed during cooking. The juice of the marinated beetroot will leach into the oranges, so plate up this dish just before serving to keep the pink and orange colours vibrant. **Serves 8.**

10 small beetroot, well washed
2 limes, juice of
4 tbsp olive oil, or oil of your choice
sea salt and freshly ground black pepper
6 oranges
to serve, finely chopped parsley

Two or three days before you need the salad, place beetroot in a deep saucepan and cover generously with water. Cover and bring to the boil, then simmer, with the lid half on, until tender, for about 30 minutes. The water may need topping up.

Drain and rinse with cold water then slip off the skins or peel with a peeler. When cool place in a dish, cover with plastic wrap and refrigerate.

To make the dressing, whisk the lime juice, oil, salt and pepper together. The day before it is required, slice the beetroot into rounds, place back in the dish and pour over the dressing. Cover and refrigerate again.

Cut rind and pith off oranges. Slice oranges, place in a bowl, adding any juice, cover and refrigerate.

When time to serve, arrange alternate slices of orange and beetroot in a shallow serving dish. Mix any orange juice into the lime dressing remaining from marinating and pour over the salad. Sprinkle with a little chopped parsley and serve immediately.

Beetroot & Rosemary Muffins

These are very tasty and can be made into mini versions for your dinner or cocktail party. **Makes 12.**

200 g cooked beetroot, coarsely grated
250 g plain flour
1 tsp baking powder
½ tsp salt
50 g raisins or sultanas
1 large egg
300 ml buttermilk or plain milk
50 g butter, melted and left to cool
50 g Parmesan, grated
2 tsp fresh rosemary leaves, chopped
to serve, goat's-milk cheese or cream cheese

Preheat oven to 200 °C/400 °F. Grease a 12-hole muffin tin with butter. Put grated beetroot into a sieve suspended over a bowl. Leave for at least 15 minutes. Sieve flour and baking powder into a large mixing bowl and stir in salt and raisins or sultanas.

With clean hands, squeeze juice from beetroot and discard. Gently fold beetroot into flour mixture. Beat egg in a separate bowl and add buttermilk and melted butter. Pour the mixture into the flour and beetroot, stir for a dozen strokes, then stop – don't over-mix.

Sprinkle one third of the grated Parmesan over the muffin holes, then spoon in batter to fill two-thirds of each hole. Mix remaining Parmesan with chopped rosemary and sprinkle over muffins. Bake in centre of oven for 15–20 minutes, until risen. Remove from oven, run a small knife around muffins and lift out. Allow to cool slightly, then serve warm topped with goat's-milk cheese or cream cheese.

Capsicums

Capsicum annuum

Technically they are classified as a fruit but we use them in savoury cooking and so associate them with vegetables. Sometimes referred to as 'bell', 'sweet' or 'bullnose' peppers, there are at least 26 capsicum species, with five main types cultivated for consumption. Closely related to chillies, they contain much less capsaicin (the active part that causes the heat in chilli peppers) than their spicy cousins. They are not, however, related to the pepper of the peppercorn variety.

In New Zealand, we call them capsicums, in the United States they are known as bell peppers. They contain high levels of vitamin C (particularly the red variety) and beta-carotene, which the body converts to vitamin A. They come in red, green, yellow, white, orange, purple-black and even a chocolate-coloured variety. The colour of the capsicum will give an indication of the flavour. Green is more raw, leading up to yellow and red which become sweeter and more pungent.

Capsicums give our food vibrancy and energy through their colour. However, beware as the skins on the capsicum are not so digestible by the human gut, so it is good practice to remove the skins by peeling or roasting.

Capsicums may be synonymous with Spanish and Hungarian cuisine, but were not used in their cooking until the 1500s when introduced by Christopher Columbus.

HOW TO GROW

Capsicums grow at their best in November to March, but are grown commercially year-round in hothouses. They all start life green, changing colour as they ripen to brown, orange, purple or more commonly, red or yellow.

Capsicums are warm-season vegetables and grow best in tropical and subtropical areas. Their seeds are quite slow to germinate. Soaking them overnight in warm water before sowing can speed up the process a little. It is often helpful to sow the seed and keep on a windowsill or warm place until well germinated and to plant out when the weather warms. Speed things up even more by buying seedlings from your local garden centre. Look for stocky, vigorous plants with deep green leaves.

Make sure the soil is rich and full of organic matter, compost and animal manure a few weeks before planting. A large wooden planter box or individual plastic pots are perfect. Plant in full sun in a sheltered position.

Capsicums don't like drying out as they will grow stunted, so keep watering. But don't over-water as 'wet feet' will stop flower production. It helps to companion-plant the capsicums near flowers such as lavender, thyme or somewhere bees will be attracted to. Pollination is important, so when bees aren't around try using a small, clean paintbrush to move the pollen from the small stamens onto the centre stigma. A small flick with the brush should be enough to pollinate each flower and allow the capsicum fruit to develop.

When fruit is setting, water with liquid fertiliser or side-dress the plants monthly with a little fertiliser, well-decayed animal manure or compost.

PICKING & STORING

Pick capsicums as soon as they are ripe, so that the plants will set more fruit. Capsicums keep ripening after picking, and have a relatively short shelf-life. Those with wrinkles or soft patches are past their best.

Fresh — Choose firm, smooth, shiny capsicums, and store in the vegetable bin of the fridge. Use within a week. Fresh capsicums can easily rot and cause a rancid taste in food.

Freeze — Cooked capsicum flesh is easily frozen. If freezing from raw, lightly blanch (see page 17) first, to help the chilling process. When thawed, the flesh will lose a lot of its integrity, so needs to be used in baked or stewed dishes.

Preserve — Chargrilling or roasting capsicums is the best way to preserve the flesh. Remove seeds and membranes and store the cooked flesh in oil. Keep well covered.

CULINARY USES

Capsicum can be grilled, roasted, sautéed, added to braises or curries, and stir-fried or stuffed.

Capsicum goes with anchovies, balsamic vinegar, basil, bay leaves, capers, caraway seeds, cheese, chicken, chicory, chorizo, coriander, courgettes, couscous, cumin, eggplant, eggs, garlic, ham, lamb, lemon, lobster, mayonnaise, olives, olive oil, paprika, pasta, pastry, pesto, preserved lemon, rice, rustic bread, saffron, tomatoes, tuna and veal.

Various spices, including the strongly flavoured cayenne pepper and paprika, are made from dried capsicum plants ground into a powder form.

Ideally, remove the indigestible skin by either peeling raw with a sharp peeler or chargrill them and remove skin. To remove their skin, cut the capsicums into quarters lengthways and grill, skin side up, until the skin is charred and evenly blistered. Place immediately into a plastic bag and close with a tie or loose knot. Leave for a few minutes and then remove from the bag and the skin will peel off easily. Alternatively, use a sharp vegetable peeler and work down the outside edge of the capsicum.

Cook's Tip

Grilling capsicums (especially red) enhances their natural sweetness. Place whole on a gas flame or hot barbecue plate and cook, turning frequently, until skin blackens and blisters, then remove from heat, peel and deseed. The capsicum can also be trimmed and halved or quartered, with seeds and membranes removed, then grilled skin side up under a hot grill until skin blackens and blisters, and then peeled. Be wary though – over-blackening can cause a burnt taste.

QUICK PICKINGS

Stuffed Capsicums With Goat's-Milk Cheese

Stuff smaller capsicums with a mixture of crumbled goat's-milk cheese, breadcrumbs, chopped oregano and a little pesto or tapenade. Drizzle with olive oil, cover with foil and roast at 200 °C/400 °F for 45–55 minutes.

Grilled Mediterranean Capsicums

Use grilled red capsicums dressed with a peppery extra virgin olive oil, scattered with anchovies and baby capers and served with ciabatta; or try it layered with slices of buffalo mozzarella, large basil leaves and drizzled with a balsamic dressing.

Italian Sausage & Capsicum Sandwich

Roasted capsicum and Italian sausages make a great sandwich filling. Barbecue or chargrill 1 kg Italian-style sausages until cooked and brown, then 2 sliced Spanish onions, then add 2 each of roasted, peeled, deseeded and sliced red and yellow capsicums. Serve immediately with rustic bread rolls.

Romesco Sauce

For a tangy sauce to be used with barbecued seafood and meats, barbecue 2 large tomatoes until skins just burst with 2 fresh long red chillies, then peel, seed and chop tomatoes. Process tomatoes and chillies in a food processor with 2 roasted, peeled, deseeded and chopped red capsicum, 60 g roasted blanched almonds, 2 cloves crushed garlic, $\frac{1}{3}$ cup olive oil, $\frac{1}{4}$ tsp sweet paprika and $1\frac{1}{2}$ tbsp sherry vinegar until a smooth purée forms. Makes about $\frac{3}{4}$ cup.

Capsicum Niçoise Salad

Barbecue or chargrill 250 g whole cherry tomatoes, turning over high heat until skins just burst. Roast, peel and thinly slice 2 yellow and 2 red capsicums, then place in a large bowl with chargrilled cherry tomatoes, 185 g can Italian-style tuna, drained and flaked into chunks, and $\frac{1}{2}$ cup pitted Kalamata olives. In a bowl, combine $\frac{1}{4}$ cup extra virgin olive oil, the juice of 1 lemon and $\frac{1}{4}$ tsp each ground caraway and ground coriander, pour over salad, season, then toss to combine. Serve topped with 3 halved medium-boiled eggs and flatbread. Serves 4.

Spicy Capsicum Paste

Sometimes called Harissa, this paste is used as a marinade for grilled chicken, lamb or fish, as a table condiment, or with North African dishes such as couscous. It will keep for up to 6 weeks. **Makes 1 cup.**

60 g red capsicums, roasted
1 red chilli
2 cloves garlic, peeled
sea salt
2 tsp coriander seeds
1½ tsp ground cumin
1 tsp caraway seeds
1 tsp fresh mint leaves, chopped
1½ tbsp extra virgin olive oil, plus extra

Remove seeds from capsicums and chilli and slice into pieces. Pound with a mortar and pestle or use a food processor. Crush garlic with a little salt. Blend all the ingredients except oil into a paste. Stir in oil. Transfer to a jar, cover with a layer of oil and refrigerate.

Pickled Roasted Capsicums

Delicious served with cold meats and olives, or used as a topping for pizza. These capsicums can be eaten immediately, but are best kept for one month before eating. Sealed jars can be stored for 4–5 months. **Makes 2 x 1-litre clip-seal jars.**

1.4 kg mixed red and yellow capsicums, halved and seeds removed
600 ml cider vinegar
1 tbsp sugar
2 tsp black peppercorns
1 tsp allspice
1 tbsp salt
2 dried red chillies
2 bay leaves

Place capsicums, skin side up, on a grill pan and cook under a preheated grill for 8–10 minutes until skin is charred. Place in a plastic food bag and allow to cool.

Meanwhile, pour vinegar into a large saucepan or preserving pan. Add sugar, black peppercorns, allspice and salt. Bring to the boil, reduce heat and simmer for 10 minutes. Allow to cool slightly.

Peel skin from the capsicums. Slice into thick strips and pack into warm sterilised jars (see page 18) with the dried chillies and bay leaves. Strain warm vinegar through a sieve into a clean jug. Pour vinegar slowly into the jars of capsicums until completely covered. Seal well and label.

Red Capsicum Salad

This salad may be served hot or at room temperature – preferably not cold from the fridge. **Serves 6.**

4 small red onions, peeled
8 red capsicums
50 ml olive oil
3 cloves garlic, peeled and chopped
5 tbsp sun-dried tomatoes, finely sliced with oil
125 g spicy Italian salami, sliced and cut in thin strips
250 g small black Niçoise olives
2–3 fresh oregano leaves

Preheat oven to 200 °C/400 °F. Place onions in a bowl, cover with boiling water and allow to stand for 2 minutes. Cut each capsicum into quarters, remove pith and seeds and cut each quarter crosswise into 2 or 3 pieces. Drain onions and cut into quarters.

Oil a shallow baking dish with olive oil and place the capsicums skin side down. Separate the onion quarters into 'petals' and scatter them over the capsicums. Add garlic and drizzle over some oil from the sun-dried tomatoes. Bake in oven for 15–20 minutes or until capsicums are just tender.

Remove from oven and scatter sun-dried tomatoes, salami and olives over the capsicums and sprinkle with some oregano leaves. Return to the oven and cook for a further 15 minutes, or until the capsicums are well cooked and beginning to colour around the edges. Allow to cool until capsicums are warm and serve on a flat platter, seasoned with salt and pepper.

Spanish Chargrilled Capsicums (pictured)

In Spanish bars and brasseries, capsicums are used in tapas meals. These chargrilled capsicums can be served as is, or folded around some fried fish, cheese or barbecued meats. **Serves 4.**

4 red capsicums
4 yellow capsicums
50 g anchovy fillets in oil, drained and halved lengthways
12 black Spanish olives, halved
salt and freshly ground black pepper
to garnish, fresh marjoram or oregano leaves
100 ml extra virgin olive oil

Cut capsicums lengthways into quarters and remove the seeds. Place capsicums, skin side up, under a preheated grill and grill until the skins have charred and blackened. Immediately place the capsicums in a plastic bag and seal with a knot. When the capsicums are cool enough to handle, remove the skins.

Arrange capsicums in a shallow dish with anchovies and olives in between. Season with salt and pepper, scatter on marjoram or oregano and pour on the olive oil. Serve at room temperature.

Brie, Red Capsicum & Leek Omelette (pictured)

Brunch or lunch will be rejuvenated by this dish. Brie can be replaced by any soft rind cheese. This is delicious eaten cold or warm, served with a tasty tomato chutney. **Serves 2–3.**

2 tbsp olive oil
1 red capsicum, peeled and cut into chunks
1 leek, thinly sliced
100 g Brie
½ cup chopped herbs, like parsley, chervil, chives, mint, etc.
6 eggs, beaten
salt and freshly ground black pepper

Preheat oven grill to high. Heat olive oil in an ovenproof frying pan and fry capsicum and leek for 5 minutes, stirring occasionally until softened. Chop Brie roughly into chunks and dot over capsicum and leeks in pan.

Stir a handful of roughly chopped fresh herbs into beaten eggs, then season well and pour over the vegetables and cheese. Cook for 7–8 minutes over a medium heat until just set around the edges.

Grill for 4–5 minutes until omelette is just set, but lightly browned on top. Cut into wedges and serve.

Stuffed Capsicums

This is a meal in itself. The ham can easily be left out for a vegetarian option. This recipe is great reward for the capsicums you grew yourself in your edible garden. **Serves 6.**

6 large red capsicums
25 g butter
1 small leek, finely chopped
250 g button mushrooms, quartered
350 g ham, chopped
2 tbsp wholegrain mustard
¼ cup fresh parsley, chopped
70 g pine nuts, roasted
1 tbsp oil

Cheese Sauce
50 g butter
80 g plain flour
600 ml milk
250 g tasty cheese, grated
150 g fresh Parmesan, grated
120 g mozzarella, grated

Preheat oven to 180 °C/350 °F. Cut tops off capsicums and put to one side. Cut a thin layer off the bottom so capsicums sit flat. Remove seeds and membrane. Heat butter in a pan, add leek and mushrooms. Cook, stirring, until leek is soft. Transfer to a bowl, add ham, mustard, parsley and nuts. Mix together well.

To make the cheese sauce, heat butter in a pan. Add flour, cook, stirring, for 1 minute. Gradually add milk, stir until sauce begins to boil. Stir in cheeses, simmer for about 10 minutes, stirring occasionally, or until sauce thickens.

Stir cheese sauce into ham mixture. Spoon into capsicums, replace reserved tops. Brush capsicums evenly with oil, place in an ovenproof dish. Cook uncovered in oven for about 25 minutes, or until capsicums are tender.

Carrots

Daucus carota

How could you survive in a kitchen without carrots? After potatoes and onions, they are one of the most commonly used vegetables. They are nutritious, sweet and provide so much flavour and colour to many dishes.

Many find carrots a challenge to grow and often we think it is easier to buy them. But there is nothing like the crispness and freshness of flavour of a bunch of sweet autumn carrots pulled from your own garden. The tops of the carrot plants can look attractive as well, draping over the side of a deep and colourful planter.

Carrots have been around forever, as remains have been found in prehistoric lake dwellings in Switzerland. Carrots have been cultivated since the seventeenth century and in fact were grown in gardens as a lace plant to fill spaces in the annual herb garden. The leaves and seeds were used far more than the enlarged roots.

When the roots were finally eaten, it was discovered they are a good source of carotene and vitamin A for good eyesight, and vitamin C for good overall health. They are a brilliant source of fibre and contain quite a lot of natural sugars, which makes the taste very appealing to all age groups. Ever met someone who didn't like carrots?

HOW TO GROW

For small-space gardening, I prefer to have a special deep tub for carrots only. Make sure the soil is rich and full of organic blood and bone, but most importantly that it is a fine soil with no lumps, or mulched up sticks. In a large tub I like to use a seed mix.

Carrots don't grow successfully from transplanting, so the better you are at sowing the seed the first time round the better the results. Sow when the weather is warm and frosts have gone. The seeds are very fine, so carefully place each seed about 2–3 cm apart. You may still need to thin them out later. Cover seeds with a thin layer of soil and water well while the seedlings appear. Some carrot seedlings can take two weeks to show.

As carrots mature you need at least 4–5 cm between each one. The wider spacing helps with the harvest. To be extra cunning, grow 2–3 tubs of seeds 3–4 weeks apart. This way, you'll have a continuing supply over the season. Don't feed carrots, it only promotes the leafy tops to become fuller. Water them when the soil is dry, but don't over-water.

PICKING & STORING

When the foliage begins to wilt and shrivel up, the carrots have reached maturity, but they can be picked early for sweeter and smaller roots. Use a fork to get the roots up, being careful not to break away the ends or pull off the top leaves and leave the root behind.

Fresh — Carrots will keep for a month in a cool dark place or fridge. Try not to put them in plastic bags – use paper bags instead.

Freeze — Peel and trim the stems. Slice the carrots into rounds, half rounds or cut into matchsticks. Whatever the cut, make sure the pieces are roughly the same size. Bring a pot of water to the boil. Plunge the carrot pieces in batches into the water and cook for about 1 minute. Remove from the water using a slotted spoon and plunge into a bowl of ice-cold water. Once cooled completely, drain well and lay the pieces on a plastic tray. Place the tray in the freezer and chill overnight. Next day, collect the pieces into a freezer bag, seal and label. The carrot pieces should last for about three months.

Preserve — Carrots are best preserved in vinegars or made into jams (see carrot and orange jam page 74). Ideally, to keep the fresh taste of carrots alive for the year, freezing is the best method of preserving, but vinegar can make smaller baby carrots tangy for an antipasto platter.

CULINARY USES

Carrots are most commonly used in soups and stews and savoury dishes. A traditional mirepoix is the combination of diced carrot, celery and onion, and is used as a flavour base for many French dishes. Because of their sweetness carrots can be baked into desserts, pies and cakes.

Carrots complement the flavours of most other vegetables, nuts, meats, grains and spices and work well with flavourings like dill, caraway seeds, parsley, coriander and chervil. The sweetness means that in Asia they are paired with sour flavours and used for jams and pickles. Most commonly they will be found grated in coleslaws, julienned in stews or diced in packets of frozen peas and corn.

Peeling a carrot is more necessary when the carrot is mature, but for some younger, smaller carrots, scrub them well and leave the skin on. Scraping the surface of the carrots with the blade of a sharp knife can be easier than peeling and wastes less of the carrot.

Oven-roasting carrots brings out the sweetness, caramelising the natural sugars and making them very tender. To roast, slice into chunks, arrange them in a single layer in a roasting dish, dot with butter or olive oil and bake covered for 45 minutes on 180 °C/350 °F.

QUICK PICKINGS

Carrot & Ginger Soup

Fry 1 onion with 2-cm piece fresh grated ginger and 2–3 cloves garlic in a little butter. Add 4 grated carrots and cook for 10 minutes. Add 1 litre of hot chicken or vegetable stock and simmer 30 minutes. Allow to cool slightly before blending. Serve sprinkled with chopped parsley and a swirl of cream.

Glazed Carrots

Steam sliced carrots for 5–8 minutes. Meanwhile melt 25 g butter with ½ cup brown sugar and 2 tbsp orange juice in a frying pan. Toss the carrots with the butter mixture and serve hot. Garnish with toasted chopped walnuts or pecans.

Mashed Potato & Carrots

Peel 750 g large carrots and 1 kg floury potatoes. Combine carrots and potatoes in a pan and add enough water to come halfway up side of pan. Add 250 g onions, chopped roughly, and season with salt and freshly ground black pepper. Bring to boil then simmer, with a lid on the pan, until vegetables are tender, about 30 minutes. Check from time to time to ensure the water has not evaporated, adding a few tbsp warm water, if necessary, to maintain the level. Drain. Mash vegetables with butter and adjust seasoning if necessary.

Carrots À l'Allemande

Peel and slice 700 g carrots. Cook in a pot of boiling water for 10–15 minutes, until tender. Drain and return to the pot. Add 50 g butter, ½ chopped onion, and 600 ml chicken stock. Cook for another 5 minutes. Drain, then stir in ¼ tsp nutmeg and 1 tbsp chopped parsley. Season with salt and freshly ground black pepper.

Carrots With Cider

Peel and slice 700 g carrots. Cook them in a pot of boiling water for 10–15 minutes, until tender. Drain off the liquid, leaving them in the pot. Add 75 g butter and when melted stir in 4 tbsp of cream gradually. Season with salt and pepper. Add 150 ml cider gradually and a few drops of lemon juice. Heat to reduce the sauce, for about 8 minutes. Serve immediately.

Carrot Coleslaw

Peel 350 g young carrots and finely grate. Peel and grate 2 eating apples, finely slice 300 g green cabbage leaves and peel and dice 1 orange. Place all in a large bowl and sprinkle with lemon juice to prevent browning. Make a dressing by mixing 3 tbsp olive oil with 4 tbsp sunflower oil, 3 tbsp lemon juice, 1 clove crushed garlic, 4 tbsp natural unsweetened yoghurt, and 1 tbsp chopped fresh parsley. Season to taste with salt and freshly ground black pepper. Pour dressing over vegetables. Toss together and serve on a platter.

Garlic & Lemon Carrots

Put 1 kg peeled and sliced carrots in a steamer basket set over boiling water. Steam for about 5 minutes, until tender. Reserve cooking water and mix 5 tbsp of it with ½ tsp Tabasco sauce. Heat 2 tbsp oil in a large frying pan over a medium heat. Add 3 cloves thinly sliced garlic, the hot sauce, juice of 1 lemon, 2 tsp toasted and crushed cumin seeds, ½ tsp salt and ½ tsp sugar. Mix well. Add carrots, then partially cover and cook over medium heat for about 10 minutes, until the liquid is reduced. Stir in 2 tbsp fresh chopped mint leaves and serve at once.

Simple Carrot Salad

Peel and finely grate 1 kg carrots. Mix together 250 g mayonnaise, 500 g raisins, ½ cup light muscovado sugar and ¼ cup cider vinegar and add to the carrots. Cover and leave overnight in the fridge for best flavour.

Asian Carrot Salad

Whisk together ⅔ cup orange juice with small piece freshly grated ginger and ½ tsp soy sauce, 2 tsp sesame oil, and 2 tbsp white wine vinegar. Season with salt and then pour over 500 g finely grated carrots. Chill. Sprinkle with toasted sesame seeds and sliced spring onions before serving.

Carrot, Apple & Ginger Juice

If you don't have a juicer, you can replace home-made apple juice with three cups of non-alcoholic sparkling cider (the flavour will be sweeter than Granny Smith apple juice). Increase carrot juice to four cups and use a good quality fresh juice (not canned). Juice ginger by finely grating, then forcing pulp through a fine-mesh sieve. **Makes about 6½ cups.**

2 kg Granny Smith apples
1.5 kg carrots, peeled and trimmed
2.5-cm piece fresh ginger, peeled
to serve, fresh mint leaves

Slice apples. Process enough slices in juicer, skimming and discarding any foam, to measure 4 cups juice, then transfer to a large jug. Process enough carrots, skimming and discarding any foam, to measure 3½ cups juice, then add to large jug with apple juice.

Process ginger, then stir 2 tbsp ginger juice into jug. Chill until cold, about 2 hours. Serve over ice, if desired. Garnish with mint leaves.

Creamy Carrot Pie

Fabulous carrots make this a great pie. Take the effort to make your own pastry and it tastes even better. A perfect meal for your vegetarian guests, or something different for your Sunday dinner or any night of the week. **Serves 6.**

Pastry
500 g flour
pinch salt
600 g butter, chilled
cold water

Filling
9 medium carrots
50 ml cream
salt and freshly ground black pepper
25 g butter
pinch of sugar
1 sprig lemon thyme, finely chopped
1 sprig parsley, finely chopped
1 clove garlic, peeled and crushed
to glaze, 1 egg yolk beaten with 1 tbsp milk

To make the pastry, put flour, salt and 100 g of the butter into food processor. Blend until it resembles breadcrumbs. Add enough water to mix to a stiff dough. Wrap the dough in plastic wrap and chill in fridge for 2 hours.

Preheat oven to 220 °C/440 °F. Roll out dough on a floured board into a square shape, and cover half with remaining butter, cut in 1-cm-thick slices. Fold over pastry to neatly enclose the butter, and roll out the dough. Fold into three layers and roll out again. Fold and roll twice more.

To make the filling, peel and wash 6 carrots, cut into chunks and boil until tender, about 15 minutes. Drain, add cream and boil for 5 minutes. Place mixture in a food processor and blend to a purée. Season to taste.

Peel and wash remaining three carrots and cut three or four little grooves down their length. Cut into 3-mm slices, place in a shallow pan with a little water, butter and sugar, and cook until carrots are soft but firm to the bite. The cooking liquid should be quite thick (if it isn't, remove carrots, reduce liquid and return carrots to the pan). Add thyme, parsley and garlic.

To assemble the pie, roll out half the pastry to 5 mm thick on a well-floured board. Line a deep 26-cm flan dish with pastry. Spoon in carrot purée and top with carrot and herb mixture. Roll out other half of pastry and spread over top of flan dish. Brush edges with beaten egg and push together with fingers to seal. Brush pastry top with egg and slice a small hole in the top to allow air to escape. Bake until puffed and brown, about 15–20 minutes.

Spiced Carrot & Saffron Soup

Enrich your kitchen with the sweet smell of saffron. The golden threads bring delight to your home-grown carrots. The saffron can be replaced by turmeric, but you won't really want to. Saffron is worth the effort. **Serves 4–6.**

450 g carrots
2 tbsp olive or sunflower oil
25 g butter
1 large onion, peeled and chopped
1 clove garlic, peeled and crushed
1 tsp ground cumin
2 tsp ground coriander
pinch (about 10–12 threads) saffron, infused in 2 tbsp warm water
1 litre chicken or vegetable stock
sea salt and freshly ground black pepper
1 orange, juice of
to serve, 1 tsp cumin seeds
150 g natural unsweetened yoghurt

Scrub carrots thoroughly and remove tops, then slice lengthways and dice. Heat oil in a deep saucepan, add butter, carrots, onion and garlic. Coat vegetables thoroughly with butter and oil, then turn heat down and allow to cook slowly, covered, until they begin to soften, about 5 minutes.

Stir in ground cumin and coriander and cook for a couple more minutes. Strain saffron-infused water, removing the threads. Add saffron water and stock to the pan and bring to the boil. Reduce heat and simmer, uncovered, for 30 minutes, or until carrots are soft.

Remove from the heat and leave to cool for 10 minutes, then push the contents of the pan through a sieve or whizz in a blender or food processor. Return soup to the pan, heat through and adjust the seasonings to taste, then add a good squeeze of orange juice.

To serve, deep-fry cumin seeds briefly in a pan until they begin to pop and turn dark brown. Ladle soup into bowls, top each with a swirl of yoghurt and scatter with a few roasted cumin seeds.

Carrot & Parsnip Tarte Tatin (pictured)

Carrots and parsnips caramelise wonderfully when cooked with honey and flavoured with soy sauce. **Serves 4.**

Pastry
200 g plain flour
pinch salt
100 g butter, cubed
1 egg yolk
cold water
2 tsp sesame seeds
1 tbsp fresh thyme, chopped
1 tbsp fresh rosemary, chopped

Topping
1 tbsp olive oil
450 g carrots, halved lengthways
450 g parsnips, halved lengthways
25 g butter
120 ml orange juice
2 tbsp soy sauce
3 tbsp clear honey
salt and freshly ground black pepper

To make the pastry, place flour, salt, and butter in a food processor. Blend until the mixture resembles breadcrumbs. Add egg yolk and enough cold water to form a dough. Finally add sesame seeds, thyme and rosemary. Wrap dough in plastic wrap and chill for at least 1 hour.

Preheat oven to 200 °C/400 °F. Heat oil in a 23–25-cm ovenproof frying pan, add carrots and parsnips and cook until golden. Add butter, orange juice, soy sauce, honey and seasoning, cook for 5 minutes until vegetables are caramelised in a syrupy sauce.

Roll out pastry on a floured board to 6-mm thick. Cut a round of pastry to the size of the frying pan. Place pastry on top of carrots and parsnips and place pan in centre of oven. Bake for 20 minutes until pastry is golden brown and crispy. Cool for 5 minutes. To serve, very carefully invert the whole dish onto a serving plate.

Carrot & Raisin Salad

Pack this salad into containers for the kids' school lunches or a picnic. The cashews can easily be left out for anyone who suffers allergies. Just add more bean sprouts to give more crunch. **Serves 4.**

4 carrots, peeled
125 g bean sprouts
120 g raisins
½ telegraph cucumber
125 g shelled, unsalted cashew nuts
2 tsp sesame seeds
150 ml orange juice
2 tsp wine vinegar
1 tsp light soy sauce
2 tsp clear honey

Grate carrots into a large bowl. Add bean sprouts and raisins. Cut cucumber into thin strips and toss together with carrot mixture. Add nuts and sesame seeds. Mix together orange juice, vinegar, soy sauce and honey and pour over the salad. Toss and serve immediately.

TART

Carrot & Vanilla Cake

This makes a shallow cake, which can be cut into shapes. Mascarpone, fromage frais or cream cheese are all perfect as the icing on this cake. **Serves 8.**

250 g unsalted butter
6 tbsp demerara sugar
1 tbsp molasses
5 eggs
300 g gluten-free flour
1 tbsp baking powder
1 whole vanilla pod
500 g carrots, peeled and grated
250 g mascarpone cheese
2 tsp icing sugar, sifted

Preheat oven to 190 °C/375 °F. Lightly grease a 20-cm round cake tin and line the base with baking paper.

Cream butter, sugar and molasses in a processor or with an electric whisk, until really creamy and smooth. Add eggs one at a time and beat well after each addition. Sift flour and baking powder and fold in. Halve the vanilla pod and scrape inner seeds out using a sharp knife. Stir vanilla seeds and carrots into the mixture.

Pour cake mixture into prepared cake tin, smoothing down on top. Bake for 40–50 minutes until well risen and firm. Cool in tin for 10 minutes or so, then turn out to cool on a wire rack. When cool, beat mascarpone with icing sugar until creamy. Spread over cake and serve.

Carrot & Orange Jam

All the sweetness of carrots comes out in this tasty jam. It is a great condiment to serve with antipasto and cheese platters, or as a filling in brown bread sandwiches. It will store well for a few months, if it lasts that long. **Makes 6 x 300-g jars.**

50 g yellow mustard seeds
50 g celery seeds
2 tbsp rice bran oil
4 large carrots, peeled and chopped
1 litre cider vinegar
350 g caster sugar
350 ml fresh orange juice
2 oranges, zest of

Gently fry the mustard and celery seeds in oil, drain on absorbent paper and set aside. Place remaining ingredients in a saucepan, bring to the boil, reduce heat and simmer until the sauce has thickened and carrots are soft. Remove from heat and cool.

In a food processor or with a stick blender, blend mixture to a purée and mix in the cold seeds. Leave to cool and pour into cold sterilised jars (see page 18). Seal well.

Pickled Carrots

Another good way of preserving carrots. These are best used in antipasto platters and salads, or just left as a nutritious snack. **Makes 2 x 1-litre clip-seal jars.**

500 g carrots, peeled
80 g sugar
500 ml white wine vinegar
2 tsp allspice
2 tsp peppercorns

Cut carrots into finger lengths, halved or quartered along the length, and blanch for 5 minutes or until just soft. Drain and set aside to cool.

Place sugar, vinegar, allspice and peppercorns in a saucepan, boil for 3 minutes, and then set aside to cool. Pack carrots into sterilised jars and pour over the cooled pickling syrup. Seal the jars and set aside in a cool place for three days before serving.

Chillies

Capsicum chinense (habanero)

Chillies are fascinating edible things. They look like harmless, colourful pods and resemble butterfly cocoons rather than the heat-packed, taste-bud destroyers that they can be. Relatively easy to grow in the right climates, it's always good to have a pot full of fresh chilli plants for eating pleasure. However, beware! Unlike the serene butterfly, these cocoons will unleash fury on the unsuspecting cook.

Many types of chillies are available and plants can be grown from the seeds of any dried chilli. The colours are deceitful, however – whereas we think red means fire, and of course some of the hotter chillies are fire engine red, the hottest of them all is the small green bird's eye chilli. Only the hardiest Thailand natives will eat a meal with more than 1–2 in a dish. Amazingly, I have seen a man eat 13 green bird's eye chillies in his green papaya salad, like we would eat honey on toast.

Chillies have health benefits – they are rich in vitamins A and C and were often carried on ships as an important source of vitamins to prevent scurvy. They can heat the blood, and many cultures believe that different chillies will give internal health to different organs in your body.

What we have to remember is to take care: care in the garden, that no unsuspecting child treats them as a sweet fruit; care in the kitchen when removing seeds and slicing; and care when eating. Start slowly, try a small amount of chilli at a time, and if you need to act tough and over-indulge, keep a large glass of cold milk to one side!

HOW TO GROW

The capsicum plant that is chilli is perfect to grow in pots. They can be moved around to the warmest part of your garden or balcony. They like deep pots with rich fertile soil. There are many types available to grow from seed. Germination will be more effective if the seeds are soaked for a couple of minutes in a bleach solution (1 part bleach: 10 parts water) and then well rinsed before sowing. Seedlings from a good plant shop will provide an easy alternative and allow you to try your hand at a few different varieties at once. Chillies are quite prolific, one or two plants will give enough whole chillies for one season.

Chilli peppers require a warm climate and warm soil to grow well, so don't rush to plant them out. Late September to early November is fine. Also, don't water young plants with cold water straight from the tap, remember they originate from very warm countries.

Once the seedlings are in flower, feed with tomato fertiliser, but less generously than recommended for tomatoes. Chilli plants are perennials and can be kept for another year, so don't pull them after one season. You may want to transfer them to a warm part of your garden or even inside.

Repot them in early September for the new growth to come again. Snails can eat the leaves and fruit (obviously silly snails are able to handle the heat!).

PICKING & STORING

Pick chillies from the plants often and they will continue to provide more and more fruit. Green pods can be picked for a strong, raw taste, or wait for the flesh to turn red for a sweeter heat.

Fresh — Pick fresh chillies when they are clean, firm and glossy. Store in a polythene bag in the fridge for up to two weeks.

Freeze — Keep in a plastic freezer bag, sealed, for up to one year – unless you want the seeds, in which case take these out before freezing.

Preserve — Chillies are great to preserve in many ways – paste, oil, vinegar, or even vodka (see quick pickings page 79). It is up to you when you introduce these flavours into your cooking. Jars of preserved chillies make excellent presents.

Dried — To dry out chillies, choose the long, thin-fleshed variety, and then string them up using a needle and long piece of strong thread. As chillies dry they give off volatile oils, which can be irritating, so don't put them in the airing cupboard next to your underwear. Rather, choose an area out of the way where lots of air can circulate around them. Use within six months.

CULINARY USES

Chillies can accompany many different flavours. They are great with acid fruits and vegetables like tomatoes and citrus. They are best served with herbs that aid digestion like tarragon, parsley and especially coriander, which is said to help the breakdown of chilli in the gut. Asian flavours like nam pla (fish sauce), sesame, ginger, soy and onions are natural companions to chillies. Sweetening up chillies by roasting or adding sugar or palm sugar doesn't take away heat but creates a wonderful flavour in many dishes.

The release of capsaicinoids, which hold the spiciness of the chilli, depends on how the peppers are cooked. Frying in oil releases all the fire but tends to vaporise some of the more interesting flavours if overdone. On the other hand, putting raw hot chillies into a blender, along with the other ingredients of a salsa, and then cooking, seems to release the characteristic flavour but only moderate heat.

Cook's Tip

Warning: Handle chillies with care – capsaicin, the burning oil in chillies, can burn sensitive areas and the heat can transfer from your hands to someone else. Always take care when preparing! The safest way is to wear thin rubber gloves, split open the chilli and scoop out and discard the seeds and white membrane (the hottest parts). Remember to wash the chopping board and any utensils used afterwards with extra hot soapy water. If your skin does come into contact with chilli and it burns, bathe the area in milk to soothe it; eyes are particularly vulnerable, so remember not to rub them (or go to the toilet!) straight after chopping chillies. If your mouth is burning after eating a hot mouthful, don't reach for cold water or beer. Dairy products like milk or yoghurt calm things down best.

TYPES OF CHILLI

Some people say small chillies are hotter than large; red are hotter than green; and thinner are hotter than fatter. But there are always exceptions, so if in doubt, use less rather than more and add extra to taste. Red chillies are simply ripe green chillies and have a sweeter, more rounded flavour. As with grapes, a fertile, nutrient-rich soil will give chillies a more intense flavour.

Jalapeño — Probably the best known chilli. It's frequently sold labelled as red or green chilli. The seeds have their own sharp flavour, so they are often not removed before cooking. Smoke-dried red jalapeños are known as chipotle chillies.

Dutch — A thick-fleshed chilli, with a sweet, hot flavour. Most commonly found in salsas, it also makes a pretty decoration – make several slits from the base to the tip, place in cold water and wait for the chilli to curl up.

Habanero — One of the hottest on earth! It has a floral flavour, making it ideal for salsas and Mexican food. Available in green, yellow and red. But beware!

Bird's eye or Thai — This fiery chilli is used in Thai cooking. It is often added to dishes whole as a finishing flavour or garnish. Look for dried or fresh ones in supermarkets and Asian shops.

QUICK PICKINGS

Green Curry Paste

With a pestle and mortar, grind together 2 deseeded and chopped fresh green chillies, 2 roughly chopped garlic cloves, 1 tsp salt, 3 roughly chopped shallots, 1 tbsp chopped lemongrass, 1 tbsp coriander seeds, 2.5-cm piece grated fresh ginger and 2 tbsp lime juice. Store in an airtight container in the fridge for up to two weeks. Add to curries, soups and stews.

Red Chilli Paste

Cook 225 g red chillies in boiling water for 2 minutes. Drain. Purée in a food processor with ½ tsp salt, 1 tbsp white wine vinegar, 2 tbsp hot water and 1 tbsp vegetable oil. Transfer to a pan and simmer gently for 8–10 minutes, stirring frequently. Allow to cool, then store in the fridge and use in place of fresh chillies; 1 tsp is equivalent to one fresh chilli. Or pour into ice cube trays and freeze. Each cube is equivalent to about 3 chillies. There is no need to thaw before use.

Chillies in Oil

Gently heat 600 ml vegetable oil, then add four halved, fresh medium-hot red chillies and cook gently for 5 minutes. Set aside overnight for the flavour and colour to develop. Next day, strain the oil into sterilised bottles and seal. Store for up to 6 months. Use the chilli oil as flavouring – add a drop to salad dressings or cooked pasta, brush over grilled fish or stir a little into tomato-based sauces. Or float a fresh chilli in the oil and serve as a condiment.

Chilli Vodka

Choose a decorative bottle that is able to go into the freezer. Prick 8 small bird's eye chillies, and 5 small thin green chillies all over with a fork and add these to the bottle. Pour in the vodka and make sure the chillies are covered. If you like to serve your vodka icy cold, put it in the freezer after a week. To finish the bottle off, tie some ribbon around the neck. This vodka will keep indefinitely. A shot of this chilli vodka added to wintery soups and Bloody Marys peps up the flavour no end. Or you could, of course, always drink it neat. Remember that the longer you leave the chillies in the vodka, the hotter it will be!

Sweet Chilli Sauce

Make your own version of sweet chilli sauce to go with all your Asian foods and to give a condiment kick to any meal. Lasts up to two weeks in the fridge. **Makes about 250 ml.**

2 tsp sesame oil
1 red chilli, finely chopped
2.5-cm piece fresh ginger root, peeled and finely chopped
1 clove garlic, peeled and crushed
8 tbsp soft brown sugar
2 tsp fish sauce
2 tbsp light soy sauce
8 tbsp water
2 limes, juice of

Place oil in a saucepan and heat gently. Add chillies, ginger and garlic and cook for 1–2 minutes until softened. Add sugar, fish and soy sauce, then bring to the boil and simmer for 2 minutes.

Remove from heat, stir in water and lime juice. Pour into a serving bowl.

Barbecue Chilli Mussels

When barbecuing mussels, make sure they all open. Mussels that don't fully open are more than likely off and not good for eating. Don't even try to prise them open. Keep plenty of moisture around the mussels so the flesh doesn't dry out. **Serves 6.**

1.5 kg live green mussels in the shells
1 tsp paprika or smoked paprika
1½ tbsp caster sugar
2 tsp salt
75 ml olive oil
1 whole fresh red chilli, seeds removed and finely chopped

Wash mussels, pulling off beards and scraping off any other debris. Discard any mussels that are damaged or don't close when tapped. Mix remaining ingredients together in a small bowl.

Tip mussels onto a hot barbecue grill or grill plate. Pour over a little water as they begin to cook to stop the flesh from drying out. Barbecue for a few minutes until they all open. If any don't open, they probably won't and these ones are not good for eating.

Dribble a little marinade mix into each mussel and cook for a further 1–2 minutes until liquid has reduced. If you're using a grill plate, you can pull off the top shell and turn them over for another minute to caramelise the marinade, but be careful not to overcook. Serve immediately with crusty bread and sweet chilli sauce (see page 79).

Chilli Roast Chicken

Chilli goes all around this chicken, so use a mild type if you can't take the heat. Whole chillies are used to flavour the potatoes, but you don't have to eat them. **Serves 4.**

8 medium-hot fresh red chillies
4 tbsp olive oil
2 tsp each coriander and cumin seeds
1 tsp ground turmeric
2.5-cm piece fresh ginger root, peeled and chopped
3 cloves garlic, peeled and roughly chopped
1 handful fresh coriander leaves
½ tsp salt
1.3–1.8 kg chicken
900 g potatoes, cut into large chunks
25 g butter, melted

Halve four chillies and take out seeds. Roughly chop the flesh. Put in a food processor or blender with oil, coriander and cumin seeds, turmeric, ginger, garlic, fresh coriander and salt. Whizz to a rough paste that is still chunky (or pound together with a pestle and mortar). Reserve 2 tbsp of the paste, cover and set aside.

Starting at the neck end of the bird, slide your hands under the skin to loosen it from the breast; take care not to pierce it. Smear half the remaining paste over breast under skin. Smooth skin back over it. Spread remaining paste all over chicken, then transfer to a non-metallic dish. Cover loosely with plastic wrap and chill for at least 2 hours or overnight.

Preheat oven to 190 °C/375 °F. Put chicken in a large roasting tin and surround with potatoes and remaining 4 whole chillies. Roast for 1 hour, turning potatoes once or twice.

Mix reserved chilli paste with melted butter and drizzle over potatoes. Return to the oven and roast for another 20–40 minutes, basting and turning the potatoes twice. Serve with steamed vegetables.

Pan-Fried Fish with Chilli & Ginger Dressing

A simple supper with oodles of flavour as well as a touch of heat. To give the fish a lovely crispy skin, make sure the oil is good and hot before adding the fillets. Also, use a large pan, so they can cook evenly in one layer. **Serves 2.**

1 tbsp flour
salt and freshly ground black pepper
4 small fish fillets, e.g. John Dory, skin on
4 tbsp olive oil
200 g spinach, stems removed and washed
5-cm piece fresh ginger root, peeled and cut into very thin slivers
1 red chilli, deseeded and sliced
½ lime, juice of
3 spring onions, cut into strips
to serve, 1–2 tsp toasted sesame seeds

Season flour with salt and pepper on a plate, and use to coat the fish. Heat 1 tbsp of oil in a non-stick frying pan and fry fillets, skin side down, for 2–3 minutes until skin is crisp. Turn and fry for 2 more minutes or until cooked. Remove and keep warm.

Add spinach to pan and stir until it wilts. The leaves will cook in the water that clings to the leaves after it is washed and will be done in no more than 30 seconds. Press lightly in a sieve to remove excess water. Keep warm.

Wipe frying pan, add remaining oil and heat. Add ginger and chilli and fry for about 1 minute until softened. Stir in lime juice. Remove from the heat and stir in spring onions. The warmth from the pan should heat them through, softening them very slightly without losing their colour and shape. Divide spinach between two warm plates. Top each with two fish fillets, skin side up, and season with salt and pepper. Pile ginger and chilli on top, then spoon dressing from pan over and around the fish. Sprinkle with sesame seeds to serve.

Mexican Chilli Pot (pictured)

Traditionally chillies are ground for this dish. It is a great dish to freeze for up to six months. Bring it out and reheat when the nights are cold and serve with hot baked potatoes and lashings of sour cream. **Serves 4.**

1 tsp hot chilli powder
1 tsp each ground cumin and paprika
1 tsp oregano
450 g lean pork, cut into cubes
3 tbsp vegetable oil
1 large onion, peeled and finely chopped
1 red capsicum, deseeded and cut into chunks
2 red chillies, seeds removed
2 cloves garlic, peeled and finely chopped
400-g can whole peeled tomatoes
2 tbsp tomato purée
1 tbsp brown sugar
150 ml chicken stock
150 ml red wine
400-g can kidney beans, drained
salt and freshly ground black pepper
to serve, sour cream and chopped fresh parsley

Mix together spices and herbs and toss with pork. Heat 2 tbsp of oil in a pan, add meat and fry for 2 minutes, and then remove from pan. Add remaining oil, onion, capsicum, chillies and garlic to the pan and fry for 4–5 minutes until golden. Return meat to the pan.

Stir in tomatoes, purée, sugar, stock, wine and beans. Cover and cook gently for 1 hour until meat is tender and stew has the consistency of a chunky soup. Season well with salt and freshly ground black pepper. Serve with sour cream and parsley.

Chilli & Green Capsicum Jelly

This jelly isn't for the faint-hearted. It packs a punch. It should be served with strong Spanish cured meats or a summer barbecue, and the serious chilli lover would eat it on their toast. To serve as a canapé, spread crackers with cream cheese and then the jelly. **Makes 600 ml.**

6 green chillies
1 green capsicum
250 ml cider vinegar
4 cups sugar
50 g pectin/jam sugar (see page 21)
green food colouring

Cut chillies in half lengthwise and remove seeds. Finely chop the flesh. Discard seeds from green capsicum and chop. Purée chillies and capsicum in a blender or food processor. Put into a saucepan with vinegar and bring to the boil. Reduce heat and simmer for 10 minutes.

Pour purée into a sieve over a bowl and leave to drain for 15 minutes. Press gently with the back of a wooden spoon to extract liquid. Remember that it is a jelly that is being made. Discard pulp. Return pepper liquid to saucepan and add sugar. Dissolve sugar over a low heat while stirring. Bring to the boil, add pectin sugar, and boil for 1 minute.

Remove from heat and carefully add 2–3 drops of green food colouring. Skim off foam, and pour into sterilised jars (see page 18), then seal.

Chilli & Pineapple Salsa

Serve with grilled fish, chicken or ham steaks or use inside flour tortillas with meat and vegetables. **Makes 2 cups.**

2 whole red Jalapeño chillies
1 small fresh pineapple
50 ml olive oil
1 tbsp runny honey
4 tomatoes
1 tbsp fresh coriander, chopped
1 tbsp fresh mint, chopped
1 lime, juice of

Place whole chillies under a hot grill for 8–10 minutes until charred, turning occasionally. Place in a plastic bag, seal and leave to cool. Peel, remove seeds and finely chop.

Peel pineapple, cut into 1-cm slices and brush with mixture of olive oil and honey. Grill until golden brown and caramelised, about 10–12 minutes, turning once. Allow to cool, then finely dice. Skin, deseed and dice the tomatoes. Mix tomatoes in a bowl with pineapple, chillies, coriander, mint and lime juice. Allow to chill before serving.

Chives

Allium schoenoprasum

Chives are related to leeks and onions and have a delicate flavour – slightly onion, slightly garlic, slightly fresh herb. They give food a sprinkle of colour and a hint of flavour. Great to have in the garden for fresh snippets, but be careful, they do need attention.

For many centuries chives have been added to food, more for medicinal use than flavour. Fresh chives have been known to boost your immune system, reduce cholesterol levels and aid digestion. They are also said to have a mild stimulant effect on the appetite. They are rich in vitamin C and iron, making them good for anaemia, but you would have to eat a lot of them to effect a cure. Bread and butter sandwiches with a generous filling of chives used to be given after fits of whooping cough as a curative.

Chives are native to China and parts of the Himalayas. They are a vital part of the Chinese traditional diet, toning up all the bodily functions, putting pink into a woman's cheeks, and were once regarded as an aphrodisiac! Chives are an ideal salt substitute for those on a low-sodium diet. All alliums (onion family) are reputed to be mildly antibiotic. Regular servings can have beneficial effects on the circulatory, digestive and respiratory systems, and this sulphur-rich food is said to make your hair grow.

HOW TO GROW

Choose a pot or a spot in your garden away from your conventional herbs. They grow well planted out in window boxes or around plants that don't attract aphids. Chives like sun, but not too much; they don't like drying out and certainly need plenty of lush soil to keep going. Healthy chives won't be attacked from sucking insects.

Chives aren't the easiest seeds to grow, often needing very mild conditions to sprout. If you can't succeed with seeds, turn to a plant nursery to buy an established plant. Feed the ground with blood and bone before sowing seeds. Cut back in autumn and add fertiliser to the soil. A light mulch of grass clippings around the bulbous roots will prevent them drying out. Trim away any flower heads to encourage growth.

PICKING & STORING

Pick leaves individually, rather than slicing off tufts at ground level, this enables the plant to grown back again faster.

Fresh — Fresh is best with chives, as the flavour is very delicate. Try not to pick the leaves until they are needed for your cooking.

Dried — Chives can be dried and stored in an airtight container for later use. Finely chopped dried chives can be reconstituted in salads, egg and chicken dishes and vegetable dishes.

Freeze — If you need chives for winter cooking, try picking the chives and snipping to small pieces. Put an amount in each of the holes in an ice cube tray. Fill with water and freeze. The ice cubes will lose flavour over time, so don't leave them too long.

CULINARY USES

Their mild flavour makes chives or garlic chives a superb seasoning for many dishes.

The flowers are milder than the leaves and can also be used in salads. Delicately flavours fish, shellfish and white meat and their accompanying sauces. Chives should be snipped or finely chopped to release the flavour. Remember: lengthy cooking destroys the flavour.

Use the leaves as a garnish for grilled fish or sprinkle into vinaigrette or salad dressing. Chives can provide a more subtle flavour in salads, dressings and sauces than their stronger cousins onions and garlic. Fresh garlic chives give a new garlicky dimension to dishes where garlic might normally be added.

Traditional fast foods like scrambled eggs, omelettes and jacket potatoes are transformed with fresh chives folded in, with or without butter or cream cheese. Cut finely and add to raw savoury pastry – the baked crust will have pleasing specks of green and delicious fresh flavour.

The sheathed flower heads and blanched stems are an important Chinese seasoning – the coarser leaves are used with pork and rice in Chinese cuisine and in stir-fries. Break up the white flowers into florets and sprinkle into salads or use as a garnish.

QUICK PICKINGS

Chive & Cucumber Salad

Peel 2 cucumbers, and remove the seeds by running a teaspoon down the middle. Slice into thin half-rings. Sprinkle with a little sea salt and squeeze a little lemon or lime juice over the top. Finely chop a handful of fresh chives. Sprinkle over the top with freshly ground black pepper. Chill for at least an hour before serving. Serve with main meal and yoghurt and mint dressing.

Baby Potatoes With Lemon & Chives

Wash and steam 450 g potatoes for 12–15 minutes until tender. If preferred, they can be cut in half before cooking. In a separate pan heat 30 g butter, add a handful of chopped chives and finely grated zest of half a lemon. Toss around to release the flavours, then pour over the potatoes and serve.

Garlic Bread

Green up your garlic bread with some freshly chopped garlic chives added to the butter and garlic mixture. Spread between slices of crusty bread, wrap in foil and bake in oven or on barbecue until butter has melted.

Smoked Oysters & Chives

Roughly chop a tin of smoked oysters with 200 g of smoked mussels and 200 g of prawns (fresh or tinned). Stir in 1 tsp Worcestershire sauce and tomato sauce and mix with 2–3 tbsp chopped chives. Serve in lettuce cups.

Bacon & Chive White Sauce

Cook and slice 2 rashers bacon. Melt 25 g butter in a microwave-proof glass jug. Add 2 tbsp plain flour and mix until smooth. Add 250 ml milk, stirring constantly. Cook uncovered in microwave for 4 minutes on high, or until thickened (stir after 2 minutes, then every 30 seconds). Add sliced bacon, 1 tbsp chopped fresh chives, ½ tsp salt and ½ tsp dry mustard powder. Stir well. Serve over vegetables. **Makes about 1 cup.**

Smoked Kahawai & Chive Pâté

Any smoked fish can be used in this quick recipe. Smoked kahawai is found at most supermarkets or good fish shops, or if you are lucky enough to have a fisherman in the family, make use of the kahawai fillets before they use it for bait. **Serves 4.**

- 175 g smoked kahawai, bones and skin removed
- 125 g cream cheese
- 125 g sour cream
- 1 lemon, juice and zest of
- 3 tbsp chives, chopped
- salt and freshly ground black pepper
- pinch cayenne pepper

Place all ingredients in a food processor and process until well blended. Taste and add salt and pepper to season. Tip into a small bowl and either refrigerate for at least 2 hours or freeze for up to 2 months. Serve on oatcakes or cheese crackers.

Chive & Gruyère Flan

Gruyère has a low melting point which often makes it ideal for pastries and tarts. It is a cheese with a very distinctive flavour, and marries well with herbs and cold meats. **Serves 6–8.**

Pastry
200 g plain flour
100 g butter
½ tsp salt
1–2 tbsp cold water
1 egg yolk

Filling
100g Gruyère, grated
1 large tomato, thinly sliced
4 tbsp fresh chopped chives
50 g Parmesan, grated
4 eggs
50 ml cream
salt and freshly ground black pepper

Put flour, butter and salt in a food processor and blend until it resembles breadcrumbs. Add cold water and egg yolk and mix until a soft dough forms. Wrap in plastic wrap and allow to chill for 1 hour in the fridge. When cold, roll out on a floured board.

Preheat oven to 200 °C/400 °F. Grease a 22-cm flan dish. Lay pastry over the top and press down the edges. Cut away any excess. Scatter over the Gruyère. Top with thin slices of tomato. Sprinkle over the chives and Parmesan. Beat eggs and cream together and season with salt and pepper. Pour egg mixture gently over the top of the other ingredients in the flan dish.

Place in centre of oven and bake for 20–25 minutes until golden brown and the egg has set. Remove from oven and allow to cool slightly before serving.

Crab & Chive Orzo Salad

Fresh crab meat is becoming more and more available in our supermarkets. If you can handle the tedium of smashing open crab shells then go ahead, but I prefer to use the ready-to-go in a pottle type. It is sweet and delicious. Of course shrimp or prawns can easily be substituted in this simple salad. **Serves 6.**

500 g orzo pasta
200 g cherry tomatoes, halved
3 spring onions, chopped
400 g crab meat
1 lemon, juice and zest of
salt and freshly ground black pepper
3 tbsp chopped chives
¼ cup mayonnaise
¼ cup yoghurt
1 tsp wholegrain mustard

Cook pasta according to packet instructions until al dente. Drain well, rinse under cold water, drain again and allow to cool. In a large bowl, mix pasta with tomatoes, spring onions, crab meat and lemon zest. Season well with salt and pepper.

Make dressing by mixing lemon juice and remaining ingredients in a small bowl. Whisk well with a fork. Pour over pasta and toss until well coated. Chill and serve.

Cheese & Herb Biscuits

These biscuits can be made 2 days ahead; store in an airtight container. The herb filling can be made ahead and kept refrigerated. The biscuits are best assembled close to serving to allow the filling to soften. **Makes 20 biscuits.**

110 g plain flour
35 g self-raising flour
¼ tsp salt
90 g butter, chopped
90 g finely grated Cheddar
3 egg yolks
2 tsp water

Herb filling
60 g butter, softened
2 tsp finely chopped chives
40 g finely grated Cheddar
salt and freshly ground black pepper

Preheat oven to 200 °C/400 °F. Sift flours and salt into a medium bowl, rub in butter then stir in cheese. Add egg yolks and water, mix to form a dough. Knead on a lightly floured board until smooth.

Roll dough on a lightly floured surface until 3 mm thick, cut out 5 cm rounds. Place rounds on baking paper-lined oven trays and prick with a fork. Bake in a moderately hot oven for about 10 minutes or until browned lightly; cool on a wire rack.

To make herb filling, beat butter with chives until creamy, stir in cheese. Season to taste with salt and pepper. Join two biscuits together with half a teaspoon of the filling, repeat with the remaining biscuits and filling.

Chive, Parmesan & Buttermilk Scones (pictured)

Buttermilk makes scones light and airy. It can be swapped for plain milk or cream but it is well worth it in traditional scones. These scones last for a few days, or can be stored in the freezer for reheating when needed. Serve these scones with lashings of butter or cream cheese. **Makes 12.**

320 g plain flour
1 tsp salt
2 tsp baking powder
50 g butter
¼ cup snipped fresh chives
50 g Parmesan, grated
½ cup buttermilk, approx

Preheat oven to 200 °C/400 °F. Mix flour, salt and baking powder in a large bowl. Rub butter into flour with fingertips until mixture resembles crumbs. Add chives and Parmesan and mix. Slowly add milk and work into a dough using a knife or fingers. The dough should be slightly tacky and sticky in your fingers but not too wet.

Turn dough onto a floured board and roll out to about 3 cm thick. Use cutters or a knife to cut out circles or triangles. Place on a baking tray lined with baking paper. Bake for 20 minutes until golden.

Creamy Salmon & Chives in Pancakes

This is a quick and simple store-cupboard meal. When there is nothing else in the house a few fresh chives will give this creamy salmon dish some fresh flavour. Canned smoked fish works equally well with this creamy sauce. **Serves 4.**

415-g can pink or red salmon
600 ml milk
50 g butter
2 tbsp cornflour
salt and freshly ground black pepper
½ tsp mustard powder
2–3 tbsp chopped chives, plus extra

Pancakes
75 g self-raising flour
25 g wholemeal flour
½ tsp salt
1 egg
150 ml milk
butter for frying

Drain salmon, and remove any bones and grey skin. Put flaked salmon in a saucepan with milk. Bring to the heat and simmer, but do not let it boil. Remove from heat. Add butter and leave to melt. Mix cornflour with a little cold milk, until dissolved. Add slowly to the salmon and milk mixture. Return to a low heat and stir until thickened. Season with salt and pepper to taste. Stir in mustard powder and chives. Keep warm while making the pancakes.

For pancakes, sift flours and salt together, then beat in egg. Gradually add milk and whisk well, until there are absolutely no lumps. Leave to rest for 30 minutes.

Heat a large heavy frying pan and lightly butter it using a paper towel. Test frying pan by dropping a tsp of the batter onto the surface. If it bubbles within a minute, the pan is hot enough. Drop about 4 spoonfuls of batter onto pan and cook on one side until bubbles start to form. With a palette knife or fish slice flip over and cook other side. Remove to a wire rack or plate and cover with a clean tea towel until all the batter has been used up.

To serve, top pancakes with creamy salmon, roll up and sprinkle with chopped chives.

Citrus Fruits

Oranges, limes, grapefruit, Kaffir limes, mandarins, clementines, tangelos

Imagine alfresco dining under a canopy of trailing wisteria with the sweet scent of oranges and lemons permeating the air – citrus trees in containers bring a fruit garden to your back door. With a huge selection of plump round fruits to choose from, all they need is care and attention and the rewards are very succulent indeed. The trees can be trained and pruned into attractive standards, or to run along a trellis. And the best part is the fruit of your labours – your own oranges for the autumn taking.

Other advantages to growing citrus trees in containers or pots are having fresh, juicy vitamin C available all the time, there are no harmful pesticides and fungicides from overseas fruit, you can move the potted plant around to catch the best sunshine, and it's a contained plant so if you move house you can take your treasure with you.

HOW TO GROW

When you buy a citrus tree from your local nursery, they usually come with good instructions on how to plant and care for them. Most trees from plant shops are grafted so will be quite hardy varieties, ready for the home gardener to care for. Old existing trees in a garden may require different care; for example they may need to be rid of pests and disease that have been attracted to their old sweet wood for a long time. Use a good gardening guide to resurrect a spindly citrus tree with not much fruit. But essentially start with a good fertiliser plan.

Not all citrus trees are created equal; they need different space, soil types and sometimes watering requirements. However, if you are going to plant a tree in a container, it needs to be large. Remember a tree is as large underground as it is on top, so for a full head of leaves and fruit setting flowers, a container of rich, fertile soil is needed. Good drainage is key, as citrus don't like 'wet feet'. Water little and often as the root structures sit close to the surface of the ground.

Feeding is also vital. Any plant shop will have an array of citrus fertilisers, designed to give the right kind of nutrients year-round to support the fruit production. Remember that is what you are aiming for, many juicy, tasty fruit off your small tree. Bees and insects are next in importance. Good flower pollination will lead to a good yield, so don't discourage bees and other flying insects circling your balcony or patio, encourage them with flowering plants and scented buds – it is good for the fruit. Regular pruning helps fruit growth and keeps pests away from the inner leaves.

PICKING & STORING

The beauty of having a potted citrus tree is that when in season there is fresh produce at your fingertips for any recipe. Instead of just using the lime in a gin and tonic, or eating a small orange, cook with them, create with them.

Fresh — Fruit, like all other produce, will taste its best when just picked and its sugars are still buzzing throughout. Keep a few oranges or grapefruit at room temperature for instant eating, and keep spare fruit in the fridge. The cold temperatures will stop the deterioration for a few weeks. If any mould appears on the fruit, get rid of them very quickly, so it doesn't spread to the others in the fruit bowl.

Freeze — The pulp and skins of citrus can be frozen easily. When thawed the texture will be very different. Marmalade makers often purée then freeze the fruit before it is ready to be made into a preserve. The skins and fruit then become slushy enough to make a perfectly palatable jam.

Dried — The outer skins are easily dried, using a dehydrator. Rehydrated into desserts or preserves, these skins bring back the citrus essence. The whole fruits may be sliced and dried and used for garnish, or in some homes placed in bowls of pot-pourri for a delicate citrus fragrance

Preserve — Citrus is highly regarded for preserves. The acidity in citrus holds pectin which is useful in jam-making to give the syrupy setting point that jams require. Often a squeeze of lemon, lime or orange juice is used instead of pectin sugar. Bottle segmented mandarins and pickle limes to preserve the citrus flavours.

CULINARY USES

The acid tang of any citrus has many partners. Savoury and sweet, the fruit can be accompanied by almost anything. The juice can be a tenderiser for meats, an essence for cakes, a zest in breads, a dressing on salads, or a squeeze on grilled seafood. The only thing that citrus may not complement is milk and dairy as the acid in it can quickly curdle milk or cream, with tummy-upsetting results.

For a higher juice yield from your fruit, microwave fruit on high for 10–15 seconds before use, or plunge into boiling water. Make long, thin strips of orange zest with a potato peeler. Dry them in a warm place and keep to crumble into casseroles.

QUICK PICKINGS

Orange Slushy

Blend 325 ml can frozen orange juice with ½ cup yoghurt, ½ cup water, 1 tsp vanilla essence, ½ cup caster sugar and 1 tray ice cubes in a food processor or blender. Serve immediately. **Serves 3–4.**

Apricot & Orange Smoothie

Place 200 g can of apricots in juice, ½ small low fat yoghurt, 100 ml fresh orange juice in a blender. Process until smooth. Chill before serving. **Serves 1.**

Cranberry & Orange Glaze For Ham Steaks

In a small bowl combine ¼ cup cranberry sauce, 1 tsp grated orange rind, juice ½ orange and 1 tsp Dijon mustard. Mix well and set aside. Place ham steaks on greased grill and brush on the glaze. Cook 5 minutes on each side brushing the glaze on as you go.

Grapefruit & Avocado Salad

Peel and pit 1 ripe avocado. Slice lengthwise. Remove peel and pith from 1 medium pink grapefruit, and cut it into segments. Arrange in layers on salad plates. In a small bowl, whisk together the juice of ½ grapefruit, 1 tbsp white wine vinegar, ¼ cup olive oil and ½ tsp coarsely ground peppercorns. Season with salt. Drizzle the vinaigrette over grapefruit and avocado. **Serves 2 immediately.**

Baked Grapefruit

Cut 1 grapefruit in half. Using a small paring knife, cut sections and loosen fruit from skin. Dot each half with 1 tsp butter and sprinkle on 1 tbsp brown sugar. Sprinkle ½ tsp cinnamon over brown sugar. Place in baking pan and bake in preheated oven at 180 °C/350 °F for 5 minutes, then grill until top is bubbly. Remove from oven and place in serving bowl with whipped cream to serve.

Bacon & Mandarin Salad

Whisk together ½ cup olive oil, ¼ cup red wine vinegar, ¼ cup sugar, 1 tbsp chopped fresh basil and ⅛ tsp Tabasco sauce. In a bowl mix together 8 mandarins, peeled and segmented, 1 bunch red lettuce, torn, 1 head of cos lettuce, torn, and sprinkle with cooked diced bacon rashers. Top with 70 g sliced almonds and toss all together with the dressing.

Steamed Courgettes & Mandarins

Cut 500 g courgettes into slices. Steam until tender. Add the segments from 6 peeled mandarins, and ¼ tsp grated nutmeg. Sprinkle with ¼ cup slivered, toasted almonds just before serving.

Grilled Lime Chicken

Combine ¼ cup chopped fresh parsley with salt and freshly ground black pepper, juice and finely grated rind of 2 limes and 1 cup dry white wine in a shallow baking dish. Add 6 skinned, boneless chicken breasts and turn to coat. Cover and marinate in fridge for 1 day. Remove chicken from marinade, reserving marinade. Heat a grill plate or barbecue and spread on a little vegetable oil. Place chicken on grill and cook 5 minutes on each side or until cooked through and juices run clear. Baste with reserved marinade as you go. **Serves 6.**

Toasted Lime Tortillas

Melt 50 g butter and stir in grated lime peel and juice of 2 limes. Brush the sides of 4 x 10-inch tortillas. Toast on a barbecue plate, turning once until golden brown. Sprinkle with salt if desired. Cool slightly and break into pieces to serve.

Grapefruit Marmalade

The fruit can easily be finely chopped in the food processor and stored in the freezer until ready to make this marmalade. **Makes 8 x 300-g jars.**

3 grapefruit
3 oranges
2 lemons
2 litres water
5 kg sugar

Place grapefruit, oranges and lemons, skins and all, into a food processor and blend until puréed. Place all fruit in a deep heavy-based saucepan or preserving pan with water. Bring to boil and boil briskly for 1 hour. Add sugar and boil for a further 20 minutes. Remove from stove if you don't want a darker colour.

Orange, Carrot & Tomato Juice

This tasty juice is packed with nutrients and tastes great poured over cubes of ice. Add more Tabasco sauce for a real flavour kick. Serve garnished with orange slices, and mint sprigs. **Serves 2.**

4 large oranges, juice of
1 large carrot, grated
150 ml tomato juice
2 celery sticks
Tabasco sauce, few drops of
ice cubes

Process orange juice, grated carrot, tomato juice, chopped celery and Tabasco sauce in a blender until smooth. Add more drops of Tabasco if you like it spicier. Pour into a tall glass over ice cubes and serve.

Persian Orange Salad (pictured on page 95)

This is an exquisite salad, based around the very traditional way that oranges are served in the Middle East. Leave the salad to chill before serving, and all the tangy flavours of herbs and onions will mingle well with the citrus. Perfect for a hot summer lunch. **Serves 4.**

3 ripe oranges or pink grapefruit, peeled, all pith removed, and sliced
1 red onion, peeled and grated
12 black olives, stones removed and chopped
1 tbsp parsley, finely chopped
2–3 sprigs mint, finely chopped
1 sprig basil, chopped
½ cup Italian vinaigrette
to serve, fresh parsley, chopped

Place oranges, onion and olives in a bowl and sprinkle with herbs. Pour over vinaigrette, toss salad, then cover and refrigerate for 1 hour. Serve sprinkled with parsley.

Lamb Stuffed with Orange, Herbs & Pistachio Nuts

Buy your lamb from your local butcher, ask nicely and they will remove the bone for you from the lamb roast. This makes it easier to stuff and slice. **Serves 4–6.**

3 tbsp olive oil
4 cloves garlic, peeled and finely chopped
100 g pistachio nuts, finely chopped
2 oranges, grated rind and juice of
4 tbsp fresh mint, chopped
2 tbsp fresh thyme, chopped
3 tbsp fresh parsley, chopped
¼ tbsp cinnamon
salt and freshly ground black pepper
1 leg lamb, bone removed, about 2 kg in weight
3 tbsp white wine vinegar
300 ml white wine
1 tbsp wholegrain mustard
1 tbsp fresh rosemary, chopped
2 tbsp clear honey
2 oranges, cut into wedges

Preheat oven to 200 °C/400 °F. Heat oil in a small frying pan, then gently cook garlic and nuts for 1 minute. Remove from heat and mix in orange rind, mint, thyme, parsley, cinnamon and salt and pepper.

Pack mixture into centre of lamb, pressing down well. Secure with a metal skewer or string and lay in a shallow roasting tin. Mix together orange juice, vinegar, wine, mustard, rosemary and more salt and pepper, then pour over top of lamb.

Roast lamb for 20 minutes, then reduce the heat to 180 °C/350 °F. Baste meat with pan juices and roast for a further 40 minutes.

Spoon 3 tbsp pan juices into a small bowl and mix with honey. Add orange wedges to pan, spoon over juices and cook for a further 15 minutes until lamb is cooked and oranges are roasted and tinged brown.

Let lamb rest for 10 minutes before slicing. Serve with caramelised orange wedges and minted mixed vegetables and orange mustard gravy.

To make gravy, place roasting tin of pan juices over a medium heat and add a squeeze of fresh orange juice, a glass of white wine and 1 tsp wholegrain mustard. Bring to boil and cook, scraping up the brown bits in the tin. Strain and serve over meat.

Semolina Citrus Cake

This is a novel recipe – instead of flour you use semolina and ground almonds; instead of butter there is oil; and there are no dairy products whatsoever. The cake will keep in an airtight container for up to four days. **Serves 8–12.**

1 lemon, zest and juice of
1 orange, zest and juice of
185 ml extra virgin olive oil
215 g caster sugar
¼ tsp salt
3 medium eggs
200 g semolina
1 tsp baking powder
115 g ground almonds
almond essence
1 tsp orange-flower water (optional)
4 tbsp Cointreau or Grand Marnier

Preheat oven to 160 °C/375 °F. Grease and line a 23-cm springform round cake tin with baking paper. Reserve a little lemon and orange zest, and put remainder in a bowl with orange and lemon juice, oil, sugar, salt and eggs. Whisk with an electric beater or hand whisk until light and fluffy and doubled in volume.

Sift semolina and baking powder into a second bowl and add ground almonds. Fold almond essence and orange-flower water into egg mixture. Pour all at once into dry ingredients, fold together, but do not over-mix. Spoon into prepared tin and smooth top with back of a spoon.

Place towards top of oven and bake for 40–45 minutes or until pale gold at edges and firm in middle. A skewer pushed into centre should come out clean. Remove from oven and let cool in tin for about 10 minutes. Drizzle liqueur over the top. Push cake out, still on its loose metal base, and let cool on wire rack for another 10 minutes. Remove base and paper. Serve in 8 or 12 wedges, warm or cool, but not chilled.

Citrus & Apricot Slice

This is a perennial favourite. No need for baking, it doesn't take long to make and has all the flavours of fresh fruit with a little sweet milk indulgence. This slice will keep well in the fridge for a week or two after making – if it lasts that long.
Makes 16 squares.

2 packets round or super wine biscuits
200 g brown sugar
397-g can sweetened condensed milk
200 g apricots, chopped
250 g butter, melted
200 g sultanas
1 tsp vanilla essence
1 orange, zest and juice of

Orange icing
100 g butter
400 g icing sugar
1 orange, zest of
4 tbsp hot water

Crush biscuits using a food processor. In a large bowl mix all ingredients together. Use your hands for this to get the best and tidiest mixing going on.

Grease and line a 20 x 30-cm brownie tin with baking paper. Put mixture into tin, pressing into corners, and flatten using the back of a spoon. Allow to chill in fridge. When firm ice with orange icing.

To make icing, melt butter. Sift icing sugar in a bowl and stir in orange zest, butter and icing sugar. Mix in enough hot water to make a paste. Spread over top of slice and chill. Cut into squares or fingers. Leave in covered container.

Lime Sorbet

Sorbet makes a great dessert to cleanse the palate after heavy main dishes. Or it can be eaten on a hot day with fruit salad! An ice cream maker is ideal and will speed up the process for this simple ice dish. **Serves 4.**

1 litre boiling water
1 kg caster sugar
5 limes

To make sugar syrup, pour boiling water into a large heatproof jug or bowl. Add sugar, stirring, until it has dissolved. Leave to cool, then cover jug or bowl. Chill until needed.

Thoroughly scrub limes in warm soapy water, then rinse and pat dry. Use a sharp vegetable peeler to remove strips of rind from three of them. Shave off any white pith as this will give the sorbet a bitter taste. Squeeze juice from all five limes, then strain.

Put rind strips in a small pan with 350 ml sugar syrup. Bring to boil, remove from heat, cover and leave to cool. When cool, add strained lime juice and 125 ml cold water, then cover again and chill overnight. The following day, remove lime strips and put mixture into a plastic container. Chill in freezer for 30 minutes, then stir with a fork. Repeat until mixture starts to crystallise and becomes solid. Alternatively use an ice cream machine to quicken the process.

Fresh Orange Terrine (pictured)

The hint of gin will make this a favourite with the adults. All you need to do is add a little yoghurt to serve. If you have problems un-moulding the terrine, dip the loaf tin or mould into boiling water for 5–10 seconds. No longer or you'll spoil the shape. Also, dip the knife in hot water to make cutting slices easier and neater. **Serves 8.**

8 oranges
175 g sugar
425 ml water
8 tsp gelatine
150 ml water
2 tbsp gin
175 g raspberries

Finely peel zest from 2 oranges in long strips. Place in a pan with sugar and 425 ml water. Heat gently to dissolve sugar, then remove from heat. Squeeze juice from two peeled oranges, strain and add to pan.

Sprinkle gelatine over 150 ml water and leave for 10 minutes to soften. Add to hot syrup with gin and stir until dissolved.

Remove zest and pith from remaining 6 oranges. Cut out individual segments and arrange a layer in bottom of a 900-g loaf tin.

Strain syrup and pour over layer of segments to cover. Chill for 15 minutes until set. Layer raspberries with remaining orange segments, cover with rest of orange syrup, then chill for 2 hours. When set, ease a flat knife round outside of tin, shake and turn out onto a platter.

Coriander

Coriandrum sativum

You either love it or hate it. It has a strong, pungent, citrus-like smell that will fill your kitchen as soon as you start chopping. Coriander, also known as Chinese parsley or cilantro, is inspirational for any dish. The feathery leaves are similar to the carrot family to which it belongs, and the long stalks and deep roots of the whole plant are used in every kind of cooking.

Coriander is said to have been used by the ancient Greeks and Romans, and the seeds have been found in ancient Egyptian tombs. It combines the effects of a sedative and a stimulant, and can become addictive if abused. The seeds may be chewed as a digestive or diuretic, while both the leaves and seeds can be used to make an infusion. Often coriander is put into Asian dishes with multiple hot chillies to calm the gut when eating. Asthma sufferers are cautioned to use coriander sparingly, as it can affect the bronchial tubes.

HOW TO GROW

Coriander is easy enough to grow, given certain conditions. It is better planted directly into the pot or ground where you want it, and in warmer areas of New Zealand will be very prolific. Transplanting plants can cause them to seed early.

It needs a light well-drained soil, plenty of moisture and not too much sun. It should be sown in early spring, once all the danger of frost is past. When the plant has flowered, the leaves alter their character and their flavour deteriorates. Unless you wish it to self-seed, this is the time to dig it up. Grow new seeds every three to four weeks for a continuous supply of fresh coriander through the summer months. Coriander flowers are great bee attractants, so grow it next to your citrus trees and around your berry fruit. Try not to over-water as this plant does not like standing in water.

PICKING & STORING

Being a delicate-leafed herb, coriander is at its best when picked fresh and used straight away. It will be pungent and full of flavour.

Fresh — Store covered, with stems in water for up to two weeks in the fridge. Beware, if too wet the leaves will turn to mush very quickly.

Freeze — Coriander leaves should not be dried, but freeze reasonably well.

Dried — There are containers of dried coriander around, but preferably only dry the seeds and ground root. The leaves, once the moisture has gone, will be a ghost of their former pungent selves.

CULINARY USES

Coriander tends to overpower other more delicate herbs so, for best results, use alone. Add to salads, soups, curries and Asian dishes. In Indonesia, they will use only the seeds as a flavouring in their curry dishes, whereas in India, a dish can't leave the kitchen without a sprinkling of these flavoursome leaves.

Coriander is grown for its seeds, leaves and roots and all are used for culinary purposes. The leaves can be used raw in salads, sandwiches and salsas, or in cooked items such as bread or curry. It complements garlic, chillies, ginger, spring onions and fresh tomatoes. Coriander works well with fish, chicken and vegetarian dishes. It can blend into curries, chutneys, soups, and the volatile oil can sometimes be used to flavour chocolates.

QUICK PICKINGS

Coriander Ginger Chicken

Combine 2 cloves crushed garlic with 2-cm piece fresh grated ginger, ¼ cup chopped fresh coriander, ¼ cup chopped fresh mint, 2 finely sliced spring onions, ¼ cup light soy sauce, ¼ cup vegetable oil and 2 tsp sugar in a large bowl. Add 2 chicken thighs, mix well and leave to marinate in the fridge overnight. Cook the chicken in a large frying pan for about 5 minutes each side until the juices run clear. Brush with marinade while cooking. **Serves 4.**

Coriander & Pea Soup

Melt 15 g butter in a medium saucepan, add 3 chopped spring onions and stir over medium heat for about 2 minutes. Add 350 g peas, 1 medium chopped potato, 1 litre water and 1 chicken stock cube to the pan and bring to the boil. Reduce the heat, cover and simmer for about 10 minutes or until peas are just soft. Blend or process mixture in a food processor until smooth. Return mixture to boil and add 1 tbsp chopped coriander leaves and 2 tbsp light cream. **Serves 6.**

Asian Lime & Coriander Dressing

In a glass jar combine ¼ cup fresh lime juice with 1 tbsp peanut oil, 2 tbsp fresh chopped coriander, 1 tsp sesame oil, ½ tsp Sambal Olek and 2-cm piece fresh grated ginger root. Season with salt and freshly ground black pepper. Shake vigorously to get a good blend. Serve with steamed vegetables.

Chilli Coriander Cream

In a blender or small food processor blend together ¼ cup sour cream with ¼ cup plain unsweetened yoghurt, 2 crushed cloves garlic and 1 fresh red chilli, seeds removed, and 1 small bunch coriander leaves. Season to taste with salt and pepper scraping down the sides of blender to incorporate it all. This may be made 6 hours ahead of time and chilled.

Coriander Dipping Sauce

Put 40 g fresh coriander leaves, 1 tbsp fresh mint, 4 finely chopped cloves garlic, juice of 1 lime, 1 tbsp caster sugar, 6 green chillies, halved and deseeded, and ½ tsp salt in a food processor or blender and process until smooth, adding 2 tbsp water if necessary to give a runny consistency. This sauce can be kept in the fridge overnight, but for the freshest, brightest flavour it's best eaten on the day it is made.

Fresh Coriander Relish

This relish can be stored in a non-metallic, airtight container for up to one week in the fridge. Delicious served with spicy poppadums, or baked potatoes and sour cream. **Makes 1½ cups.**

- 50 g ground almonds
- 1 medium onion, peeled and finely chopped
- 1 clove garlic, peeled and chopped
- 1–2 green chillies, deseeded and finely chopped
- 100 g fresh coriander, coarsely chopped
- 3 tbsp lime juice
- 3 tbsp vegetable oil
- 2 tsp sugar
- salt and freshly ground black pepper

Line a baking tray with foil. Spread ground almonds over foil and toast under a medium grill for 3 minutes until lightly browned. Leave to cool.

Place onion, garlic, chillies and ground almonds in a mixing bowl. Stir in chopped coriander. Add lime juice, oil and sugar. Season well with salt and pepper and mix well to combine. Cover and leave at room temperature for 1 hour before serving.

Avocado & Coriander Toast

Avocado has to be the perfect food – convenient, delicious and good for you. The dark, warty-skinned Hass variety has the best flavour and texture. It goes well with many herbs, but the pungency of fresh coriander is especially good to complement the subtle taste of the avocado. **Serves 4.**

- 2 avocados, halved and pitted
- 1 lime, juice of, plus extra for sprinkling
- 2 tbsp virgin olive oil, plus extra for sprinkling
- Tabasco sauce, to taste
- sea salt and freshly ground black pepper
- 4–8 slices bread, such as ciabatta or gluten-free loaf
- bunch of fresh coriander, thoroughly washed and drained, stems removed

Using a teaspoon, scoop the avocado flesh into a food processor. Add lime juice, olive oil, Tabasco and seasoning. Process briefly. Alternatively, scoop the avocado with a teaspoon into a bowl and mash with juice, olive oil and Tabasco.

Chargrill or toast bread on both sides and sprinkle with a little salt and olive oil. Spread avocado thickly over the toast, sprinkle with olive oil, a little more lime juice, sea salt and cracked pepper. Pile coriander leaves on top and serve immediately.

Mango & Coriander Salad (pictured)

A simple salad bringing together all the flavours of South East Asian cuisine. Serve with barbecued prawn skewers or as a side to whole baked snapper. Or prepare for a delicious packed lunch and keep in the fridge. The flavours combine well when left to chill for a while. **Serves 4.**

2 ripe mangoes
1 bunch fresh coriander, chopped
1 lime, grated rind and juice of
3 tbsp sunflower oil
2.5-cm piece fresh ginger root, peeled and grated
few drops sesame oil or chilli oil
salt and freshly ground black pepper
to serve, 100 g salted peanuts, chopped

Peel mangoes and slice flesh from stones. Cut into thin slices. Arrange mangoes and coriander on a serving plate. To make dressing, place remaining ingredients in a screw-top jar and shake together, or whisk together in a bowl. Drizzle over the salad and serve, topping with chopped peanuts at the last minute.

Pork & Coriander Kebabs

Pork fillet is lean, tender and requires little preparation, and it tastes delicious with lemon and coriander. Serve with a simple accompaniment of coriander and Greek yoghurt. **Serves 4.**

900 g pork fillet
1 bunch spring onions
3 lemons, juice and finely grated zest of
25 g bunch fresh coriander
3 tbsp olive oil
salt and freshly ground black pepper
200 g Greek yoghurt

Cut pork into about 16 cubes and put into a shallow dish. Cut onions into short lengths and add to dish. Finely grate the zest and squeeze juice from one lemon. Roughly chop coriander.

Sprinkle lemon zest and juice, half the coriander, olive oil, salt and pepper over pork and stir well to mix.

Cut remaining lemons into wedges, and then cut each in half. Thread pork, onions and lemon alternately onto four large or eight small skewers. Cook under a hot grill for 10 minutes, turning occasionally until browned.

Mix reserved coriander into yoghurt. Season with salt and pepper to taste. Serve kebabs with coriander yoghurt.

Courgettes

Cucurbita pepo

Courgettes are perfect plants for your small veggie garden – they are glossy, dark green beauties and they grow abundantly. Also known commonly as zucchini, courgettes are classified as a small summer squash. Rewarding and easy to grow, a single plant can feed a family for quite some time over summer in glorious Mediterranean dishes. Grow more than one plant and there is potential to create many different zingy pickles and chutneys for the winter months.

Courgettes can be green, yellow or variegated vegetables and are best cooked, rather than served raw. Even the delicate yellow/orange flowers can be stuffed and cooked, and are a delicacy in the finest kitchens. Courgettes are low in calories with useful folate and potassium minerals.

HOW TO GROW

Courgettes are easy to grow. What a great vegetable to have in your garden. Choose seedlings from your local plant shop and put in the ground in October or November for a bumper summer crop. Grow a seedling in a large pot filled with healthy, composted soil, but remember these plants can grow large and can produce a healthy yield. For best results find the sunniest patch in your garden and dig a hole. Fill with compost and good garden mix and plant a seedling. Courgette plants will thrive if mulched well with pea straw, pine needles or even newspaper. The fruit of the plant will sit better on this mulch and not rot in the soil. Water well and they will thrive. Bees are essential for pollination of the fruit, so stay away from insecticides.

PICKING & STORING

For the perfect food, wait until the courgettes are over 20 cm long, but you don't want to leave them any longer. They can become fibrous and not very pleasant to eat. Pick them at their peak for a sweeter and moister vegetable.

Fresh — Try not to store courgettes for longer than three days. They are prone to chilling damage and can become a huge mess in your veggie bin.

Freeze — Cut courgettes into rings. Dip in boiling water for 20 seconds and then remove with a slotted spoon and plunge immediately into ice cold water. Leave to cool then drain well. Lay flat on a plastic tray and place in freezer. When icy, put into freezer bags, label and secure with tie. Freeze for up to six months.

Preserve — Great in chutneys or chargrilled and kept in oil.

CULINARY USES

Courgettes originated in the Americas and are now traditionally grown in warmer areas. Many of the recipes you will find for these green cylinders come from the Mediterranean. Courgette is a great match with olive oil, tomatoes, garlic and Parmesan. Courgettes are a key ingredient in ratatouille so are great growing companions to tomatoes. Any cheese or salty foods like capers and anchovies complement this vegetable. It is also used commonly in India as a base for 'rajas'.

QUICK PICKINGS

Stir-Fried Courgettes

Stir-fry courgette sticks with fresh asparagus and a few pine nuts. Use lemon juice and chives to dress the stir-fry.

Blanched Courgettes

Blanch courgette strips (see page 17) and toss with fresh beans, red capsicum, red onion rings, black olives and feta for a great summer salad.

Grilled Courgettes

Cut courgettes lengthways. Sprinkle with a little crushed garlic, crumbled feta and freshly ground black pepper. Sprinkle with olive oil and grill in the oven on high for 5 minutes until cheese starts to brown.

Barbecued Courgettes

Slice courgettes lengthways. Brush liberally with a good olive oil, sprinkle with sea salt and freshly ground black pepper. Lay on a hot barbecue grill plate and cook 2–3 minutes each side until the lengths begin to soften. Serve immediately.

Pan-Fried Courgettes

Cut courgettes into lengths about ½ cm thick. Dip in egg and fresh breadcrumbs and fry the strips in a little rice bran oil. Add minced garlic to the egg mixture and plenty of salt and pepper for extra flavour.

Stuffed Courgettes

Halve the courgettes and sprinkle with salt to rid them of some of the moisture. Scoop out pulp from centre of each half and mix with equal quantity of blanched, drained and chopped spinach. Add a little Parmesan, garlic and chopped parsley. Sprinkle with breadcrumbs. Pour over olive oil and brown in a hot oven.

Courgette & Apple Relish

This simple relish will accompany any summer meat dish or be a favourite in an old-fashioned cheese sandwich.
Makes about 6 cups.

750 g courgette, grated
1½ tbsp sea salt
600 g apples, peeled and chopped
4 medium onions, peeled and chopped
500 ml white wine vinegar
250 g raisins, chopped
150 g brown sugar
½ tsp garam masala
½ tsp ground coriander
½ tsp turmeric

Place courgette in colander or sieve, sprinkle with salt and stand for 2 hours. Rinse under cold water and then drain on absorbent paper or through a sieve.

Combine courgette, apples, onions, vinegar and raisins in large saucepan. Bring to boil, simmer, covered, for about 20 minutes or until mixture is pulpy. Stir in sugar and spices. Stir over heat until sugar is dissolved. Bring to the boil, simmer, uncovered, stirring occasionally, for about 20 minutes or until mixture is thick. Pour into hot sterilised jars and seal when cold. (see page 18).

Courgette & Mustard Pickle

Gherkins or pickling cucumbers will complement the courgettes in this recipe. If unavailable ordinary cucumbers can be used. This is a home-made version of piccalilli which goes well with cold meats and cheese. **Makes 8 x 300-g jars.**

100 g sea salt
1.2 litres water
500 g courgettes, diced
300 g celery, diced
1 onion, peeled and diced
2 gherkins, diced
600 ml vinegar + 3 tbsp
25 g plain flour
1 tbsp mustard powder
½ tbsp turmeric
2 tsp ground ginger

Dissolve salt in water by heating in a saucepan. Place all vegetables in a large bowl, pour over the brine, cover and leave for 24 hours.

Boil vinegar for 10 to 15 minutes. It will then be less than 600 ml but will be the right consistency. Blend the 3 tbsp cold vinegar with the flour, mustard powder, turmeric and ginger in a good size bowl. Strain vinegar onto this, stirring well. Pour sauce into a saucepan and stir over a low heat until adequately thickened. This is important, the sauce should be sufficiently thick to coat the spoon without running off rapidly.

Lift vegetables from the brine, drain well but do not rinse in cold water. Put into mustard sauce and simmer for 5 minutes only. Stir lightly to ensure a good blend, then spoon into sterilised jars (see page 18) and seal well.

Courgette & Brie Soup

A creamy soup that brings comfort to summer and beyond. It pays to freeze courgettes in summer. Bring out your frozen courgettes if soup is your choice for winter meals. **Serves 4–6.**

- 25 g butter
- 250 g onion, peeled and finely chopped
- 200 g potato, peeled and cubed
- 1 clove garlic, peeled and finely chopped
- ¼ cup white wine
- 300 ml vegetable stock
- 550 g courgettes, chopped
- 200 ml milk
- 200 g Brie, plus extra slices to garnish (optional)
- 3 tbsp cream
- 15 basil leaves, torn, plus extra to garnish
- salt and freshly ground black pepper

Melt butter in a heavy-based pan and fry onion for 2–3 minutes, until softened. Add potato, garlic and wine, and cook for a further 5 minutes.

Stir in stock and courgettes and bring to boil. Reduce heat, then cover and simmer gently for 20 minutes, or until potato is cooked. Pour in milk, add Brie and gently heat through until melted.

Stir in cream and torn basil leaves. Season and serve with extra slices of Brie on the top, if you like, and sprinkle with basil.

Courgette & Feta Fritters (pictured)

For a picnic, antipasto or even brunch, these fritters go well with cold meats, olives and a few caper berries. Greek yoghurt is a good complement to the saltiness of the fritters. **Serves 4.**

- 2 medium courgettes
- 1 tbsp sea salt
- 160 g plain flour
- 4–5 anchovy fillets
- 1 tbsp capers
- 200 g feta, crumbled
- 2 cloves garlic, peeled and crushed
- ½ tsp Sambal Olek or chilli paste (optional)
- salt and freshly ground black pepper
- 3 eggs

Grate courgettes and place in a colander. Sprinkle with sea salt and leave for 1 hour. Let moisture drain from courgettes. Squeeze out any remaining moisture and place courgettes in a large bowl.

Stir in flour, anchovies, capers, feta, garlic and Sambal Olek. Season to taste. Mix in egg until it makes a nice paste. Leave to rest for 20 minutes in the fridge.

Heat a pan with butter and olive oil. Drop a tablespoon of mixture into oil and cook for 2–3 minutes then turn. Place on a kitchen towel to remove any excess oil. Serve warm or cold with an antipasto platter and a crisp green salad.

Stuffed Beef & Coriander Courgettes

The courgettes soak up the flavours of the spicy beef beautifully in this recipe, creating a nifty way to get vegetables into the family meal. **Serves 6–8.**

1 cup wild rice
1 tbsp peanut oil
1 onion, peeled and diced
2 cloves garlic, peeled and finely chopped
3-cm piece fresh ginger root, peeled and grated
1 small red chilli, finely chopped
500 g lean beef mince
1 tsp cumin
1 tbsp mild curry powder
420-g can tomato pasta sauce
½ bunch fresh coriander
salt and freshly ground black pepper
4–6 large courgettes

Coriander sauce
2 tbsp sour cream
2 tbsp Greek yoghurt
1 lemon, juice of
1 bunch fresh coriander, chopped
2 tbsp sweet chilli sauce

Preheat oven to 180 °C/350 °F. Bring a medium pot of water to boil, then cook wild rice for 20 minutes, until firm but tender. Drain rice and run under cold water (to halt the cooking process). Set aside.

Heat oil and sauté the onion, garlic, ginger and chilli until onion has softened and mixture is aromatic, about 3 minutes. Add minced beef and cook over a high heat stirring constantly to break it up. Continue cooking until meat is cooked through and liquid has evaporated. Add cumin and curry powder and stir well.

Add tomato sauce and simmer for 10 minutes until mixture is thick and fairly dry. Remove from heat and fold in fresh chopped coriander and cooked rice. Season to taste.

Wash courgettes, then cut lengthways and scoop out centre seeds. Fill with beef mixture, mounding the beef slightly. Place in a baking dish, nestling them next to each other. Bake in oven for 20 minutes, then serve warm drizzled with the coriander sauce.

To make sauce, process all ingredients together and chill until ready to serve.

Courgette & Walnut Cake

This is a great picnic cake, rich and full of goodness. Keep chilled to keep it for a long time. **Serves 8–12.**

- 350 g plain flour
- 380 g sugar
- 3 tsp baking soda
- 2 tsp baking powder
- 2 tsp ground cinnamon
- 1 tsp each of ground cloves, nutmeg and allspice
- 1 tsp salt
- 320 ml olive oil
- 6 eggs
- 400 g courgettes, finely grated
- 200 g walnuts, finely chopped
- 240 g sultanas
- 420-g can mango slices, drained

Cream cheese icing

- 400 g cream cheese
- 50 g butter, melted
- 500 g icing sugar, sifted
- 1 lemon, juice and zest of

Grease and line 2 x 23-cm springform tins with baking paper. Preheat oven to 180 °C/350 °F. In a large bowl, whisk together dry ingredients until all lumps are removed.

In the bowl of an electric beater, mix together olive oil and eggs. Beat well on a low speed. Add dry ingredients to oil and eggs. Then slowly beat in the courgettes, walnuts, sultanas and mango.

Divide batter between two tins and spread evenly. Bake for 30–35 minutes or until a skewer comes out clean. Leave to cool on a wire rack for 10 minutes. Ice with cream cheese icing.

To make the icing, mix cream cheese and butter in a large bowl until well blended. Add icing sugar and lemon juice and zest and stir well. Use half the icing to fill centre of cake and the remainder on top. Sprinkle with extra chopped walnuts if desired.

Dill

Antheum graveolens

They say dill has a subtle flavour, but when you pick a handful of dill from the tall, feathery plant and taste it, it has a distinct aniseed flavour. Not so subtle, but delicate and piquant at the same time. Dill's green frond leaves grow beautifully among other herbs, but be careful it doesn't spread and make the garden its own. The seeds, which are contained in yellow seed heads or 'umbels', are just as important in cooking and carry the same dainty aniseed flavour. The name itself comes from the Greek 'anethon graveolens', meaning strongly scented, usually muskily or aromatically so.

Dill has long been sought after for its aphrodisiac properties. Steeping a few sprigs in hot wine and drinking half a pint was said to excite the passions! Alternatively it was said that adding dill to your bath made you irresistible to your lover. Nowadays, it is more commonly used to make food irresistible.

HOW TO GROW

Dill is a summer crop, and isn't the easiest to get right. It's sometimes better to buy an established plant from the nursery. It goes to seed very fast and doesn't transplant well, but don't let this put you off. Grown from seed sown in spring, dill plants like a sunny, sheltered position, and soil that is well-drained yet able to hold water during summer. Add plenty of organic matter to soil before planting, and water regularly but never let the soil dry out completely.

PICKING & STORING

The leaves are harvested when young, before the plant comes into flower.

Fresh — Dill should be snipped from the plant and chopped to release the flavour. Fresh leaves can be kept in a plastic bag in the fridge.

Freeze — Chop finely, mix with water, and freeze in ice cube trays.

Dried — To dry, hang bunches in a warm, dry, well-ventilated place. Keep in airtight jars in a cool, dark place. Dried leaves do not retain much flavour, so use generously.

CULINARY USES

Two parts of the dill plant are used in cookery – the sweet green leaves and the seeds. The flower of dill is reminiscent of caraway, with the seeds more pungent than the leaves. It brings out the aroma of mild foods. Dill can be added to most fish and meats, to white sauces and a variety of vegetables, especially potatoes and cucumber. The fresh leaves make a flavoursome garnish. Use, too, in cottage cheese dips and spreads, in dressings and sprinkled over salads.

Dill has a natural affinity with all sorts of fish. Either stuff or wrap fish in dill fronds before cooking, or sprinkle it with finely chopped dill after cooking. Fresh dill is the essential herb for curing fresh fish, especially salmon. In Scandinavia vast quantities of chopped dill are used to preserve salmon and create gravadlax. This is usually accompanied by a fresh dill and mustard sauce.

It also brings out the flavour of many vegetables and pulses – again, sprinkle it on after cooking. I actually think dill is best used on its own, or with a mild herb such as parsley; use it as a definite flavour, rather than just a background enhancer.

QUICK PICKINGS

Dill Butter

Mix chopped dill with butter to make delicious herb butter for poached trout, asparagus, grilled tomatoes or new potatoes. Instead of garlic butter in garlic bread make herb butter adding chopped fresh dill, fresh parsley, fresh garlic chives and fresh thyme. Spread through the loaf, wrap in foil and bake until butter melts.

Dill & Crab Sandwich

Sprinkle chopped dill on crayfish or crab with mayonnaise to make the ultimate seafood sandwich.

Dill & Smoked Fish

Chop equal quantities of fresh garlic chives and fresh dill over smoked fish, smoked meat and smoked cheeses, for a lively, refreshing starter.

Dill Pickles

Pickling cucumbers are another plant that can easily be grown in your garden. If you don't have such ambition, then a good vegetable store will have pickling cucumbers when in season. This recipe is an excellent way to preserve the flavour of fresh dill. **Makes 1 x 2-litre clip-seal jar.**

10 pickling cucumbers or gherkins, scrubbed clean
1 bunch fresh dill
5 cups water
75 g coarse sea salt
1 tsp dill seeds
½ cup white wine vinegar
1 tsp black peppercorns
1 tbsp pickling spice

Put cucumbers and fresh dill, either sliced or whole, in a 2-litre sterilised, clip-seal jar. In a saucepan, combine water with salt, dill seeds, vinegar, peppercorns and pickling spice. Bring to boil over high heat for 3 minutes. Leave to cool. Pour cooled mixture over cucumbers; if there is excess liquid, be sure to add all spices to the cucumbers and discard any remaining liquid. Seal jar and store in a cool, dark place for 3 weeks before serving. Refrigerate after opening.

Dill Mayonnaise

With fresh egg yolks this delicate mayonnaise deserves to be served immediately with fine poached salmon or steamed fish. Refrigerated and in a covered jar it will last for 1–2 days. **Makes 1 cup.**

- 2 egg yolks
- 1–2 tbsp fresh lemon juice or white wine vinegar
- ¼ tsp salt
- 250 ml vegetable oil
- 3 tbsp fresh dill, finely chopped
- salt and freshly ground black pepper

Whisk eggs, lemon juice or vinegar and salt in a medium glass or ceramic bowl. Make sure it is smooth and light. Slowly add oil, a few drops at a time, until mixture starts to thicken. You need to be very vigorous with whisking to incorporate the oil well. Add dill and stir in until well combined. Season to taste.

Dill & Smoked Cheddar Muffins

Smoked Cheddar is my personal favourite for this recipe, but a mature full-flavoured cheese may be used instead. Make sure it is a strong flavour because the dill is a strong-flavoured herb. Serve these with a soup or as a side to a meat dish. **Makes about 16.**

- 250 g plain flour
- 1 tbsp baking powder
- salt and freshly ground black pepper
- 125 g smoked Cheddar, grated
- 2 tbsp fresh dill, chopped
- pinch of cayenne pepper
- 1 egg
- 250 ml milk
- 50 g butter, melted
- 25 g Cheddar, grated, for topping

Preheat oven to 190 °C/375 °F. Sift flour and baking powder together into a bowl, then season with plenty of salt and a little pepper. Add cheese, dill and cayenne. Make a well in the centre of the bowl.

In a bowl, whisk together egg, milk and butter, then pour into the well. Work quickly together with a knife, to mix, but do not over-mix. Spoon mixture into about 16 greased muffin tin holes. Top with remaining grated cheese. Bake in oven for about 20 minutes, or until well risen and golden on top.

Poached Salmon Fillets with Dill & Cucumber Vinaigrette (pictured)

The convenience of having a good fishmonger is that they can do the work for you. Either buy a whole fish or just the prepared long fillets. It makes easy work of preparing salmon for a special meal.
Serves 8 as a main course.

2 filleted sides of fresh whole salmon
olive oil, for brushing
salt and freshly ground black pepper
1 small lemon, sliced
5–6 fresh parsley sprigs
5 black peppercorns, coarsely crushed
100 ml white wine or water
1 whole telegraph cucumber
1 bunch dill
1 lemon, juice of
100 ml olive oil
to garnish, lemon slices and dill sprigs

Preheat oven to 180 °C/350 °F. Using the back of a knife held at an angle, scrape scales from fish, working from tail to head. They will scatter, so work over sink or with plenty of newspaper around. Rinse salmon fillets under cold water, then pat dry with paper towel.

Carefully run your fingers along flesh to check for small bones and lift out any you find with tweezers. Rinse flesh with cold water, then pat dry using paper towel.

Line a shallow roasting tin with a double layer of foil and brush base with a little oil. Season flesh side of salmon evenly with salt and pepper, then lay it on foil and tuck lemon slices and parsley sprigs underneath. Scatter over peppercorns and pour over wine or water.

Gather foil together and seal at top to form a loose parcel so the fish can poach inside. Place in oven and bake, allowing 8–10 minutes per 450 g. To test if salmon is done, press a knife into the thickest part – the flesh should flake easily and the fish should also feel firm to touch.

While fish is cooking prepare the vinaigrette. Use a vegetable peeler to thinly slice strips off cucumber. Place in a bowl with dill and squeeze over lemon juice, olive oil and season with salt and pepper. Allow to stand for 20 minutes.

Using two fish slices, carefully lift salmon fillets from tin, allowing them to drain, then place on a board to cool. The flesh should fall away from skin for removal. Remove back ridge of any bones, then gently scrape off any dark flesh. Transfer to a serving plate and garnish with dill and cucumber vinaigrette. Use cucumber strips to garnish top and sides of the salmon fillets. Pour over any extra dressing to coat salmon. Garnish with slices of lemon and sprigs of dill. Serve at room temperature.

Marinated Raw Fish with Dill & Red Capsicum

A Pacific island-inspired recipe. Dill is a natural accompaniment to fish and imparts a subtle flavour to the fish as it marinates. Serve the fish in lettuce cups or cocktail glasses, or less formally, with pita bread as a perfect protein snack. **Serves 4–6.**

500 g fresh white fish, like snapper or tarakihi
2 lemons, juice of
50 g bunch dill
2 spring onions
salt and freshly ground black pepper
1 red capsicum, deseeded
400-ml can coconut cream
to serve, lettuce cups, lemon wedges and dill sprigs

Cut fish into cubes and remove any bones. Put cubes in a shallow dish and sprinkle over lemon juice, dill and spring onions. Leave covered in the fridge for 2–3 hours until fish has turned opaque; you may need to carefully turn with a spoon. Don't leave for too long, as it will begin to disintegrate. Season to taste with salt and pepper.

Dice red capsicum and add to fish. Stir in coconut cream. Serve in lettuce cups or cocktail glasses with wedges of lemon and a sprig of dill.

Dill & Potato Salad

A quick salad to throw together when guests gather. Fresh herbs at your back door allow you to easily add flavour to a bland ingredient like potatoes. **Serves 8.**

900 g large waxy potatoes, scrubbed but not peeled
300 ml dry or medium-dry white wine
salt and freshly ground black pepper
3 tbsp extra virgin olive oil
3–4 spring onions, finely chopped
6 tbsp fresh dill, chopped

Cut potatoes into 1-cm cubes and cook in a pan of boiling, salted water for 10–15 minutes until tender (test them with the point of a knife). Meanwhile, measure wine into a separate small pan and boil vigorously for about 10 minutes until reduced by half.

Drain potatoes, then transfer to a bowl and sprinkle over wine while it's still hot. Season with salt and pepper, toss gently, then carefully stir in olive oil, spring onions and half the chopped dill. Leave to cool. Taste and season if necessary, then sprinkle over the rest of the dill. Mixing the dressing into the still-warm potatoes helps them absorb the flavours even better. Leave to chill for about 1 hour before serving.

Edible Flowers

Marigolds, nasturtiums, rose petals, geraniums, pansies, viola, borage and lavender

Planting flowers in your garden takes on a whole new meaning if you can eat them too. Many summer blooms, which seem to pop up all over the garden, can provide colour and flavour to a salad or sweet pudding. Some flowering plants have edible seeds, leaves and blooms. Marigolds not only have edible petals, but the peppery scent from these annuals will deter some insects. The petals are rich in vitamin C and were once eaten to ward off scurvy and settle the stomach.

Nasturtiums are climbing flowers that pop up in the spring and summer with prolific abundance. Thomas Jefferson sowed them at his mountaintop home, Monticello, and Claude Monet grew heaps at Giverny. During the late nineteenth century, as more dwarf varieties became available, gardeners worked them into their plots to cover walls and scale fences. Nasturtiums can, in fact, be a pest as they spread over the side of roadways and down embankments in ways that highlight their sprawling or clambering habits.

For fragrance and beauty alone, roses have no equal, and this 'gift of angels' was also popular for its healing power. The delicate flavour of rosewater is excellent in elegant foods and preserves. They are very hardy shrubs, and provide many benefits to the small-time gardener. One or two plants help attract helpful bees and give a sense of beauty to all around.

Geranium flowers can be used in salads or in cooking. The leaves themselves have a strong aroma, and are often dried for tinctures and teas, but the petals bring colour to fruit salads and sorbets.

There are many more, like flowers from rosemary, or sage lemon balm and pineapple sage. They offer a slightly bitter, colourful bite to any salad.

HOW TO GROW

Most flowering plants have simple needs – sun, fertile soil and plenty of water. Planted in pots and planters around the garden they not only provide edible blooms, but are helpful for bees, and just generally make the garden a delight.

PICKING & STORING

Be careful to use only edible blossoms. Some plants are poisonous, so know your flowers well. Keep your flowering plants free of pesticides and other chemical sprays. Flowers from florists are often treated to keep the blooms 'alive' for longer.

Fresh — When gathering fresh flowers from the garden, pick early in the day and in dry weather. Rinse well under cold water to remove any pollen. Take out the pistils and stamens and the bitter white part of the petal.

Dried — The obvious use of dried petals is in pot-pourri to give fragrance to the air. Dry petals on pieces of newsprint paper or in a dehydrator. The petals can also be used in sugars or reconstituted in jams.

CULINARY USES

Some flowers such as lavender, rose, nasturtium, jasmine and orange blossom can lend their delicate flavour to sorbets, custards, jams and jellies, liqueurs, wines and teas. Other blossoms like geraniums, chrysanthemums and marigolds, for example, have a duller flavour but add beautiful, splashy colour to the plate as garnishes for desserts, fruit salads and cakes.

QUICK PICKINGS

Flower Sugars

Sugar can be flavoured with flower petals, such as rose, lavender or rose geranium and accompanied by vanilla pods, cinnamon sticks or cardamom pods. Layer the dry petals in the sugar canister or jar with white granulated sugar crystals. Use these sugars to add extra flavour to custard sauces, cakes and other baked goods.

Cherry & Rose Petal Brandy

Pit 750 g sour cherries and crack the stones. In a jar, combine cherries, stones, and 500 g caster sugar. Add petals of 6 scented roses and 60 g dried jasmine or lavender flowers and 1 litre of brandy. Stir well and seal jar. Infuse in a dark place for at least 1 month. Strain into bottles and store in a dark place.

Kulfi

Boil 450 ml milk in a saucepan then simmer until reduced to one third original quantity. Gradually add 20 g rice flour to milk, stirring well. Pour in 150 ml evaporated milk and continue to stir. Lower heat, add petals from 2–3 stems of lavender and 1–2 rose petals and simmer for 10–15 minutes. Add 50 g sugar and stir well until it dissolves. Set aside to cool and then stir in ½ tbsp chopped almonds and ½ tbsp pistachio nuts. Transfer mixture to a freezer-proof container and freeze until icy but not solid. Remove container from freezer and beat mixture until the ice melts, then return the Kulfi to the freezer until firm. Scoop into serving bowls, sprinkle with a few chopped nuts and rose petals and serve.

Floral Syrup

Place about 500 g flower petals (white heels removed) in a saucepan and add 2½ cups water, or more if necessary to cover. Bring to boil, cover and infuse for 30 minutes. Strain and return to pan with 375 g sugar, or to taste. Simmer for 10 minutes. Infuse the petals alone or create floral infusions like violets and honey or elderflowers and orange.

Summer Cocktail

A fruity drink for warm days. The tequila gives it a special kick and the flower petals garnish beautifully, and provide a unique peppery flavour. Serves 2.

2 very red tomatoes, cores removed and quartered
4 medium carrots, scrubbed
50 ml tequila
salt and freshly ground black pepper
to garnish, nasturtium flowers and leaves

Using a juice extractor or food processor, process tomatoes and carrots. Transfer to a small jug. Stir in tequila, and season with salt and pepper. Pour mixture into two tall ice-filled glasses, garnish with nasturtium flowers and leaves, and serve immediately.

Crystallised Flowers

Crystallised flowers, petals or leaves are wonderful treats, which both look pretty and taste great. Choose a suitable selection from the garden – ensuring of course that there is nothing poisonous. Violets, nasturtiums, roses, geraniums, marigolds, currant leaves and elderflowers are just some of the wonderful edible flowers and leaves that can be crystallised.

1 egg white
flowers, petals and leaves
caster sugar

Whip egg white lightly until fluffy. Separate flowers, petals or leaves, leaving a short piece of stalk if possible. Paint both sides of each with egg white, using a small brush, and then sprinkle both sides with caster sugar and leave to dry. If necessary sprinkle a second time with sugar to ensure they are evenly coated. Leave to dry completely before storing in an airtight jar. These will keep for 1–2 months in an airtight container.

Tomato Salad with Flowers

Petals provide a great garnish to this salad. Tomatoes and cucumbers from your own garden are complemented by the sweet serenity of your own garden petals. Serves 4.

3 large ripe tomatoes
200 g cherry tomatoes
1 whole apple cucumber
¼ cup fresh parsley, finely chopped
100 g baby rocket leaves
250 ml French vinaigrette (see page 222)
salt and freshly ground black pepper
handful of geranium, marigold and nasturtiums petals

Peel and remove cores from large tomatoes, then dice into small pieces. Peel cucumber, remove seeds and dice. Put all tomatoes and cucumber in a bowl with parsley and rocket leaves. Toss through vinaigrette and season to taste with salt and pepper. Finally add petals and toss quickly. Serve as a side or in individual salad bowls.

Rose Pavlovas with Raspberry & Petals (pictured on previous page)

The rosewater in this dilutes the sweetness of the pavlova, but leaves behind the most sensual of fragrances. A delicious complement to a traditional favourite. **Serves 6–8.**

6 egg whites
500 g caster sugar
2 tsp white vinegar
4 tsp rosewater
2 tbsp cornflour
to garnish, whipped cream, fresh raspberries and assortment of fresh edible petals

Preheat oven to 180 °C/350 °F. Line an oven tray with baking paper. Draw 8 x 5-cm diameter circles on the baking paper.

Using an electric mixer or hand beater, beat egg whites until fluffy. Slowly add caster sugar for 10–15 minutes or until thick and glossy. Mix vinegar, rosewater and cornflour together. Add to meringue. Beat on high speed for a further 5 minutes, until the sugar has been well dissolved and you can't feel any grains of sugar left in the mixture.

Spread the pavlovas within edges of circles, keeping as round and even as possible. Smooth edges and swirl a pattern into surface. Place tray in oven then turn temperature down to 100 °C/200 °F. Bake for 1 hour. Turn off oven. Open door slightly and leave pavlovas in oven until cold. Carefully lift onto serving plates. Decorate with whipped cream, raspberries and flower petals.

Petal Pie

A pretty petal pie, prepared for special occasions or when life needs beautifying. Flowers needn't exist solely in the garden. **Serves 6–8.**

250 g pre-prepared puff pastry
300 ml cream, whipped
150 ml plain yoghurt
2 tbsp caster sugar
1 egg yolk, beaten
2–3 tbsp rosewater
4 roses, crystallised petals (see page 126)

Preheat oven to 190 °C/375 °F. For pastry base, line a 25-cm flan ring with the pastry sitting above the edge. Fold pastry over to make a double edge slightly above the ring. Prick bottom of pastry well and bake in oven for 10 minutes.

To make filling, whip cream, add yoghurt, sugar and egg yolk. Mix together and add rosewater. Pour into prepared flan case and bake at 190°C/375 °F for about 20 minutes. Allow to cool, cover carefully and place in fridge to set. To serve, place the crystallised petals in circles on top of pie.

Feijoas

Feijoa sellowiana

Every year offers come thick and fast from neighbours trying to offload bags of feijoas. As the fruit drop to the ground, helpless gardeners do their best to use up the plentiful fruit. It's not that they are not liked, it's just that the trees are abundant in this country and when they fruit they are extremely prolific.

Feijoas have a gritty, jelly-like pulp encased in a lime-green, bitter, banana-like skin. If that doesn't sound appealing, the distinctive taste is. Every year kids in the neighbourhood wait in anticipation for the hedged plants and overloaded neighbour's tree to bear, and the fruit to fall to the ground. They bite them in half, suck out the pulp and chuck the skins back over the fence. That is how I remember feijoas. They are also commercially grown in New Zealand and the flavour of feijoa appears in many manufactured products like drinks and cereals.

These fruit are native to Brazil and Argentina, and cope well growing in warm coastal areas. Sometimes called the 'pineapple guava', the trees appear similar to our native pohutukawa, especially when they flower in the early summer.

What is common with feijoas is that they will grow everywhere in New Zealand and in abundance. So if you don't grow your own plant, there will always be someone in the area who has a fruiting plant and wants to use up the fruit.

HOW TO GROW

You will not be able to enjoy the rewards of a feijoa plantation quickly – it may take up to five years before your tree bears fruit. But once they do, they are prolific fruiters and a great plus to any edible garden, big or small. Feijoas seem to thrive in most gardens without constant feeding, pruning and attention. One tip though: don't plant just one, it is important to have two or more trees in your garden to help with pollination. Bees and insects are the best pollinators, so don't scare these beautiful creatures from your small garden. They will be encouraged by the beautiful red stamens that appear in late spring. The trees grow best in full sun in well-drained soil. The trees grow well in hedges for larger gardens, to replace more boring ornamental plants, or equally well in wooden pots or concrete tubs. A good prune once the fruit has fallen will encourage good fruiting the following year. Add plenty of compost and sand for good drainage.

PICKING & STORING

The fruit of the feijoa tree is ready when the first ones start to fall to the ground, which is about April to May. The season will finish quickly once the cold weather sets in, as the fruit will brown and rot with excess rain about.

Fresh — Ripe feijoas may be refrigerated, but they don't have to be. Placed in a brown paper bag at room temperature is usually a sufficient way to store. If the fruit is not so ripe put an apple in the bag. Ripe feijoas will last about 3–5 days. If storing the pulp only, lemon juice may be added to any feijoa mixture to stop browning.

Freeze — Feijoas freeze really well. Peel and dice into small pieces and boil for 5 minutes with a few squeezes of lemon juice. Put pieces in a plastic container or freezer bag, or purée the feijoas in a blender or food processor and pour the pulp into an ice cube tray, again with a little lemon juice. When frozen, remove from tray and put the cubes in a freezer bag.

Preserve — Feijoas are ideal for chutneys, and with their raw, earthy flavour they partner well with apples, mangoes, figs, prunes or apricots. They can be made into jams, drinks or liqueurs, or added to flavour vodka.

CULINARY USES

Ripe feijoas have a unique and distinctive taste and aroma. The flesh can be eaten raw or used to tenderise meat, make into pickles or cold or hot desserts. The flesh can also be pulped down to make a concentrate for drinks.

Feijoas best complement other fruits, especially tropical flavours like mango, passion-fruit, rambutans or dragonfruit. They will work well in baking as a tart equivalent to apples and pears and quinces. Because of the feijoas' quizzical taste, they handle spices like cinnamon, allspice, nutmeg and ginger really well. The feijoa fruit has a high pectin content which makes it a perfect fruit for jam and chutney making.

Cook's Tip

Feijoa pulp will oxidise and turn brown quickly. Use the pulp quickly or add a squeeze of lemon juice to avoid the browning.

QUICK PICKINGS

Feijoa Salsa

Peel and finely chop 3 large feijoas and mix with 1 red onion, peeled and finely diced. You could also use the diced flesh from an apple cucumber. Stir through 1 tbsp brown sugar, juice of 1 lemon and freshly ground black pepper and serve with barbecued steak or chicken.

Feijoa & Strawberry Dessert

Halve 2 large feijoas, scoop out pulp and discard skins. In a blender or food processor purée feijoa pulp with 1 cup fresh or frozen strawberries and juice of ½ lemon. Add ½ cup white sugar and pulse. In a small saucepan combine ½ cup milk with 2 tsp gelatine, let stand for 1 minute until gelatine has moistened. Combine with fruit pulp and stir in 1 cup plain low-fat yoghurt. Freeze in an ice cream maker or plastic tray and keep stirring until a frozen dessert forms.

Feijoa Jam

Place 1 kg feijoa pulp in a preserving pan or large, wide saucepan and add ½ cup water, and the juice and zest of 1 lemon. Bring mixture to a boil over medium heat and cook until fruit is soft, about 15 minutes. Add 1 kg white sugar and stir until it dissolves. Bring jam to a rapid boil and cook without stirring until mixture reaches the setting point (see page 18), about 20 minutes. Pour jam into sterilised jars (see page 18), cool and seal. Jam can be eaten immediately. **Makes 6–8 cups.**

Feijoa & Banana Bran Muffins

Preheat oven to 200 °C/400 °F. Sift 320 g self-raising flour into a bowl and mix with ½ cup baking bran. In another bowl, mash together 6–8 peeled feijoas with 1 banana. Pour in ½ cup warm milk and ½ tsp baking soda. Melt 100 g butter, and add 1 cup brown sugar and 2 eggs. Stir well. Combine fruit mixture with butter mixture, then mix liquids into flour and bran. Do not over-mix, it should still have a few dry bits. Spoon mixture into a 12-hole muffin tin. Bake for 18–20 minutes, until muffins are golden brown and spring back when touched.

Feijoa Chutney

When feijoas come into season, pinch and plunder as many as you can to make chutneys and jams. This chutney is perfect with winter roast meats or for the summer barbecue. Add spoonfuls to your crockpot curries for extra flavour as well. **Makes 6 x 300-g jars.**

1 kg feijoas, peeled and roughly chopped
3 onions, peeled and finely diced
320 g dates, soaked and chopped
340 g raisins, roughly chopped
500 g brown sugar
1 tbsp ground ginger
½ tsp ground cloves
½ tsp cayenne pepper
1 tbsp curry powder
750 ml white vinegar
500 ml water

Combine all ingredients in large preserving pan or heavy-based saucepan. Stir over a medium to low heat, without boiling, until sugar is dissolved. Bring to boil, simmer, uncovered, stirring occasionally, for about 1½ hours or until mixture has thickened. Make sure it does not catch on the bottom of the pan.

The chutney is ready when a spoon run across the bottom of the pan parts the chutney and it doesn't move back. Remove any scum from top of pot with a slotted spoon. Pour chutney into hot sterilised jars (see page 18). Seal well with jar lids when cold.

Minted Feijoa Sauce

This sauce is better made ahead of time for dinners or barbecues. Fresh-off-the-tree feijoas make this sauce work well with chicken or pork steaks. **Makes 350 ml.**

3 tbsp caster sugar
60 ml water
2 tbsp fresh mint, chopped
1 tbsp orange juice, freshly squeezed
½ lemon, juice of
4 feijoas, peeled and diced

In a small saucepan, bring sugar and water to the boil, and cook for 2–3 minutes, stirring frequently. Don't let it burn. Remove from heat, stir in the mint and citrus juices, and leave for 30 minutes. Gently stir in feijoas, and let sit for 30–60 minutes before serving.

Feijoa Curry

Full of flavour, the feijoa fruit can take on strong curry spices well. It is common in India to add fruit to curries. When the fruit is falling all over the ground, use them in this brew to bring a unique flavour to the chicken. Accompany with minted yoghurt, rice and naan bread for a real touch of India. **Serves 4.**

¼ cup olive oil
4 chicken breasts, skinned, boned and cut into bite-size chunks
2 carrots, peeled and thinly sliced
2 red, yellow or green capsicum, diced
1 onion, peeled and thinly sliced
1 clove garlic, peeled and crushed
4–5 ripe feijoas, peeled, halved lengthwise and cut into thick slices
1 tbsp curry powder
½ tsp salt
¼ tsp allspice
⅛ tsp ground black pepper
1 litre chicken stock
1 tbsp cornflour mixed with 2 tbsp cold water

In a heavy-based frying pan, heat a little olive oil. Sauté chicken for 3 minutes, or until just starting to brown, and remove from pan. Heat remaining oil in frying pan and sauté carrots, capsicums, onion and garlic for 5 minutes or until carrots are nearly tender.

Add chicken back to frying pan with feijoas, curry powder, salt, allspice and pepper. Heat chicken stock in a separate saucepan and when simmering add to chicken and vegetable mixture. Bring to boil, then reduce heat. Add cornflour and water to thicken, and simmer, covered, for 20 minutes. Serve with basmati rice.

Feijoa Crumble

This is a quick and easy dessert and best served with lashings of custard and cream. The riper the feijoas the better, but not too brown. **This recipe makes four individual desserts or can easily be made in one medium Pyrex dish as a whole dessert.**

10–14 medium-sized feijoas
1 orange, finely grated zest of
4 tsp brown sugar
4 tbsp water
100 g butter
160 g plain flour
80 g wholemeal flour
4 tbsp brown sugar
2 Weetbix, crumbled

Preheat oven to 160 °C/325 °F. Peel and slice feijoas and place in four individual dessert-sized ramekins. Sprinkle over orange zest and a tsp of brown sugar and a tbsp of water on top of each.

In a separate bowl, combine butter, flours, second measure of sugar and crumble in the Weetbix. Mix with a knife or fingers until it resembles fine breadcrumbs. This can be done in a food processor, but has a better texture if crumbled with your fingers.

Sprinkle topping over fruit and press down slightly. Bake for 30 minutes, until the fruit is stewed and the topping crisp. The fruit will begin to bubble through the topping, which will tell you when it is cooked.

Feijoa Sponge Cake

This very moist cake can be kept in a sealed cake tin as a delicious snack. Or serve it warm with cream and custard for a gorgeous autumn dessert. The cake will freeze well if not intended for eating on the same day. When you remove from freezer, thaw and return to oven for 15–20 minutes and serve with cream and custard. **Serves 8–10.**

6–8 fresh feijoas, peeled and halved
4 tbsp granulated sugar
300 g butter
320 g caster sugar
3 eggs
½ lemon, finely grated rind of
1 tsp vanilla essence
250 ml milk
600 g high grade flour, sifted
1 tsp baking powder

Preheat oven to 180 °C/350 °F. Grease and line a 25-cm springform cake tin with baking paper. Place feijoas in a bowl and sprinkle with first measure of sugar. Toss and leave to sit while preparing cake.

Cream together butter and second measure of sugar. Add eggs one at a time, beating well after each addition. Add lemon rind and vanilla essence. Stir in milk, flour and baking powder.

Pour batter into tin. Arrange feijoas on top. Bake in oven for 60–65 minutes. The fruit will sink into the cake as it cooks.

Lemongrass

Cymbopogon citrates

It is not hard to see why this plant is called lemongrass. It looks like a grass, but has a particularly stunning lemon scent at the bulbous ends. The long, razor-edged leaves carry some of the scent, but it's the pale stem, actually tightly-rolled leaf bases, that is the big culinary prize. Hidden inside the fibrous stems are hundreds of minuscule oil sacs that release the lemon scent. Associated mainly with Thai and South East Asian food, it is used mostly where the citrus tang is needed to complement the heat of chilli and the saltiness of fish sauce. It is best known for its use in the Thai Tom Yam soup.

Don't be without this plant in your small garden. Not only is it an attractive textural-looking plant, in a tall pot or semi-sunny patch of the garden, it is also beautifully scented and makes for easy access to great cooking.

A native to South East Asia, where it grows very well because of the plentiful rain and sunshine, lemongrass is known to the Thais as 'takrai'. In Thailand it is usually grown on small-scale farms and collected from the farms by an agent before being exported. This plant is new to New Zealand, and the flavour of the stalks has made a huge impact on our fusion-style cuisine.

The Thais believe growing lemongrass in the garden helps to keep snakes away and it is often planted to control soil erosion. We don't have snakes in this country, but another of its properties is as a fly and insect repellent when used in an oil burner. Lemongrass is a close relative of citronella and is used to scent insect-repelling candles.

HOW TO GROW

Lemongrass is propagated by taking detached parts of established clumps and transplanting them. This plant rarely flowers, so there is little chance of seed production. Roots soon develop and the plant grows arching, cane-like stems with pale blue-green leaves up to 90 cm long. As the clump spreads, the outside canes are the ones that are sliced off at the base and used for cooking.

It is best grown in a big container, which drains well. You will know when the plant is not happy and needs more water, as the long leaves curl up. The plants like to be moist but not sit in soggy puddles. Typically in Asia you would find lemongrass growing next to ponds and creeks. These plants don't like the cold. If you live in a frosty place, bring the pot inside during the winter. Keep the plant well fed with organic liquid fertiliser such as a seaweed mix.

Preserve — Lemongrass pastes and marinades are a good way of using an abundance of stalks. A good oil will be needed to purée the stems and to cover the paste before sealing in jars. Lemongrass vinegar is a good way to introduce the flavour to salsas and sauces. Bruise and slice several stems and pop into a clean bottle along with a chilli or two for heat, then add enough rice or white wine vinegar to cover generously. Seal and leave on a sunny windowsill for at least a week before using.

Dried — The stalks can be dried and ground into flakes or shredded into pieces. Dried pieces need to be kept in airtight containers with no humidity. Dried lemongrass needs to be soaked overnight before being used.

PICKING & STORING

Use a sharp knife or cutting tool to take the outer stems from the plant. It is the bulbous, dense stems at the bottom that hold the flavour, so trim the top leaves. Cats like the leaves to clean their teeth with, so don't throw them out. The leaves can also be kept and cut up into mulch for your herb garden.

Fresh — Fresh lemongrass will keep if you stand it up in a small glass of cold water and place it in a cool place. It will also last for a few weeks wrapped tightly in plastic wrap and refrigerated.

Freeze — Lemongrass can be frozen, wrapped in a plastic bag, for up to a year. Most imported lemongrass we buy has been frozen. If you chop it into thin rings before you freeze it, you can use it straight from the freezer. Like anything though, freezing will decrease flavour. Fresh is best.

CULINARY USES

Only the bottom 15–20 cm of the plant is of use in the kitchen. Any roots or upper leaves should be trimmed off. Hard outside layers should be peeled away, leaving the soft inner leaves.

There are a number of ways to prepare lemongrass. It can be used whole, or cut diagonally into four or five large chunks. It will need to be bruised if used like this, to help release the essential citrus oils. Use the blunt edge of a cleaver, rolling pin or heavy knife to smash the fibrous stem apart. Otherwise it can simply be used as a seasoning, in which case you would remove it before serving the dish.

Lemongrass is indigestible, so long stems are used for flavour and then discarded. Thai people often leave pieces of lemongrass in their dishes. They pick up the pieces with their fingers and suck the lemony flavour out to refresh their palates.

In Thailand, lemongrass is ground into curry pastes, used to flavour broths and to add its wonderful fragrance to fresh, vivid salads. It can be used in puddings, or infused in a sugar syrup, perhaps with a hint of fresh ginger. Drizzle the syrup over vanilla ice cream, stir into whipped cream or use it to liven up fruit salad or strawberries.

Lemongrass goes well with fish and shellfish, or with a tomato-based sauce for a fish stew. Or it can be infused in oil to scent home-made mayonnaise. Flavour clear honey with finely chopped lemongrass; store for a few days, then use in baked custards or drizzle over Greek yoghurt.

An essential oil from lemongrass leaves is used in aromatherapy to reduce fever, help the immune system fight infections, as a painkiller for headaches and muscular pain, as an anti-depressant and to help reduce lethargy and stress. Chopped lemongrass can be made into an infusion that is believed to be effective against the flu, and as an aid to digestion. Chinese and Thai women sometimes bathe in lemongrass-scented water after giving birth to help with their hormones and menstrual cycle.

QUICK PICKINGS

Chicken With Lemongrass

Process 1 tbsp finely chopped lemongrass, 2-cm piece fresh grated ginger, 3 cloves chopped garlic, ¼ cup chopped coriander and ¼ cup chopped mint in a food processor. Add 2 tbsp peanut oil, season to taste and process until a fine paste forms. Combine 500 g chopped chicken thigh fillets with paste and marinate for 30 minutes. Stir-fry over high heat for 4–5 minutes and serve with steamed rice and sweet chilli sauce.

Lemongrass Tea

Allow one bruised stalk of trimmed lemongrass for each cup of tea. Boil in a pan with some water for several minutes, then transfer to a jug to serve.

Prawn & Lemongrass Noodles

Cook 100 g vermicelli rice noodles according to directions on packet, then drain. Heat 1 tbsp peanut oil in a large saucepan, add 2 cloves chopped garlic, 1–2 chopped fresh, small red chillies and cook over medium heat for 30 seconds, then add 6 cups chicken or fish stock. Bruise 1 stick lemongrass with a pestle, tie into a knot, add to soup with 2 Kaffir lime leaves and simmer for 5 minutes. Add 300 g peeled and de-veined green prawns and ¼ cup lime juice and simmer for 3–5 minutes. Add drained noodles and season to taste with fish sauce and more lime juice. Discard lemongrass and serve immediately.

Lemongrass With Fruit & Coconut Ice Cream

Combine 220 g caster sugar, 125 ml lime juice and 300 ml water in a saucepan. Add 1 bruised lemongrass stick tied in a knot and 1 cinnamon stick and stir over low heat until sugar dissolves. Increase heat and simmer for 5–10 minutes, or until slightly syrupy. Cool for 20 minutes, then remove lemongrass. Combine sliced mango, peeled lychees and halved strawberries in a bowl, pour syrup over, cover and refrigerate until cold. Serve with coconut ice cream.

Lemongrass Marinade

This marinade may be made in advance and kept in the fridge for 5 days. It is best used for marinating beef pieces, fish, pork or chicken before putting them in a stir-fry. Also great for spreading over raw vegetables before grilling on a barbecue. **Makes 1 cup.**

- 4 stalks lemongrass, cut into pieces and bruised
- 2.5-cm piece fresh ginger root, peeled and grated
- 4 cloves garlic, peeled
- 2 shallots, peeled and roughly chopped
- 2 tbsp brown sugar
- ½ cup Mirin or Japanese cooking wine
- 2 tbsp fish sauce
- 6 tbsp canola oil

Push lemongrass, ginger, garlic and shallots through feed tube of a food processor with motor running. Process until very finely chopped. Add sugar, Mirin or cooking wine and fish sauce. Process until puréed, scraping sides as needed to incorporate all the pieces. With motor running, slowly add oil. Process until well emulsified. Keep in a sealed container in the fridge.

Lemongrass Paste

This paste can be used to flavour fish dishes, chicken, pork or any stir-fry. Try using it as a flavour base to a coconut cream curry or rice pilaf dish. **Makes 1 cup.**

- 2 tsp extra virgin olive oil
- 6 shallots, peeled and finely chopped
- 3-cm piece fresh ginger root, peeled and grated
- 3 cloves garlic, peeled and crushed
- 1 stalk lemongrass, cut into pieces and pounded
- ¼ cup water

Heat oil in a medium saucepan over medium to low heat. Add shallots, ginger, garlic, lemongrass and water. Cover and cook until very tender, for about 8–10 minutes. Remove cover and cook until liquid has evaporated, about 1 minute more. Transfer to a food processor and purée to form a smooth paste. Keep refrigerated in a jar or sealed container for up to 5 days.

Lemongrass Crab Cakes

Very tasty finger food for your summer barbecue or Thai-style dinner party. These crab cakes can be made ahead of time and then cooked fresh just before serving. **Makes 24.**

1 tbsp oil
4 spring onions, finely chopped
1 clove garlic, peeled and crushed
2.5-cm piece fresh ginger root, peeled and grated
1 small red chilli, deseeded and finely chopped
1 stalk lemongrass, very finely chopped
350 g fresh or frozen crab meat
2 tbsp fresh coriander, chopped
1 tsp fish sauce
75 g white breadcrumbs
3 eggs
freshly ground black pepper
50 g plain flour
sunflower oil, for deep-frying
to garnish, coriander sprigs and shredded red chilli

Heat oil in a small pan and add spring onions, garlic, ginger, chilli and lemongrass. Cook gently for 2–3 minutes or until soft. Transfer to a bowl, cool and stir in crab meat, coriander, fish sauce, 6 tbsp of breadcrumbs and one egg. Mix and season with black pepper only.

Shape tablespoonfuls of mixture into 18 balls, flatten the crab balls into cakes with the palm of your hand and shallow-fry in a little oil. Place on a baking sheet and chill for 20 minutes. Coat each cake lightly with flour, roll in remaining beaten eggs, then the remaining breadcrumbs.

Shallow-fry in batches in hot oil for 3–4 minutes or until golden. Drain on absorbent paper towel and keep warm while frying the remaining cakes. Garnish with coriander and shredded red chilli, and serve with sweet chilli sauce (see page 79).

Lemongrass & Sweet Basil Pilaf

This pilaf is packed full of fragrant flavours. Basil leaves can be swapped for mint leaves or even parsley in this dish. It is best served with grilled vegetables and a mild curry. **Serves 4.**

1 tbsp olive oil
1 large red onion, peeled and finely chopped
2 garlic cloves, peeled and crushed
1 tbsp mustard seeds
2 stalks lemongrass, very finely chopped
1 tbsp cumin seeds
1 lemon, finely grated rind and juice of
350 g jasmine rice
1.6 litres vegetable stock
450 g sugar snap peas
1 small bunch sweet basil leaves
salt and freshly ground black pepper

Heat oil in a large frying pan and sauté onion, garlic, mustard seeds, lemongrass and cumin seeds for 3–4 minutes. Add lemon rind, juice and rice and stir until rice is translucent, about 3–4 minutes. Stir in stock and simmer, uncovered, for 15 minutes until rice is tender and stock has been absorbed.

Remove rice from heat. Scatter over sugar snap peas and cover pan with a tight-fitting lid. Leave to stand for 5 minutes. Fluff up rice with a fork and stir in basil leaves. Season to taste and serve immediately.

Lemongrass Salad

All the flavours of the Pacific brought to your house. Grow your own lemongrass, chillies and salad ingredients, and the salad takes on a life of its own. The coconut is optional, but gives a gorgeous nutty and creamy texture. Serves 8.

Lemongrass Dressing

2 stalks lemongrass, very finely chopped
3 limes, juice of
⅓ cup chilli sauce
¼ cup fish sauce
50 g sugar

Salad

2 tsp oil
500 g prawns, shelled and de-veined
1 cup shredded coconut (optional)
300 g cabbage, shredded
20 green beans, cut into 2.5-cm lengths and blanched
1 cup roasted peanuts, coarsely chopped
1 cup fresh coriander leaves, chopped
1 red onion, peeled and thinly sliced
1 bunch mint leaves, roughly chopped
¼ cup Kaffir lime leaves, finely chopped

To make lemongrass dressing, combine ingredients in a bowl.

Heat a grilling pan over medium-high heat until hot. Brush pan with 1 tsp oil. Grill prawns until flesh turns pink, about 2 minutes on each side. Brush prawns with a little oil during grilling to prevent sticking. Remove and set aside. Spread coconut in a small pan, toast over medium heat, shaking pan frequently, until lightly browned, 4–5 minutes. In a large salad bowl, combine cabbage and beans with other salad ingredients. Add dressing and toss well. Transfer to a serving platter, top with grilled shrimp and toasted coconut and serve.

Tom Yam Kung (pictured)

In Thailand there are many variations to this soup, also known as sour prawn soup. Regional and cultural variations will add vegetables, extra chillies or more sour lime depending on their family traditions. Fish can be substituted for prawns, and lemon rind can be used instead of Kaffir lime leaves if unavailable. Serves 4–6.

1 lemon or lime, cut into quarters
2 cloves garlic, peeled and finely chopped
2 red chillies, deseeded and finely chopped
2 Kaffir lime leaves
2 stalks lemongrass, cut into pieces and bruised
1 tsp fish sauce
2 tsp ground coriander
1 tsp chilli paste
¼ tsp white pepper
1.5 litres chicken or fish stock
750 g prawns, peeled and de-veined
4 spring onions
2 lemons, juice of

In a large saucepan put lemon or lime, garlic, chillies, lime leaves, lemongrass, fish sauce, coriander, chilli paste, pepper and stock.

Bring to a rapid boil then reduce heat and simmer for 20 minutes. Add prawns and cook 5–7 minutes or until the prawns have changed colour. Trim spring onions and chop finely.

Add spring onions to soup with lemon juice. Remove lime leaves and pieces of lemon. Serve hot.

Lemons

Citrus medica

A lemon tree is perfect to grow in anyone's garden. They will nestle into the sunniest of spots, next to decks and verandas or as a centrepiece in a container on a balcony. Lemons are the fruit of the citron tree. They are very acidic and highly scented. The trees originally came from India, but now grow outdoors in temperate areas of the world.

Lemons are one of the most commonly used fruits we grow in our garden. A tree is invaluable to provide you with citrus juice on tap. Look after it and it will look after you with prolific, sweet, tangy fruit.

Lemons, like most citrus, provide us with a valuable source of vitamin C. Whole trees were grown on sailing ships to give the crew a source of vitamins to prevent scurvy. The fruit, which was taken from India to the Mediterranean by the wandering Romans, has become a staple in the European and Arab cuisine. The lemon was rare and expensive in days gone by and treated as a delicacy for any cooking. Now even though we have an abundance of these acidic fruit growing in our own back yards, they still need to be treated with respect.

Classic lemon dishes include the French tarte au citron, or lemon tart. Then there is Middle Eastern lemon sherbet, which is where lemonade comes from. Chicken tagine with preserved lemons is historically one of the oldest dishes in Moroccan cuisine, and of course where would we be without lemon meringue pie?

HOW TO GROW

Lemon trees will love the sunniest spot of a sunny garden. They are bushy and full of lush green foliage so can be a useful border plant, as well as growing in large pots and containers. They require a warm, sunny, protected position out of cold winds. They don't like frosts or extremely cold weather. The container with soil should have good drainage. Improve drainage of your soil by digging in extra sand and use a good container mix.

Buy grafted plants from a nursery for hardy stock. Plant your tree no deeper than it is already set in the bag. Treat the roots carefully, as citrus trees do not like their roots to be disturbed. The roots grow close to the surface, so mulch the base of the plant to keep in moisture and suppress weeds. As well as compost, add a slow-release citrus fertiliser. Lemons plants are big feeders, they require regular feeding for optimal fruiting and growth. Apply citrus fertiliser monthly.

Citrus will need watering during spring and summer, but not usually in winter. Water your plants when the top soil is dry. For container plants, this will probably mean daily watering during summer. Insufficient water will result in poor plant growth, and bitter fruit.

Remove fruit buds in the first year of the tree's life to assist your young tree to establish, and leading to better fruiting in the second year. Lemon trees are heavy croppers, often setting more fruit than they can sustain. Early removal of approximately one third of the crop will result in improved fruit quality.

PICKING & STORING

Choose lemons that are heavy for their size and have no soft brown spots. Lemons do not ripen off the tree, so if you grow your own tree, pick only as much as you need. Twist the lemon when picking to take it easily from its stalk, alternatively cut the stalk. Pruning off the stalk helps with the fruit production for the next year. Lemons that fall to the ground are already half way to rotting.

Fresh — Lemons will keep at room temperature for up to seven days, or you can extend their storage time for up to two weeks in the fridge. Avoid storing damp lemons as they will become mouldy quickly and deteriorate rapidly.

Freeze — The frozen fruit is only really good for making marmalade or such things. Freeze the lemon juice in ice cube trays or small bags for all-year-round supply.

Dried — Grated lemon rind can be added to caster sugar, spread on a tray until dried, then stored to make a fragrant sugar for sprinkling on berries, cakes or pancakes. Or peel off strips of lemon rind, and place on brown paper. Allow to dry in hot water cupboard overnight. Next day, blitz in the food processor and seal in a jar to use in candies or desserts.

Preserves — There are many ways to preserve lemons. The Greek way is to combine with salt and oil and place in jars (see page 147), or try making a lemon confit (see page 150), lemon jam, crystallised lemon zest, candied peel or lemon curd. Any one of these will preserve the zesty flavours all year round.

CULINARY USES

Lemons can be found in nearly every cuisine in the world. The only exception may be Asian cuisine where limes are usually used. They are indispensable in cooking, as they have the ability, like salt, to bring other flavours to life. They blend well with sugar and salt and are a valuable source of pectin when making preserves and jams. The citric acid is also a valuable tool when cutting fruits and vegetables such as artichokes, pears and apples, to stop them from browning.

While the juice of the lemon holds the flavour, it is the oil in the rind of the fruit that contains the perfume. When removing the rind with a grater or small sharp knife, it is important to remove as little of the white pith below as possible, as it is very bitter. When preparing whole lemons for cooking or for making candied rind, blanch them first in several changes of water. This removes bitterness and softens the fruit, which counteracts the hardening effect of cooking in sugar.

Lemons are great company for anchovies, chicken, chilli, cream, eggs, fish, garlic, lamb, leeks, mint, pasta, potatoes, rice, ricotta, rosemary, sage, shellfish and thyme. In fact most herbs are complementary and most meats have some kind of recipe with lemon flavouring.

Preserved lemons can be used for many different dishes, again because they take on new characteristics from their preservation. Preserved lemons can be used to stuff chickens; with tiger prawns on skewers; thinly sliced in tagines; or finely diced and added to mayonnaise, hollandaise and guacamole.

Cook's Tip

To extract the maximum juice, before squeezing, roll the lemon around on a chopping board for a few minutes or hold it under warm running water or put the whole lemon in the microwave on high for 5 seconds only.

Cook's Tip

To save on the pain of scrubbing the lemon grater, press a sheet of greaseproof paper onto the teeth before grating. Also, place a piece on the chopping board to easily pick up all the zest from the board. Use a pastry brush to extract as much of the rind from the grater as possible.

QUICK PICKINGS

Candied Peel

Peel wide strips of lemon rind, leaving a little white pith attached, then blanch three times in boiling water. Drain, then cover with a sugar syrup and simmer gently until rind is tender and almost translucent. Drain and cool completely on wire racks. Finely chop and use in fruit cakes or biscuits.

Crystallised Lemon Zest

With a zester, remove zest from two lemons and place shreds in a saucepan with enough water to cover. Bring to boil, remove from heat, drain zest, and then repeat the process twice more. Place a cup of caster sugar and a cup of water in a saucepan with blanched zest and simmer gently until it is translucent. Strain off liquid, allow zest to cool and place in a container with a handful of caster sugar. Seal container and shake until zest is covered with sugar.

Lemon Jam

Peel the skins from 24 lemons. Blanch the skins (see page 17). When they are soft, drain them. Chop up the lemon skins and rub half of them through a sieve. Cut the rest into thin strips. Mix these ingredients and moisten with the juice of 8 lemons. Add an amount of sugar equal in weight to the lemon skins. Cook in a preserving pan in the same way as other jams.

Preserved Lemons

Wash and dry 20 lemons. Cut each lemon into quarters from the top to within 1 cm of the bottom, taking care to leave the four pieces joined at the stem end. Place them in a plastic bag in the freezer for 24 hours. Remove from freezer and allow to defrost. Stuff the insides of lemons with a heaped tsp of sea salt. Arrange them neatly in a 5-litre jar, sprinkling each layer of lemons with salt and crushed coriander seeds. Add extra freshly squeezed juice and honey mixed with warm water to almost the top of the jar. Leave some airspace before closing the jar. Place a piece of cardboard on the bottom of a large pot and sit the jar on top. This stops it vibrating. Add warm water to cover the jar completely and slowly bring it to the boil. Boil for 6–7 minutes then remove from heat. Gently lift jar from pot.

Let the lemons sit in a warm place for 1 month before opening, turning the jar upside down periodically to distribute salt and juices. Once opened, keep refrigerated. If lemons are not frozen first, then the maturation process will take at least three months. To use the lemon, remove from brine and discard pulp. Wash rind and use. Some white crystals will form on the top lemons, which is normal, so do not discard them.

Home-Made Lemonade

Squeeze 4 lemons and reserve juice. Put juice and 1 cup sugar into a saucepan and place on the stove. Heat through until sugar has dissolved. Be careful not to let it boil over and burn. Remove from heat and leave to cool. In a large jug, place lemon slices and plenty of ice. Pour over lemon syrup and fill up with ice-cold or soda water. Give mixture a good stir and then serve. The syrup can be made ahead of time and kept in a jar in the fridge. Spoon into jugs and fill with water when needed. **Makes 3 litres.**

Lemon Curd (pictured)

This is a classic recipe but it is important in preserving the flavour of lemons and can be used almost anywhere. I like to double this recipe and use it on everything from ice cream to fruit salad to soufflés, muffins or just plain old toast. **Makes 4 x 200-ml jars.**

4 lemons
125 g butter
2 cups sugar
4 eggs, beaten

Grate rind of the lemon. Avoid white part as it is bitter. Squeeze lemons and drain the juice, removing all pips and pith.

Melt butter in a large glass bowl, over a pot of boiling water. Stir in sugar and lemon juice until sugar is well dissolved, for about 5 minutes. Remove from heat. Add eggs and lemon rind.

Replace over boiling water and cook, stirring all the time until mixture thickens. Pour into hot sterilised jars (see page 18). Once opened, store in fridge.

Lemon Confit

(pictured on previous page)

This is a different way to preserve lemons, but uses a similar salted method to achieve the end result. These lemons are ideally used on pancakes, or in cheesecakes, baked tarts, fruit salads or in baked breads and muffins. **Makes 900 ml.**

850 g lemons, washed
770 g caster sugar
8 lemongrass stalks or lemon thyme sprigs

Bring a large saucepan of heavily salted water to the boil over high heat, then add lemons and return to boil. Drain, refresh in cold water and drain again.

Cut lemons widthways into 5-mm thick slices and remove seeds. Place 1.25 litres water and sugar in a large saucepan, then bring to boil over medium heat, stirring until sugar dissolves. Add lemon slices and lemongrass stalks or lemon thyme sprigs, reduce heat to low and simmer for 1½ hours or until lemons are soft and translucent and liquid has reduced to a thick syrup. Remove from heat and cool to room temperature. Pack into 1-litre sterilised jars (see page 18), seal. Keep the lemons covered and they will keep for up to 1 month.

Fennel, Anchovy & Lemon Spread

Accompanied by salty condiments like prosciutto, capers and queen olives, this dip is a perfect companion to any antipasto platter. Serve with toasted sourdough or sesame crackers. **Makes about 2 cups.**

1 small bulb of fennel, trimmed and chopped
70 g blanched almonds, roasted and finely chopped
70 g pistachios, finely chopped
8 anchovy fillets, finely chopped
1 tsp salted capers, rinsed
½ lemon, juice of and finely grated rind
⅓ cup extra virgin olive oil
2 tbsp fresh basil, chopped
sea salt and freshly ground black pepper
to serve, extra virgin olive oil and sourdough baguette

In a food processor or blender, process fennel, nuts, anchovies, capers and lemon rind until a coarse purée forms. With the motor running, add lemon juice and olive oil and process until combined. Transfer purée to a bowl, add basil, season to taste and stir to combine. Drizzle with olive oil and serve with toasted bread.

Lemon Sauce

I would have this sauce on just about anything – from fresh spring asparagus, steamed cabbage or fish, pork or chicken steaks or drizzled all over barbecued mussels. It will go a long way in any household. **Serves 6–8.**

4 large egg yolks
1 tsp caster sugar
3 lemons, juice of, strained
½ tsp finely grated lemon zest
½ cup chicken or fish stock
generous pinch salt
generous pinch cayenne pepper
1–2 tbsp cream (optional)

Place egg yolks into a metal or glass bowl. Add sugar, lemon juice and zest and beat with a whisk or electric hand beater until light and creamy. Place bowl over a saucepan of gently simmering water. You don't want the bowl to touch the water and the water should never boil. Continue to whisk or beat for 5 minutes until well aerated and thick.

Gradually add stock and continue to whisk or beat over low heat until mixture thickens, about 12–15 minutes. The sauce should be the consistency of thick cream and will thicken as it cools. When cool, season with salt and cayenne pepper and if a richer sauce is desired, fold in cream. Cover and refrigerate until required. Will last 2–3 days in the fridge.

Lemon Chicken Soup

This is a fabulously easy soup to make, with tart tastes to inspire the palate. A quick soup for dinner or lunch. It is quite amazing how the zesty lemon can show off the flavours of many other ingredients so well. **Serves 4.**

25 g butter
1 small onion, peeled and finely chopped
25 g plain flour
850 ml chicken stock
1 lemon, finely grated zest and juice of
1 skinless, boneless chicken breast, cut into small cubes
2 tbsp sour cream
salt and freshly ground black pepper
2 tbsp fresh parsley, chopped

Melt butter in a saucepan. Add onion. Cover and cook on a very low heat until soft, but not coloured, around 10 minutes. Stir in flour. Cook for 1 minute. Increase heat, pour in stock and stir until boiling, to dissolve all the flour.

Add lemon zest, one tbsp of lemon juice and chicken. Cover and simmer for 15 minutes. Stir in sour cream and remaining lemon juice to taste. Season and sprinkle with parsley.

Lemon & Oregano Pork

If I had my way I would put lemon into everything. It has a way of cutting through and making dull food taste scrumptious. Make a regular schnitzel meal into something a little bit special by adding the yellow zest and fragrant herbs to the pork. A rather simple dish for the whole family. **Serves 4.**

1 lemon, finely grated zest and juice of
2 cups dried breadcrumbs
2 tbsp fresh oregano, finely chopped
1 clove garlic, peeled and finely crushed
4 pork schnitzels
2 tbsp sunflower oil
to serve, lemon mayonnaise

On a plate, mix together lemon zest, breadcrumbs, oregano and garlic. Pour lemon juice onto another plate. Dip each pork schnitzel first into lemon juice and then into breadcrumb mixture until well coated.

Heat oil in a large frying pan over a high heat and fry pork for 3–4 minutes on each side, until crumbs are crisp and pork is cooked through. Serve each schnitzel with a spoonful of lemon mayonnaise, new potatoes and steamed green beans.

Lemon Biscotti

These biscotti become somewhat addictive. You won't want to keep the biscuit tin empty for too long. They work well with herbal teas in the afternoon after gardening, or as teething biscuits for young infants. Keep the biscotti in airtight containers, and they will keep their freshness for a long time. **Makes about 48.**

500 g plain flour
1 tsp baking powder
½ tsp salt
2 large eggs, at room temperature, plus 1 extra for brushing
250 g caster sugar
60 ml extra light olive oil
3 large lemons, finely grated rind of
125 ml milk

Preheat oven to 180 °C/350 °F. Line 2 baking trays with baking paper. Combine flour, baking powder and salt, then sift into a bowl.

Place eggs in another bowl and beat with an electric mixer until foamy. Gradually add sugar, beating constantly until mixture is pale and thick, about 3–4 minutes. Beat in oil, then lemon rind.

Add flour mixture and milk to egg mixture, alternating, beginning and ending with flour. Combine until it forms a sticky dough. Transfer dough to a well-floured surface and divide into 2 equal parts. Shape into logs, about 3 cm thick. Carefully, place logs 5 cm apart on one of the prepared trays. Combine extra egg with 2 tsp water and brush over logs. Bake until golden and firm, about 25 minutes, turning baking tray for even baking. When cooked, place tray on a wire rack and cool for 10 minutes. Leave oven on.

Using a bread knife, cut logs diagonally into 1-cm-thick slices. Lay slices on baking trays and bake again for 10 minutes. Turn slices over and bake for another 8–10 minutes or until golden. Cool on wire racks.

Lemon Shortbread Biscuits (Gluten-Free)

If you are a slave to your bowels and follow a gluten-free diet, or even if you are looking for a more nutty shortbread, this is the recipe for you. Work quickly with dough and keep it chilled and you shall receive crispy biscuits at the end of the cooking process. **Makes 35.**

175 g butter
75 g caster sugar
3 lemons, finely grated rind of
175 g rice flour
75 g ground almonds
to decorate, 200 g white chocolate buttons, melted

Preheat oven to 180 °C/350 °F. Cream butter until soft. Add sugar and lemon rind and beat until light and fluffy. Add rice flour and ground almonds and mix until well combined.

On a rice flour-covered surface, knead lightly until dough is smooth. Cover with plastic wrap and refrigerate for about 1 hour, which will make dough firmer and easier to handle. Roll out dough on a rice-floured work surface to a thickness of 5 mm. Stamp into rounds with a 4-cm cutter.

Place on several baking sheets covered with baking paper and bake, in batches if necessary, for 10–15 minutes until golden. Leave biscuits to cool for a few minutes on the baking sheet before transferring to a cooling rack. Decorate with melted white chocolate before serving.

Individual Lemon Cheese Tarts

A goat's-milk cheese is usual for these traditional Mediterranean tarts, but here I've found a mixture of smooth cottage cheese and mascarpone works best. These tarts are usually eaten cold with fresh summer melons and grapes. **Serves 6.**

Pastry
100 g plain flour
pinch of salt
50 g butter
1 small egg, beaten

Filling
250 g cottage cheese, sieved
250 g mascarpone
2 eggs
2 lemons, juice and zest of
100 g caster sugar

To make pastry by hand, put flour and salt in a bowl, then rub in butter and egg to bind. Or, put everything except the egg into a food processor and blend, then add egg and blend to make a ball. Wrap in plastic wrap and chill for 30 minutes.

Preheat oven to 180 °C/350 °F. Press pastry out into 6 x 9-cm tartlet tins (with vertical and not sloping sides) and prick the bottom. Line with baking paper and fill with baking beans, and bake blind for 15 minutes. Remove the paper and beans.

To make filling, blend cottage cheese and mascarpone with eggs, lemon juice, sugar and half the zest until smooth. Pour into the tart cases and sprinkle with remaining zest. Bake for 25 minutes until set. The tarts will sink a little but will taste fantastic.

Greek Lemon Pie

This recipe originates from the islands of Greece – the combination of almonds and honey in this dessert makes for a great flavour with the lemon. Perfect for an autumn meal or alfresco lunch. The effort taken is totally worth the treasure at the end. **Serves 8.**

Pastry
150 g plain flour, plus extra for dusting
40 g icing sugar
1 tsp lemon rind, finely grated
150 g cold unsalted butter, finely chopped
2 egg yolks
1 tsp vanilla extract
½ tsp ground nutmeg

Filling
150 g unsalted butter, softened
¼ cup honey
5 egg yolks
165 g ground almonds
60 ml cream
2 lemons, juice of
to serve, Greek yoghurt

Syrup
100 g caster sugar
2 lemons, rind of, cut into thin strips
½ cup water
1 lemon, juice of

To make pastry, blend flour, icing sugar and lemon rind in a food processor until combined. Add butter and process until mixture resembles fine breadcrumbs. Add egg yolks, vanilla and nutmeg, and process until mixture just comes together. Form into a solid lump, then wrap in plastic wrap and refrigerate for 1 hour.

Preheat oven to 180 °C/350 °F. To make the filling, use an electric mixer to beat butter and honey until pale and creamy. Add egg yolks, one at a time, beating well after each, then add ground almonds, cream and lemon juice and stir until combined.

Roll out pastry on a lightly floured surface until 5 mm thick and use to line a 22-cm tart tin with removable base. Cover pastry with baking paper, then fill with baking beans or rice and bake at 180 °C/350 °F for 10 minutes. Remove paper and beans and bake for another 5 minutes or until pastry is dry and golden.

Pour filling into pastry shell, then bake at 160 °C/325 °F for 30–40 minutes or until filling is set. Meanwhile, to make syrup, place sugar, lemon rind and water in a saucepan and bring to the boil, then simmer over medium heat for 5 minutes or until syrup thickens, and leave to cool slightly. Add lemon juice to warm syrup and stir to combine. Spoon warm syrup over warm pie. Serve slices of warm lemon pie with Greek- style yoghurt.

Mint

Mentha

The family of mint plants is large and varied. There is spearmint, apple mint, false apple mint, ginger mint, pineapple mint, water mint, bergamot mint, Japanese mint, Vietnamese mint, red mint, peppermint, penny royal, and so on and so on. Spearmint is what we will commonly find in our gardens, and without much effort at all it grows, just about anywhere. It is completely invasive and crawls its way through open soil so readily it is often thought of more as a weed than a helpful herb.

Mint is amazing. The pure volatile punch you get from the scented leaves, and the essence it imparts to food, make it a necessity to have around. It can be used successfully for sweet and savoury dishes, complements lamb like they were meant to be together forever, and when you think you've had enough, it is the common ingredient in chewing gum.

Mint originally had a medicinal background. Witches in medieval times gave concoctions of mint for pep and exhilaration, or as an aphrodisiac. Greek brides wore wreaths of mint for similar reasons, while children carried bunches of mint to stimulate their minds.

Greeks and Romans introduced spearmint to Britain and it has spread since then. Most importantly, it is known that rats and mice detest mint, which is why it was strewn on floors, churches and in pantries in medieval times. Perhaps that is why some household detergents seem today to still carry the fragrance of mint.

HOW TO GROW

Mint plants grow vigorously, and you are advised to restrict them by burying pots or sinking barriers, such as pieces of slate, around the roots. A small piece of stem, planted in soil, will usually take root. The many varieties of mint can be bought from good nurseries, which may encourage a pot-pourri of flavours. Perfect for pots and containers, or hanging baskets, the trick is to keep pruning the stems back to encourage soft growth and fine tips of leaves. Do not allow to flower, as this will harden the stock and the mint plant loses its flavour.

Keep your mint pot in semi-shade, semi-sun to get the best flavour. Water the plants often and give the soil a few drops of liquid fertiliser every month and you can enjoy fresh mint even in the winter.

PICKING & STORING

Pick the new leaves from the tips of the stems, which will hold more flavour and are less woody in texture than the old growth.

Fresh — Mint leaves will keep in plastic bags for a couple of days, before turning black.

Freeze — Finely chop it and put into ice cube trays and top with water, then freeze; this will give you mint ice cubes for soups and stews when your plant has died down. Whole mint leaves frozen in water will make a refreshing addition to summer drinks, like iced tea or home-made lemonade.

Dried — Dried mint can also be very effective. Because of the strength of oils in mint leaves, dried mint holds the flavour well. Dry the leaves on paper, then crush and seal in jars or plastic bags.

CULINARY USES

Mint is best with lamb, shellfish, chocolate and oranges. With its clean fresh flavour, added to its undoubted digestive properties, mint is a versatile herb. Mint sauce, whatever the French might think, can be superb if you use just a very little white wine vinegar, instead of malt. A bowl of fragrant tabouleh, made with bulgur wheat, spring onions, tomatoes, parsley, lemon juice, olive oil and plenty of fresh mint, is a marvellous salad. Very finely chopped mint goes wonderfully with dark chocolate – stir some into a mousse or icing for a chocolate cake.

QUICK PICKINGS

Minted Ice Tea

Put 10 tea bags in a 4-litre jug and add about 1 litre of hot water. Allow to soak for 20 minutes, until the flavour of the tea comes through. Add to this 100 ml sugar syrup, 2–3 sliced lemons, and a big bunch of mint leaves. Chill and serve over ice cubes. Use apple mint or spearmint leaves for a difference in flavour.

Mint & Grapefruit Sorbet

Make a sugar syrup by combining 1 cup water with ½ cup sugar in a saucepan. Bring to the boil. Simmer for 5 minutes. Remove from heat, add ½ cup fresh mint leaves and let steep for 20 minutes. Strain syrup and discard mint leaves. Juice 2 large pink grapefruit and measure out 1 cup of juice. When syrup has cooled, combine with grapefruit juice. Pour mixture into a plastic container and freeze. After half an hour stir with a fork. Replace in freezer. Keep doing this until soft sorbet forms. Garnish with mint leaves.

Apple & Mint Salsa

Place ½ cup raisins in a small bowl, cover with boiling water, leave to plump up. Drain well. Peel 2 large Granny Smith apples, remove cores and chop. In a bowl toss apples with 2 tbsp lemon juice, 4 finely chopped spring onions, and the leaves of a bunch of mint, finely chopped. Stir in raisins and 1 tbsp honey and stir well. Garnish with extra mint leaves and serve with chicken or duck.

Candied Mint Leaves

Froth up 2 egg whites with a little water. With a small brush, paint fresh leaves of apple or pineapple mint with the egg white and dust both sides with caster sugar. Set each leaf on a sheet of greaseproof paper and allow to dry. They will dry with a frosty crystallised coating and make a nice garnish or a pleasant candy treat.

Chilled Melon & Mint Soup

Place 2 kg ripe, peeled rock melon with ¼ cup fresh mint leaves, ¼ cup lemon juice and 2 tbsp sugar into a food processor or blender and process until smooth. Taste, and add more sugar or lemon juice if desired. Refrigerate until thoroughly chilled. Stir well and serve in chilled bowls. **Serves 6.**

Fresh Mint Chutney

Place 2 bunches fresh mint, 3 limes, peeled and seeds removed, 1 tsp salt, 1 tsp garam masala, 3 tsp sugar, 6 shallots and the flesh of fresh green chillies to taste in a food processor and process to a paste. You may need to add some water. Spoon into a bowl and serve at once.

Mint Chutney

This is excellent with rye bread and Cheddar. To make coriander chutney, simply substitute chopped fresh coriander for chopped fresh mint.

Makes about 1 litre.

- 500 g cooking apples, peeled, cored and chopped
- 250 g onions, peeled and coarsely chopped
- 2 cloves garlic, peeled and finely chopped
- 1 yellow capsicum, deseeded and chopped
- 450 ml white wine vinegar
- 2.5-cm piece fresh ginger, bruised
- 1 tsp whole coriander seeds
- 4 black peppercorns
- 4 whole allspice berries
- 250 g brown sugar
- ½ tbsp sea salt
- 4 tbsp fresh mint, chopped

Put apples, onions, garlic and capsicum into a heavy preserving pan with the vinegar. Bring slowly to boil and simmer until soft, about 30 minutes. Tie together the ginger, coriander seeds, peppercorns and allspice in a piece of muslin. Add to pot along with sugar and salt. Heat gently until sugar has melted, then simmer until thick. This may take as long as 1 hour.

When done, remove from heat. Discard muslin bag with ginger and spices and stir in chopped mint. Spoon into warm sterilised jars (see page 18) and leave to cool. Then close jars tightly, wipe with a damp cloth and label clearly.

Mint Jelly

The leaves of sage, tarragon, thyme or lemon thyme may be substituted for mint. Use half as much sage as mint, but equal amounts of the others. **Makes approx 750 ml.**

- 1 kg Granny Smith apples
- 1 large bunch fresh mint
- ¼ cup lemon juice
- 2 tsp grated lemon rind
- 2 tsp white wine vinegar
- 300 ml water
- 1 kg white sugar, approximately
- ¼ cup finely chopped mint, extra
- green food colouring

Chop unpeeled apples roughly. Put into a deep pan with mint, lemon juice, rind and vinegar. Add water and cover. Bring to boil and simmer for about 30 minutes, until apples are soft and pulpy. Scald a jelly bag or fine cloth by dipping it in boiling water, then pour in apples and mint. Suspend bag over a bowl to drain overnight. Do not push the mixture through the cloth as it will make a cloudy jelly.

Next day measure the juice and add 500 g sugar for every 600 ml of liquid. Bring to boil in a heavy pan and boil steadily until setting point is reached (see page 18). This will probably take 20–30 minutes. Skim off scum and remove pan from heat. Stir in chopped mint. Add enough drops of green food colouring to achieve the desired colour. Pour into sterilised jars (see page 18) and leave to cool completely, then seal jars tightly.

Mint Mojitos

For a taste of Cuba, a mojito, pronounced mo-hee-toh, is a very popular cocktail. Mint and rum make a great combination – best sipped whilst reclining near a sun-drenched beach. Mint is the main flavour in this drink, so fill every glass with many leaves. Use ice cubes and not crushed ice. This keeps the true mojito flavour from being diluted as the ice melts. **Makes 1.**

- water
- sugar or palm sugar
- 1 lime, quartered
- plenty of ice cubes
- a bunch of fresh mint leaves
- 50 ml clear rum, e.g. Bacardi
- soda water
- to garnish, lime wedges and mint sprigs

To make the sugar syrup, put equal parts of water and sugar or palm sugar into a pot and heat on high, stirring all the time. When sugar has dissolved and before it boils, remove from heat and allow to cool.

In a cocktail shaker or large glass, place the lime, ice cubes, mint leaves, 2 tbsp sugar syrup and rum. Give the glass a good stir or the shaker a very good shake, with the lid on. Pour ingredients from the shaker into a tall glass and top with soda water. Garnish with a lime wedge, mint sprig and a swizzle stick or straw.

Parma Ham with Mint & Mango Relish

Parma ham is thinly sliced cured ham. Exquisite in taste, a small amount is an ideal complement to the tropical taste of the mangoes. Prosciutto, or another thinly sliced smoked ham, is just as good. **Serves 6 as a starter.**

3 ripe mangoes
1 passion-fruit
4 tbsp grapeseed oil
3 tbsp lemon juice
salt and freshly ground black pepper
5 tsp fresh mint, chopped
75 g Parma ham

In a processor or blender, purée flesh of one mango with pulp of passion fruit. With motor running, slowly add oil and lemon juice. Season to taste with salt and pepper. Fold in fresh mint.

Thickly slice remaining mangoes and arrange on serving plates with Parma ham. Divide the mint and mango relish among individual dishes or ramekins to accompany and serve.

Rack of Lamb with Mint & Olive Crust

(pictured on previous page)

Feel like a gourmet cook when you put this dish together. It is simple yet totally effective. The lamb presents well under its crumbly topping and the juicy cutlets are tantalising with fresh steamed beans and asparagus. **Serves 6.**

2–3 trimmed racks of lamb
50 g butter
½ cup breadcrumbs
1 bunch fresh mint, chopped
½ cup black Kalamata olives, stones removed
2 cloves garlic, peeled
salt and freshly ground black pepper
2 tbsp wholegrain mustard
to serve, French beans or asparagus

Preheat a roasting tin in oven at 220 °C/425 °F. Trim excess fat from racks of lamb. In a food processor, combine butter with breadcrumbs, chopped mint, olives, garlic, salt and black pepper. Spread meat side of lamb with grainy mustard, then with breadcrumb mixture, pressing it on to lamb well.

Place lamb in roasting tin and cook for 25–30 minutes, basting with pan juices frequently for medium-rare lamb. Remove from oven, cover with foil and stand for 10 minutes before serving. Serve with French beans or asparagus.

Mint & White Chocolate Cheesecake

I have a standard cheesecake recipe that I pull out for nearly every occasion, and it works well. It is the one pudding in the world I can't resist and a sweet and fresh mint-flavoured one like this makes me giddy. It doesn't last long in our house.
Serves 6–8.

250-g packet malt biscuits
1 tsp grated lemon rind
1 tbsp lemon juice
75 g butter, melted

Filling
1 bunch mint leaves, finely chopped
2–3 drops mint essence
½ cup sugar
2 tbsp lemon juice
1 tsp lemon rind
4 tsp gelatine
4 tbsp water
250-g pot cream cheese
250-g pot sour cream
150 g white chocolate, melted
to garnish, grated white chocolate and candied mint leaves (see page 159)

Finely crush biscuits in a food processor. Combine biscuit crumbs, lemon rind, juice and butter. Line base of a 22-cm springform tin with biscuit mixture. Leave to chill while preparing filling.

To make filling, in a bowl mix mint leaves and essence with sugar, lemon juice and rind. Combine gelatine and water. Leave to swell for 10 minutes. Beat cream cheese until soft. Add sour cream and melted chocolate and beat until well combined. Beat in mint mixture, until sugar has dissolved. Add gelatine to the cheese mixture. Pour filling into prepared base. Chill until set. Serve garnished with grated white chocolate and candied mint leaves.

New Potatoes

Solanum tuberosum

The potato has transcended the days of Sir Walter Raleigh and the Irish potato famine. For centuries the starchy root tuber has been an integral part of our diets. We mash, roast, bake and fry with great gusto. And we can't even begin to discuss the serious number of varieties of potatoes that exists in the world and in our country.

When spuds are planted and harvested slightly earlier than the usual 20-week stage, a smaller, sweeter variety is created. New potatoes, or 'earlies', are just that – the early, straight-out-of-the-dirt approach to potatoes. No sitting around in cold storage, no waiting for the intricate starches to develop over the autumn and winter. New potatoes are the summer crop we wait for.

Relatively easy to grow in contained gardens, these potatoes can actually provide a centrepiece to your pottager garden, or are happy in a semi-sunny spot of the patio. Garden purists will say you can't grow great spuds in wine barrels, but the proof is in the trying. New potatoes are rich in vitamin C, so don't over-cook or deep-fry, which will leach away the goodness. These baby spuds need to be treated with respect.

HOW TO GROW

There are many ways to grow potatoes, in troughs and mounds throughout your garden. But for a small space, potatoes can also be successfully grown in pots and barrels. Select a wine barrel free of mould and mildew, and drill a few holes in the bottom or sides to allow for drainage on rainy days. Place newspaper in the bottom for drainage. Half-fill the barrel with compost. Press three or four potatoes into the soil. It is best to buy seed potatoes from your plant shop, but that doesn't mean the potatoes from your local grocery store won't do. Make sure the stems and eyes are pointing upwards, and preferably make sure that there is only one main stem that will grow from each potato.

Cover with a 3–4-cm layer of soil. The seed begins to sprout after a week, sending up lush shoots of green. As the plants grow it is a simple task to add more soil to mound them up, but wait for there to be more than 5 cm of growth before covering. Always leave a little leaf showing. The soil needs to stay moist in the growing process, but not waterlogged. Rot will quickly set in. Old black rubber tyres are another way of building a potato stack in your garden and deep wooden planters work too.

Gardener's Tip

Potatoes will grow well in any soil, but most importantly, don't grow potatoes in the same soil two years in a row. Similarly, don't grow potatoes in the same soil you used for tomatoes. They are from the same family so share the same diseases.

PICKING & STORING

About 13–17 weeks after planting the seed the junior potatoes will be ready. The plants will have flowered and the tops will begin to die back. Dig down into the earth, pull out a potato and brush your finger over the skin. If the skin comes away easily, the potatoes are ready for plucking. Simply tip out the contents of the barrel and harvest the crop.

Fresh — New potatoes can be stored easily in paper bags, or ideally in something like a flax kete. Keep in a dark, cool place and the potatoes will last for months.

Freeze — Potatoes store so well fresh, that there is no need to freeze. However, potatoes will freeze very well. Peeled and cut into chunks, or mashed or puréed, the potatoes need to go into a vacuum-packed bag and be well sealed.

CULINARY USES

Where do you begin with the potato? There is not a lot they don't match. In many different contexts, the potato needs the support of strong flavours to make it more palatable. Often the potato is used as the supporting act on a plate – holding up the piece of meat or sauce.

New potatoes are fresh and crisp, and have a greener, more citrus flavour compared to the deep-earth matured starch taste of older potatoes. Full-flavoured cheeses, butter, citrus juice, subtle and piquant herbs, strong chillies, mild flavoured fish and fragrant vegetables can all marry a new potato.

New potatoes are better cooked in their skins, so simply scrub them gently to remove dirt and any loose skin before cooking. Place the potatoes, halved if necessary, in a pan and cover with the minimum of boiling water. Cover with a lid and simmer gently for approximately 20 minutes, until just tender. Once cooked, drain immediately.

QUICK PICKINGS

New Potato & Feta Salad

Cook 500 g new potatoes in a pan of lightly salted boiling water. Cover and simmer for 15 minutes or until just tender. Drain and allow to cool slightly. Toss with 225 g washed baby spinach leaves, handful halved cherry tomatoes, 70 g toasted pine nuts and 200 g crumbled feta. Season to taste with salt and freshly ground black pepper and drizzle over extra virgin olive oil and serve. **Serves 4.**

Pesto New Potatoes

Cook 500 g new potatoes in a pan of lightly salted boiling water. Cover and simmer for 15 minutes or until tender. Drain and allow to cool slightly. Toss drained potatoes with 2–3 tsp pesto (see page 32), season with salt and freshly ground black pepper to taste and serve immediately garnished with grated Parmesan.

Spicy New Potato Salad

Cook 500 g new potatoes in a pan of lightly salted boiling water. Cover and simmer for 15 minutes or until tender. Drain and allow to cool slightly. Toss drained potatoes with 2–3 tsp spicy capsicum paste (see page 59). Add 1 red onion, peeled and finely sliced. Serve garnished with roughly chopped mint leaves and black olives.

Pan-Fried New Potatoes

If there are leftover cooked new potatoes, they can be made into another great meal by slicing and cooking in a non-stick frying pan with a knob of butter, seasoned with salt and freshly ground black pepper. For extra flavour add a pinch of dry mustard and fresh snipped chives. Serve with tomato chutney and poached eggs for a great breakfast.

Garden Salad

Cook 500 g new potatoes in a pan of lightly salted boiling water. Cover and simmer for 15 minutes or until tender. Drain and allow to cool slightly. Blanch 1 small cauliflower, broken into florets, and 150 g green beans, trimmed and halved, for 5 minutes then refresh under cold running water. Combine potatoes, cauliflower, beans and 2 red-skinned apples, quartered, chopped, and tossed in lemon juice. Toss together, with some tarragon cream dressing (see page 256). Serve immediately.

Chilli-Roasted New Potatoes

(pictured over)

A brilliant spicy accompaniment to grilled or roasted meats. Top with spoonfuls of sour cream for a cool contrast. **Serves 4.**

700 g new potatoes, scrubbed
2 tbsp olive oil
2 tbsp tomato purée
2 garlic cloves, peeled and finely chopped
1 red chilli, seeds removed and finely sliced
sea salt and freshly ground black pepper

Preheat oven to 200 °C/400 °F. Tip potatoes into a roasting tin. In a bowl, mix together oil, tomato purée, garlic and chilli. Season with salt and pepper. Spoon chilli oil over potatoes, toss well until potatoes are completely coated.

Transfer to oven and roast, turning them occasionally, for about 50 minutes until cooked and skins are crisp. Sprinkle with extra sea salt and serve immediately.

Parchment-Baked New Potatoes with Garlic Chives

This is a very simple way to cook your home-grown spuds, which reveals the versatility of baking paper. It steams new potatoes easily and helps with the washing up. **Serves 3–4.**

500 g new potatoes, scrubbed
50 g butter
2 tbsp fresh chives, roughly snipped
coarse sea salt

Preheat oven to 190 °C/375 °F. Cut out two large heart-shaped pieces of baking paper 33 cm across at the widest part and approximately 28 cm long.

Divide potatoes between the paper hearts to cover one half of each. Dot with butter and sprinkle with chives and coarse sea salt. Fold the other half of the heart over and, starting at the pointed end, seal the edges by folding them over and over again. Work your way around each package to enclose potatoes neatly and snugly.

Bake for 35 minutes and serve immediately in their parcels, so that they can be opened at the table.

Shepherd's Pie with New Potatoes

Scrap the idea of using starchy, floury old potatoes for your shepherd's pie. Reap all the rewards of the skins of new potatoes by mashing them into the topping. It is a fresh taste to an old classic. The family will love it. **Serves 4–6.**

1 tbsp olive oil
1 onion, peeled and chopped
2 cloves garlic, peeled and chopped
1 carrot, peeled and chopped
1 celery stick, chopped
450 g minced lamb
150 ml red wine
400-g can peeled, chopped tomatoes
salt and freshly ground black pepper
750 g new potatoes, scrubbed
5 tbsp fresh mint, chopped
85 g butter, melted
2 tbsp fresh coriander or parsley, chopped

Preheat oven to 200 °C/400 °F. Heat oil in a frying pan, add onion, garlic, carrot and celery and sauté for 5–10 minutes until softened and just beginning to colour. Add lamb and fry, stirring until evenly browned.

Stir in wine and chopped tomatoes. Bring to boil, lower heat and simmer very gently, uncovered, for about 20 minutes, until lamb is tender and sauce is thickened. Season with salt and pepper to taste.

Meanwhile, cook potatoes in their skins until very tender, about 15–20 minutes, depending on size. Drain very well, return to pan and lightly crush with a fork until falling apart. Stir in 3 tbsp of the mint and half the butter, then season with salt and pepper.

When the lamb is cooked, stir in the remaining herbs, and spoon into a 1.2-litre pie dish. Carefully cover the surface of meat with spoonfuls of potato. It should look very rough. Drizzle with remaining melted butter. Bake for about 25 minutes, until top is golden brown. Allow to sit for a minute or two before serving.

Smoked Salmon & New Potato Salad (pictured)

New potatoes are tender nuggets of delight. If you grow a barrelful, treat them to a special friend like smoked salmon. They share the same, delicate yet creamy flavour. Tart them up with a few tangy gherkins and you have a very exquisite relationship indeed. **Serves 10.**

1 kg new potatoes, scrubbed
100 g pickled gherkins
200 g smoked salmon, cut in fine strips
2 tbsp snipped fresh chives

Dressing
2 tsp wholegrain mustard
1 lemon, juice of
6 tbsp olive oil
salt and freshly ground black pepper
3 tbsp mayonnaise

Slice potatoes into quarters. Cook them in a pan of boiling salted water for about 15 minutes until tender, drain well and put in a bowl. Slice gherkins diagonally and add to bowl with salmon strips.

Whisk together mustard, lemon juice and olive oil, with some salt and pepper, until thick and emulsified. Whisk in mayonnaise. Stir into potato and salmon until mixed well, then spoon into a serving dish and sprinkle over the chives.

New Potato Skewers with Chive & Yoghurt Dressing

Any way to freshen up vegetables and get kids to enjoy them is well worth putting in your dinner-time repertoire. Get small hands to help with dinner. Threading small potatoes onto skewers could create a small amount of excitement at meal time. **Serves 4.**

8 bamboo skewers
600 g new potatoes, scrubbed
2 tbsp olive oil
1–2 tsp sea salt
250 g natural unsweetened yoghurt
¼ cup fresh chives, chopped
2 tbsp lemon juice
½ tsp honey

If using wooden skewers, soak them in water for 30 minutes. Cook potatoes in a saucepan of lightly salted water. Bring to boil then reduce heat to a steady simmer and cook for about 10 minutes, until just cooked through. Drain well.

Thread potatoes onto skewers, drizzle with a tbsp of oil and sprinkle with salt. Place on a preheated barbecue grill and cook for five minutes each side, or until browned.

To make dressing, combine yoghurt, chives, lemon juice, honey and remaining tbsp of oil and salt to taste. Chill until needed. Serve with the hot potato skewers.

Parsley

Petroselinum crispum

As the *Oxford Companion to Food* states: 'Parsley is the most popular herb in European cookery'. Say no more. We use it so much that half the time we probably don't even realise it is flavouring our food. Why? Because fresh and dried parsley, while not rich in distinct flavour, provides colour and garnish to our drab foods. Where would we be without a garnish of parsley and a slice of orange on our plate?

Parsley has such a subtle flavour. We liken it to celery or coriander although it is not the same. Believed to have originated in southern Europe, it is so widely used in Middle Eastern and Mediterranean food, argument breaks out as to who claimed it first. What is known is there are two varieties available quite commonly – curly parsley and flat-leaf parsley. As names go, they describe exactly the plants' differing attributes. Some may say the flavours are stronger in the curly, but who can really tell?

Parsley does have one particular attribute that may explain why we use it to garnish our food: it is known that eating a sprig of parsley after rich garlicky food will cleanse the palate and rid the breath of any lingering odours. It is rich in iron, and parsley tonics are given to anaemia sufferers. Parsley tea is also good for urinary infections such as cystitis.

The one thing we can be thankful for is that the habit of sprinkling parsley over the edges of our dinner plates is, hopefully, a trend belonging to the past.

HOW TO GROW

Parsley can easily be grown from seed. Seedlings can take up to six weeks to appear. Plant seedlings 20 cm apart in rich compost soil, well-drained but with adequate moisture in summer.

PICKING & STORING

Parsley grows from the centre out, so pick sprigs from around the outside, otherwise the plant will die.

Fresh — Roughly chop the leaves to sprinkle, or store the leaves as whole bunches. Keep in a plastic bag in the fridge or sprinkle with water and wrap in paper towels.

Freeze — Pick off all the bushy parsley tops and freeze in a large plastic bag. Once frozen, scrunch the bag and you'll be left with a large bag of ready-chopped parsley.

Dried — Dry with a paper towel before chopping. Keep in an airtight container away from light and moisture.

CULINARY USES

The curly variety is best for fine chopping or as a garnish, and the flat-leaf variety for flavouring food. Use with chopped mint to flavour bulgur wheat for a tabouleh salad. Parsley works with egg dishes such as omelettes or with any type of salads, stews, soups, sauces, rice or pasta. Just about anything can handle a sprinkling of parsley.

QUICK PICKINGS

Parsley Tea

Put a few sprigs of parsley into a cup with a slice of fresh ginger. Pour over boiling water and allow to steep.

Gremolada

Combine 1 tbsp grated lemon zest with 1 tbsp grated orange zest, 2 cloves finely chopped garlic and 2 tbsp chopped flat-leaf parsley. This is a common Italian flavouring often added to cooked osso buco.

Parsley Sauce

Melt 100 g butter in a saucepan, blend in 2 tbsp flour, then gradually add 500 ml milk. Stir until smooth and cook until it thickens. Season to taste with salt and freshly ground black pepper. Just before serving, add ¼ cup fresh chopped parsley and 2 finely chopped hard-boiled eggs. Sprinkle on a little nutmeg. This is good on salmon, chicken, new potatoes or any vegetable dish. **Makes 2½ cups.**

Bacon & Parsley Pinwheels

Combine 2 cups fresh snipped parsley with 500 g finely chopped cooked crispy bacon, 1 cup mayonnaise, 1 tbsp Worcestershire sauce. Lightly butter 20 pieces of white sandwich bread with crusts removed. Spread a tsp or so of the parsley mixture over the butter. Roll slices and wrap in foil and freeze. Cut into thin rounds and then thaw. Serve toasted as a finger food.

Parsley Relish (pictured)

A relish like this is halfway between a relish and a pesto. It will make light work of the abundance of parsley that one plant gives. The distinct, earthy taste of parsley punches through all the other flavours. **Serves 10.**

1 large bunch flat-leaf parsley
2 tsp sugar
1–2 tsp salt
2 cloves garlic, peeled and crushed
2 spring onions, very finely chopped
1 lemon, juice of
60 ml olive oil

Pick off leaves from parsley stems, chop finely with a knife. In a bowl mix parsley with sugar, salt, garlic, spring onions, lemon juice and olive oil. Scrape into a small bowl and serve with a platter of cured meats and cheeses.

Tabouleh

You can't really talk about this herb without mentioning how well it works in tabouleh. A really traditional way to use parsley. This salad goes a long way, and there will always be some left over for a healthy and nutritious lunch for work or school. **Serves 6.**

225 g bulgur wheat
1 cucumber, peeled and deseeded
450 g tomatoes, peeled and deseeded
8 spring onions, finely diced
2 large handfuls chopped parsley
6 tbsp lemon juice
8 tbsp extra virgin olive oil
salt and freshly ground black pepper

Liberally cover bulgur wheat with boiling water and soak for 30 minutes. Finely dice cucumber and tomatoes. Place in a large bowl with spring onions and parsley. Drain bulgur wheat and squeeze dry. Add to cucumber mix, dress with lemon juice and olive oil, season with salt and pepper to taste and serve.

Spaghetti with Parsley Pesto (pictured)

I think the unique thing about parsley is that it doesn't need a lot of work to bring a dish to life. It has colour and plenty of flavour. I choose pecorino cheese to complement the flavour of the parsley and not override it. Other cheeses will do. The important part is to chop the parsley well and remove any unnecessary stalks first. **Serves 4.**

375 g spaghetti
1 large bunch parsley leaves
2 tbsp toasted pine nuts
2 cloves garlic, peeled and finely chopped
50 g pecorino cheese, finely grated
125 ml extra virgin olive oil
salt and freshly ground black pepper
to serve, $^{1}/_{3}$ cup flaked pecorino cheese

Cook pasta in a large saucepan of boiling, well-salted water, uncovered, until just tender, about 8–10 minutes. Drain and drizzle with a little olive oil.

Roughly chop parsley by hand and combine with pine nuts, garlic and grated pecorino in a mixing bowl. Gradually add oil in a thin stream and stir well until combined.

Combine pasta and pesto in a large saucepan. Toss gently to combine. Season to taste with salt and pepper. Serve sprinkled with the extra pecorino cheese.

Parsley & Lemon Couscous

We all need a repertoire of good recipes that go with the main meals we conjure up. You can't go wrong with couscous. An essential store cupboard staple, it can be ready to eat pretty quickly. This would have to be the quickest dish to make and uses all the fresh flavours from your garden. **Serves 4 as a side dish.**

- ¼ cup couscous
- 60 ml water
- 1 lemon, juice of
- 2 tbsp extra virgin olive oil
- ¼ cup fresh parsley, finely chopped
- 2 tbsp fresh mint, finely chopped
- 2 tsp preserved lemon rind, finely chopped (see page 147)
- 1 tbsp pine nuts, toasted
- salt and freshly ground black pepper
- 1 small tomato, peeled, deseeded and diced

In a medium bowl, combine couscous with water and lemon juice. Let stand 10 minutes. To the softened couscous add olive oil, parsley, mint, preserved lemon rind, pine nuts, salt and pepper. Mix well with a fork, separating the grains as much as you can. Mound the couscous in the centre of a serving platter. Top with diced tomato and extra chopped parsely.

Smoked Fish & Parsley Mousse

Warning – this recipe contains uncooked eggs. But it is delicious, so it is well worth hunting out good-quality eggs from a reliable source. The mousse can be made a day ahead and kept covered in the fridge. **Serves 6.**

- 900 g smoked cod, bones removed
- 1.2 litre mixture milk and water
- 1 onion, peeled and cut in half
- 2 celery sticks, broken in half
- 3 tsp gelatine
- 3 tbsp fresh parsley, finely chopped
- 6 tbsp mayonnaise
- 150 g sour cream
- freshly ground black pepper
- 2 egg whites
- to serve, green salad leaves and warm grainy bread

Cook fish in a large pan with milk and water mixture, onion and celery, over a moderate heat, until liquid just begins to heave under skin, then leave to cool completely. Measure 150 ml of cooking liquid into a small pan and sprinkle in gelatine granules. Warm, but don't boil, until gelatine has dissolved, then leave to cool.

Remove fish from its liquid, then flake it, removing bones and skin. Mix with parsley. In a seperate bowl combine mayonnaise and sour cream. Stir in the gelatine mix and season with pepper. Fold into fish and parsley. Whisk egg whites until stiff, then use a metal spoon to fold them quickly, carefully and thoroughly into the fish. Scrape mousse into a bowl, cover and chill. Serve with salad and bread.

Lamb & Parsley Patties

A burger patty is one of those quintessential recipes we should all make from time to time. Why get take-out when a recipe like this takes no time at all, and fresh herbs from your garden give so much more than preservatives in a manufactured version. Build a burger with lettuce, carrot and beetroot and it is all Kiwi! Or serve it with a yoghurt sauce and couscous for a Middle Eastern theme.
Serves 4.

500 g minced lamb
¼ cup fresh parsley leaves, chopped
1 tbsp coriander, finely chopped
1 tbsp fresh mint leaves, finely chopped
½ onion, grated
a pinch of cinnamon
⅛ tsp ground cumin
salt and freshly ground black pepper

Sauce
½ cup plain yoghurt
1 tsp fresh mint leaves, finely chopped
1 tbsp fresh parsley leaves, finely chopped
salt and freshly ground black pepper
to serve, fresh lettuce leaves and pita bread toasted

Preheat oven to 220 °C/440 °F. In a bowl, combine lamb, parsley, coriander, mint, onion, cinnamon and cumin. Season to taste, knead mixture with hands until well combined, and then chill, covered, for 15 minutes. With moistened hands, form into eight oval patties, about 2 cm thick.

On a grill plate or heavy-based frying pan, cook patties for 3–4 minutes each side. Alternatively, line a baking tray with foil and grease with oil. Place each patty on tray and bake at 220 °C/440 °F for 10–15 minutes, until cooked through.

Make sauce while lamb is cooking. In a bowl whisk together yoghurt, mint, parsley and salt and pepper to taste. Divide patties between four plates lined with lettuce leaves and serve them with yoghurt sauce and pita breads.

Passion-Fruit

Passiflora edulis

The trouble with passion-fruit is the fruits don't usually make it to the kitchen to be cooked. Eating the succulent nectar-like fruit straight off the vine is one of those special things about summer.

Like pomegranates, which they resemble, these fruit are best in any number of cool desserts. To smell the fruit evokes thoughts of a tropical paradise. Commercially grown in South America, Hawaii, Israel and Australia, we are very lucky that these tropical vines can grow successfully in New Zealand, and with great ease.

A vine will grow in a large concrete pot, crawling around a dividing fence line or trellis. As the flowers bloom you'll notice what a different bud they are to a simple rose – and then they metamorphose into the fruit. To the observer, that is half the fun and, luckily, we get to eat the end result.

Passion-fruit grow better in warm climes, as the vines originate from the tropical isles of South America and South Africa, where they are known as granadilla. Passion-fruit are a good source of vitamins A and C, as well as potassium and iron. One passion-fruit has only 16 calories. When eaten with the seeds, a serving is an excellent source of fibre. But don't eat the purple hard skins – they contain traces of cyanogenic glycosides, which can release poisonous hydrogen cyanide.

HOW TO GROW

Passion-fruit vines grow well in sub-tropical and temperate climates, which are free of frost. They are perennial, so once the vine is there it can be trained around a support to produce fruit-bearing laterals. Vines need a sunny spot in the garden and prefer light soils with good drainage. Insects are invaluable for good fruit production, and ants and bees are needed for pollination because of the heaviness and stickiness of the pollen.

Vines can be trained on fences, the railings of balconies or terraces and pergolas. Provide wires or wire netting for the tendrils to cling to. Growing the plant against a balcony or wall will help protect against frost. One well-grown vine will give sufficient fruit for an average-sized family.

Passion-fruit respond well to generous feeding. Apply a complete fruit fertiliser when growth starts in spring. Regular watering is needed because roots are quite shallow. Mulching is useful too, but keep away from stems as this may cause rot.

After the tree fruits, cut vines back if they are too dense. This allows better air movement and encourages new laterals on which fruit is formed. Vines may become weak and spindly after four or five years so it pays to have new ones coming on as replacements.

PICKING & STORING

When the fruit is ripe, it changes from shiny green to wrinkled, dimpled, deep-purple skin. It will usually fall from the vine, and needs to be harvested quickly before the birds and insects get hold of the sweet insides. The skin is old-looking, but this does not mean the fruit is rotten. If the fruit is slightly green when it falls, leave on a sunny window ledge to ripen.

Fresh — Once ripe, the fruit can be stored in the fridge for up to 1 week.

Freeze — The pulp of passion-fruit is a delicate thing. It breaks down quickly in cold conditions. If there is an abundance of fruit pulp, scoop out the insides and freeze the seeds in ice cube trays. The pulp should be used quickly, however, to avoid too much degradation.

Preserve —Passion-fruit preserves well as jam, jelly and wine. You need a lot of fruit for the process, so if your vine is super prolific, then well done, you have got access to a dream flavour that can be bottled.

CULINARY USES

In other countries passion-fruit is harvested for commercial production. The pulp is canned or made into syrups that are used worldwide for desserts and ice creams. In Brazil, they make a passion-fruit mousse and a special passion-fruit drink. In Indonesia and Hawaii, like New Zealand, the fruit is prized for eating raw, but also used for passion-fruit syrup, common in drinks.

Passion-fruit is generally eaten fresh but may be cooked in sauces, fillings and desserts. Begin by cutting the fruit in half and scooping out the fleshy pulp with a spoon. Leave behind the waxy interior. To remove seeds from the pulp, strain in a non-aluminium sieve, or use cheesecloth or muslin, squeezing to extract the juice. The seeds can be dried and kept, for further planting or even crushed for sprinkling over desserts.

QUICK PICKINGS

Passion-Fruit Pina Colada

Pour 30 ml Bacardi into blender with 120 ml pineapple juice, pulp from 2 passion-fruit, 30 ml coconut cream (or Malibu) and 15 ml sugar syrup. Top with ice cubes and blend until smooth, then pour into a tall serving glass. **Serves 1.**

Passion-Fruit Syrup

Mix equal quantities of sugar and water in a saucepan, and bring to boil. Boil for 2–3 minutes, until sugar has dissolved. Add pulp of some passion-fruit, equal quantity to the weight of the sugar. Stir and let stand for a couple of hours. Pour syrup through a sieve and remove seeds. The syrup can be poured over fresh fruit salad or vanilla ice cream.

Passion-Fruit Curd

Make a lemon curd (see recipe page 148). Near the end of cooking as curd begins to thicken, add pulp from 6 passion-fruit. Stir well to combine. Pour into sterilised jars and seal. Keeps well.

Passion-Fruit Smoothie

In a blender add 150 g unsweetened yoghurt to 2 scoops ice cream, 1 banana, 1 tsp honey and a handful ice cubes. Scoop in the pulp of 2–3 passion-fruit and blend well until puréed. Add melons, strawberries or other berry fruits to sharpen the taste of your tropical smoothie.

Passion-Fruit Meringues

Preheat oven to 120 °C/250 °F. Beat 2 egg whites until very stiff, add half of 125 g sugar and beat with a wooden spoon. Add remaining sugar and beat again. Place spoonfuls on greased trays and bake slowly, about 1 to 1½ hours. When cold place on a serving platter and top with whipped cream and fresh passion-fruit pulp.

Passion-Fruit & Peach Jam

I am somewhat reluctant to use valuable fresh passion-fruit in jams, but the peaches and passion-fruit collide incredibly well in this recipe. Golden queen peaches are the best for their juicy succulence. **Makes about 3 cups.**

- 4 large peaches (800 g)
- 4 lemons, juice of
- 125 ml water
- 420 g sugar, approximately
- ¾ cup passion-fruit pulp, about 9
- 2 tbsp peach liqueur

Peel and halve peaches, discard stones, chop peaches finely. Combine peaches, lemon juice and water in large saucepan. Bring to boil, simmer, covered, for about 20 minutes or until peaches are soft.

Measure fruit mixture, allow ¾ cup sugar to each cup of fruit mixture. Return fruit mixture and sugar to pan, stir over heat, without boiling, until sugar is dissolved. Bring to the boil, boil uncovered, without stirring, for about 10 minutes or until jam gels when tested. Stir in passion-fruit and liqueur. Stand 10 minutes, stirring occasionally, before pouring jam into hot sterilised jars (see page 18). Seal when cold.

Passion-Fruit Wine

If you have so many passion-fruit you don't know what to do, imbibe some of the wine from this recipe. Hugely rewarding of the effort it takes to make, this delicious sweet wine is the perfect accompaniment to any dessert.
Makes 6 litres.

- 72 ripe passion-fruit
- 4½ litres water
- 2 kg sugar

Halve and pulp fruit. Add water, let ferment 6–8 days, strain through muslin cloth then add sugar. Let sit for three weeks, strain, and then let stand for a few days more. Strain again and put in a sealable keg. Let stand about seven months in a cool, dark place, then it is ready to use. Stir it well, several times a day.

Passion-Fruit Posset

Possets were traditionally taken as medicinal drinks in medieval Britain. This recipe has been adapted into a very similar popular Irish dessert. **Serves 6.**

600 ml cream
165 g caster sugar
6 passion-fruit, pulp strained
to serve, berries such as blueberries or raspberries, icing sugar and almond biscuits

Place cream and sugar in saucepan, slowly bring to boil over low heat, stirring continuously until sugar dissolves. Boil for 3 minutes. Remove from heat and whisk in strained passion-fruit juice, then pour into 6 x $^2/_3$ cup-capacity ramekins and cool to room temperature. Cover with plastic wrap and put in fridge for 4 hours or overnight. Serve desserts topped with berries and dusted with a little icing sugar, with almond biscuits.

Passion-Fruit Biscuits (pictured)

It's not hard to make biscuits with melt-in-the-mouth characteristics, and these are some of the best. They are an easy and passionate way to use fresh passion-fruit. **Makes about 24.**

185 g butter, softened
½ orange, finely grated rind of
120 g icing sugar
¼ tsp ground cardamom
3 passion-fruit, pulp of
110 g rice flour
185 g self-raising flour

Passion-fruit icing
50 g butter
200 g icing sugar
1 passion-fruit, pulp of

Preheat oven to 220 °C/440 °F. Process butter, orange rind and icing sugar in a food processor until creamy. Add cardamom and passion-fruit pulp and pulse to combine well, then fold in combined sifted flours. Cover closely with plastic wrap and refrigerate for 30 minutes.

Roll tablespoonfuls of mixture into balls, then place on greased and baking paper-lined oven trays and flatten to form 6-cm rounds. Bake in oven for 12 minutes or until golden, then transfer to wire racks to cool.

Meanwhile, to make icing, place butter, sugar and passion-fruit pulp in a heatproof bowl over a saucepan of simmering water and stir until smooth and glossy. When biscuits have cooled, dip half of each biscuit into passion-fruit icing, then transfer to a wire rack. Stand for 30 minutes or until icing sets.

Passion-Fruit Charlotte (pictured)

A light dessert that is quick to make with fresh passion-fruit straight off the vine. A warning for those who don't eat raw eggs – this contains raw egg whites, but oh ... how delicious. **Serves 4.**

2 tsp gelatine
2 tbsp cold water
100 ml cream
4 eggs, separated
5 passion-fruit
1 tsp vanilla essence
75 g sugar
to serve, whipped cream

Passion-fruit coulis
6 passion-fruit
6 tsp caster sugar
4 tbsp water

Soak gelatine in cold water. Heat cream until just beginning to foam. Remove from heat. Add beaten egg yolks, stir well and return to low heat. Stir well until mixture thickens, do not let boil or it will curdle. Remove from heat.

Add gelatine and stir in well to dissolve. Let mixture cool, add passion-fruit pulp and vanilla essence and cool slightly. Beat egg whites and sugar to make a light meringue, combine two tbsp egg white mixture with custard, folding in well. Add balance of egg white and fold in carefully using a metal spoon or a rubber spatula. Pour mousse into decorative mould or individual glasses, leave to set. Serve topped with whipped cream and a spoonful of passion-fruit coulis.

To make passion-fruit coulis, combine passion-fruit pulp with sugar and water. Bring to boil then sieve to remove pips.

Peas

Pisum sativum

There is nothing wrong with buying frozen peas. They are cheap and sweet and ready to go. But after growing, shelling and tasting your own fresh peas straight out of a summer garden, it makes you wonder why we can't have them fresh all year round. Of course, they are seasonal and not going to last all year long, but summer freshness comes in a pod.

Peas have been traced back to Switzerland in 3000 BC, and then quickly moved through Europe and China to become a favourite vegetable. Their ability to dry well and be moved about made them a staple food of many cultures. They were cheap, filling and a good source of protein.

They grow well through the summer months, although are not a fan of high temperatures. The fruits of a summer crop are nowadays frozen to be enjoyed all year round. We have come a long way from having the summer's harvest dried or brined, and can now enjoy the fresh taste all year round. But nothing, repeat nothing, will compare to a freshly picked pea.

HOW TO GROW

Peas love growing in New Zealand. We grow some of the best in the world. The plants like cooler temperatures, in fact over 20 °C is too hot for them.

Plant the seeds directly into healthy, fertile organic soil either in a plot of garden or well-drained pots. Make sure there are stakes or wire for them to crawl up against as they grow quickly and need support. Seedlings can also be transplanted, but be careful to handle the growing peas gently, so as not to break them. They like sunshine but can handle some shade, especially in the hottest part of the day, so they will grow well on a balcony or veranda.

Water well, especially through summer days. Mulching the bottom of plants with pea straw or newspaper helps keep moisture in the all-important roots. In fact, the best part of the pea plant is in the roots. Because they are nitrogen-fixing legumes – they extract nitrogen from our atmosphere, which forms nodules on the roots – remove the tops of the plants at the end of the pea season and dig the roots in for the next crop of leafy vegetables.

PICKING & STORING

Garden peas are best picked when slightly immature. They are sweeter and not too hard. Pick from the vines regularly, which will encourage further growth of more pods. As a rule, the pods are ready for picking three weeks after flowering.

Fresh — Peas will lose their flavour very quickly after picking, so from vine to pot to table is highly recommended. If you have to store them, try the fridge, but better still just eat them straight from the garden.

Freeze — This is an excellent method of sealing in the flavour of the fresh pea. We buy so many that we take it for granted that as soon as they are harvested they are quickly podded, blanched and snap-frozen. For home preservation, freezing is the best too. Blanch them in water for 1 minute only, then spread on a plastic tray and freeze individually before placing in airtight plastic bags.

Preserves — Peas can be stored in brine and sealed in a tin. This does, however, break down the chlorophyll in the pea, creating a yellowy, insipid-looking pea. These travel well, but will often be used for soups and stews, rather than for their beautiful colour.

Dried — Peas can be successfully dried in a dehydrator, for rehydration later or for crunchy snacks. Dried peas are quite common in Indian cuisines in curries and vegetarian ragus.

CULINARY USES

As a cheap source of protein, dried peas are often rehydrated into thick porridge-like meals. Pease pudding, dhal and pease meal were some more common old-fashioned meals. The French made immature fresh green peas famous in their cuisine and called them petits pois. They even ate the immature pod and called it mange-tout, or what we know as sugar snap peas.

The flavour of peas is sweet and crisp. They complement any other vegetable and work well with chicken, pork and fish. They will happily be a side vegetable on just about any meal, or can be used to bulk up a vegetarian curry. The sweetness of the pea also accompanies the saltiness of bacon and cured meats, and a standard favourite is pea and ham soup. However, fresh peas, straight out of the garden, need fresh flavours. Lemons, delicate herbs, salmon, or egg dishes all accommodate the humble garden pea. Adding mint to the water while cooking peas brings out all the sweetness and complements the more immature peas well.

Fresh peas are best cooked quickly in rapidly boiling water. Cook until they are just tender, 3–5 minutes, add a little salt and a little sugar just before they finish cooking, then drain and toss them with chives, lemon zest and freshly ground black pepper. Add a little butter before serving for extra indulgence.

QUICK PICKINGS

Peas À la Française

Place 8 peeled and sliced shallots and 25 g butter in a small frying pan, add enough water just to cover shallots, then cook over medium heat, stirring occasionally, for 10 minutes, or until shallots are just tender. Increase heat to high and cook until liquid evaporates and shallots caramelise slightly. Trim a butter leaf lettuce core and remove outer leaves for another use.

Combine lettuce heart, fresh chopped chervil, parsley, chives or tarragon, 650 g podded fresh peas and shallots in a saucepan. Add enough chicken stock to come two-thirds of the way up the side, then dot with about 80 g butter, chopped. Cook over high heat for about 5 minutes, or until peas are tender and liquid is syrupy. Serve with lamb cutlets.

Mrs Beeton's Peas With Ham

Cook 500 g shelled peas and drain well. Fry ½ small onion in 25 g butter until lightly browned. Add 1 tsp flour and 100 g diced ham, stir over heat for a minute or two, then add peas, 300 ml chicken stock, pinch caster sugar, pinch of grated nutmeg. Simmer until peas are thoroughly reheated, about 10 minutes. Season and serve. **Serves 6.**

Confetti Peas

Heat a frying pan with 2 tbsp olive oil. Cook ½ cup red capsicum, ½ cup finely chopped celery, 1 finely chopped red onion on a medium heat for 2–3 minutes. Stir in 125 ml chicken stock. Add 1½ cups fresh shelled peas and continue to stir, cooking over medium heat for 5–6 minutes, just until vegetables are tender and liquid reduces. Season to taste with salt and freshly ground black pepper.

Creole Green Peas

Melt 30 g butter, add 1 finely chopped onion and fry until transparent. Add 1 tbsp plain flour and brown. Be careful not to burn. Add 400 g fresh shelled peas and ½ cup chicken stock. Cook about 15 minutes. Serve immediately.

Peas With Rice

Finely chop 4 spring onions. Sauté gently in 60 g butter in a deep saucepan with lid. Add 500 g shelled peas and cook 1–2 minutes, stirring constantly. Add 1 litre hot chicken stock, cover and simmer for 8–10 minutes. Add 1 cup arborio rice and 2 tbsp finely chopped parsley, stir once, bring to a boil, cover and reduce heat to a simmer. Cook about 15 minutes. Season to taste with salt and pepper. Remove from heat and stir in ½ cup grated Parmesan.

Pea & Lettuce Soup

You can serve this delicious spring soup either hot or chilled. If you decide to serve it chilled, it might be too thick for your liking, so add some water or light stock to thin it down a little. **Serves 6.**

100 g butter
1 lemon, peeled rind and juice of
1 bay leaf
1 onion, peeled and finely chopped
600 g fresh peas, shelled
1 iceberg lettuce, washed and finely shredded
1 tsp caster sugar
salt and freshly ground black pepper
900 ml boiling water

Lemon cream
150 ml cream
200 g fresh peas, cooked for 1 minute in boiling water and drained
1 lemon, finely grated rind and juice of
to garnish, thin strips of lemon rind

To make soup, melt butter in a large saucepan. Tie together lemon rind and bay leaf and add to melted butter with onion. Cook over a low heat for 10 minutes or until onion is soft and golden. Add peas, lettuce, sugar, salt and pepper, and stir until coated with butter. Carefully pour in boiling water, return to boil and simmer for 10 minutes or until peas are very soft. Remove from heat, take out lemon rind bundle and discard. Allow to cool a little, then pour into a blender and purée until smooth. Add lemon juice.

To make lemon cream, heat cream in a small pan and allow to bubble for 5 minutes. Add peas and grated lemon rind, season to taste with salt and pepper and cook for 2 minutes. Add lemon juice and stir through. Reheat soup, season to taste if necessary. Ladle soup into individual bowls and drizzle some lemon cream over each one. Garnish with lemon rind strips and serve.

Minted Pea Omelette

Let the fresh taste of peas come through in a simple dish. This takes no time at all – cooks in under 8 minutes in one pot, so there is no excuse for not serving quick and nutritious meals. **Serves 2.**

5 eggs
1–2 sprigs fresh mint, chopped
100 g fresh peas
salt and freshly ground black pepper
25 g butter
50 g Cheddar, grated
to serve, crusty white bread and a green salad

Preheat grill. In a bowl lightly beat eggs with a fork until just frothy. Stir in mint and peas, and season with salt and pepper.

Heat butter in a frying pan, swirling it round so it coats the base and sides. When it starts to froth, pour in egg mixture, swirling pan to spread it evenly. Cook over a moderate heat for 3–4 minutes. Sprinkle over cheese, then grill for 2–3 minutes, until cheese has melted.

Tilt pan onto edge of plate, then with a fork fold omelette in half and slide onto plate. Cut in half and serve with crusty bread and green salad.

Pea Pancakes with Smoked Salmon

Perfect finger food for your guests, and an attractive starter for any meal. The horseradish zing complements the sweet pea taste and smokiness of the salmon. The pancakes and dip can be made ahead of time and assembled just before your guests arrive. **Makes 24.**

- 100 g plain flour
- 1 egg
- 100 ml milk
- 2 tsp fresh chives, snipped
- salt and freshly ground black pepper
- 200 g fresh or frozen peas
- vegetable oil for frying
- 6 tbsp sour cream
- 1 tbsp creamed horseradish
- 200 g smoked salmon slices
- to garnish, fresh chives, snipped

To make pancake batter, mix together flour, egg, milk, chives and season to taste with salt and pepper. Steam peas for about 5 minutes if fresh or 2 minutes if frozen, and put into a bowl. Using a potato masher or fork, roughly mash peas and add to pancake batter.

In a frying pan, heat a little oil until it's smoking hot. Turn heat down and add small tbsp of batter, making about three pancakes at a time. When small holes appear on the top of the pancakes, flip them and cook the other sides for about 30 seconds. Keep warm on absorbent paper towel. Cook remaining batter in same way.

To make the dip, mix together sour cream and creamed horseradish. Top each pancake with a teaspoonful of dip and then top with a slice of smoked salmon and sprinkle with chives.

Pea & Smoked Fish Cakes

Smoked fish is one of the most underrated protein sources. It is tasty and adds a distinct flavour to meals. Mix it up with tender, sweet new-season peas and you have a winner. **Makes 6.**

- 450 g potatoes, peeled and cut into chunks
- 200 g smoked fish, skin and bones removed
- 4 tbsp milk
- 25 g butter
- salt and freshly ground black pepper
- 2 eggs, hardboiled
- 175 g fresh peas, cooked
- 2 tbsp fresh parsley, finely chopped
- 100 g white breadcrumbs
- 2 tbsp vegetable oil
- to serve, lemon wedges and fresh lettuce leaves

Preheat oven to 200 °C/400 °F. In a large saucepan, boil potatoes in salted water for 10–12 minutes. Meanwhile put fish, milk and butter in another saucepan. Season, cover, and simmer 4–5 minutes. Strain and reserve milk. Flake fish.

Drain potatoes and mash. Add eggs and continue to mash. Add reserved milk and stir in fish, peas and parsley. Shape mixture into six even-sized balls with your hands, then press down to form a cake. Press each cake into the breadcrumbs, coating evenly.

Pour oil into a roasting tin. Heat for 5 minutes in oven. Add fishcakes and coat in hot oil. Cook 25–30 minutes, turning once or twice. Serve immediately with wedges of lemon and fresh lettuce leaves.

Herb Pasta with Peas & Bacon (pictured)

Very quick and very simple. If you can't find a Boursin cheese, cream cheese will do, or a soft goat's-milk cheese. **Serves 4.**

- 350 g dried pasta, such as penne
- 350 g fresh peas, shelled
- 1 large red capsicum, deseeded and cut into chunks
- 8 rashers rindless streaky bacon
- 150 g soft cheese with herbs and garlic (such as Boursin)
- 300 ml milk
- salt and freshly ground black pepper

Cook pasta according to packet instructions. Five minutes before the end of cooking time, add peas and red capsicum. Bring back to boil and continue to cook.

Meanwhile, preheat grill to hot and grill bacon until crispy. When cool enough to handle, cut into bite-sized pieces.

Add soft cheese and milk to a large saucepan. Warm through, stirring continuously until smooth and thickened. Drain pasta and vegetables, and toss with cheese sauce and bacon. Season with salt and freshly ground black pepper and serve immediately.

Pea & Kumara Tortilla

This is an ideal light lunch or small dinner. I like to mix it up with new potatoes and parsnips instead of kumara. Tortilla originates in Spain where they sell pieces as a supper snack. **Serves 4.**

- 350 g kumara, peeled and cut into chunks
- 200 g fresh peas, shelled
- 2 tbsp olive oil
- 1 small onion, peeled and finely chopped
- 1 clove garlic, peeled and crushed
- 200 g cherry tomatoes, halved
- 6 eggs
- to serve, green salad

Cook kumara in boiling water for 5 minutes. Stir in peas, return to boil and cook for another 5 minutes. Drain well.

Heat oil in a medium non-stick frying pan. Fry onion and garlic for 2 minutes, stirring. Stir in kumara, peas and tomatoes.

Lightly beat eggs, pour over the kumara mixture, and cook for 4–5 minutes over a medium heat until almost set. Cook 2–3 minutes under a preheated grill until beginning to brown. Remove from oven and cool slightly. Cut into wedges. Serve with a green salad.

Prawn & Pea Risotto

If you master the art of risotto, it is an easy dish to add to your family's dinner repertoire. A few good ingredients will make a quick and creamy meal. Prawns in this dish are a great complement to peas, but mussels, shrimps or squid rings can all be an ideal substitute. **Serves 4.**

750 g medium prawns, in shell
1.75 litres water
salt and freshly ground black pepper
250 g fresh peas
¼ cup fresh chives, chopped
½ lemon, finely grated zest of
1 medium onion, peeled and finely chopped
50 g butter
300 g arborio rice
200 ml dry white wine
to serve, grated Parmesan

Peel shells and remove veins from prawns. Put shells and water in a saucepan and bring to a simmer and keep covered. Toss prawns with ½ tsp salt, then chill, covered. Toss together peas, chives, zest and pepper in a bowl. In a wide, heavy-based saucepan or sauté pan, cook onion in butter over a low heat. Stir until onion is softened, about 3–5 minutes.

Add rice and cook, stirring, 2 minutes. Increase heat to medium, then add wine and cook, stirring 1 minute, until absorbed into rice. Stir in a ladleful of simmering shrimp broth. It is best to pour through a sieve, then discard shells. Cook, stirring constantly and keeping at a strong simmer, until most of broth is absorbed. Continue cooking and adding broth, ladlefuls at a time, stirring constantly and allowing each addition to be absorbed before adding next, until rice is tender and creamy-looking but all'onda (see page 18), about 18 minutes in total.

Add prawn and pea mixture and continue to cook, stirring and adding more broth if necessary, until prawns are just cooked through, about 3 minutes. Season to taste and serve risotto immediately, sprinkled with Parmesan.

Rhubarb

Rheum rhabarbarum

In the UK it is a vegetable, in America it is a fruit, but technically rhubarb has all the characteristics of a herb and is therefore in that category. In Germany it is called 'pie plant'.

It grows from a rhizome, and likes a good drought. It is a peculiar plant with a peculiar flavour, but we like growing it in our gardens because it grows easily, and is a steadfast favourite for warm winter comfort food.

Luckily for the home gardener, rhubarb will tolerate an awful lot of neglect and still thrive. But beware, rhubarb leaves are poisonous, very poisonous. They need to be cut off before any cooking. The leaves are good for keeping bugs away, but not good for wandering hands around the garden. It does not even pay to put the leaves into your compost as they can cause toxicity in the soil. But the stalks are delicious.

HOW TO GROW

Rhubarb grows in organic fertile soil. Rhubarb can be grown from seed, but it does take a long time to be ready to cut from. The best way is to take cuttings from the rhizome.

It grows well in shaded areas of the garden and can easily be planted into containers and moved in and out of the sun as needed. The plant will be most prolific in the winter under colder, darker conditions.

Fertilise well and rhubarb will reward you. Cut the stalks on a regular basis and they will flourish with more and more shoots. Try not to pick the stalks from the rhubarb in the first year of planting, as the stems need to build up reserves that give the herb its distinctive tang. Cut away any flowers that appear, they will destroy the plant for the future.

PICKING & STORING

Cut the stalks away from the plant at the very bottom of the stem. The sweeter, pinker, juicier bit is the stem closest to the dirt.

Fresh — Fresh stalks will be best cooked straight from the garden. The fibrous stem will lose moisture very quickly. The cut stalks can be wrapped in paper and kept in the fridge.

Freeze — The cooked pulp is great for freezing. Even though it will break down in the thawing process, that is a benefit to rhubarb. It can then be made into pies, tarts and crumbles.

Preserve — Rhubarb is made for jam. It has a naturally high pectin level, so will complement any other fruit it is put with.

CULINARY USES

Choose fairly thin red stalks. The red colour holds the flavour and sweetness. There is no need to peel rhubarb, simply wash the stalks well. Prepared rhubarb should have any leaves and the white scraggy ends removed.

If you don't want rhubarb to turn to mush, cook it in the oven. Pack the cut-up rhubarb into an ovenproof dish in a single layer. Add sugar (about 50 g per 250 g rhubarb) and whatever flavourings you like, then add a little liquid (orange juice, sweet wine or water), cover tightly and cook for about 15–20 minutes at 180 °C/350 °F. Leave to cool and firm up before using.

Try rhubarb with pears, papaya, apples, pineapple, strawberries and sharp flavours such as orange, lime and grapefruit. Also pair with ginger, lemongrass, orange flower, rosewater or even aniseed.

Don't restrict rhubarb to sweet dishes. A close relative of rhubarb is sorrel, it works in soups and sauces for trout, mackerel and salmon. Stew it with a little sugar and serve with pork, duck or goose instead of apple sauce.

QUICK PICKINGS

Stewed Rhubarb On French Toast

Cut 300 g rhubarb into 2 cm pieces. Put in a saucepan with about 1 cup sugar. Cook on a medium heat until rhubarb breaks down and is slightly pulpy. Meanwhile, dip 2–3 slices of thick-cut bread, or half a croissant, in an egg and cream mix. Fry bread in melted butter in a frying pan. Turn and cook both sides. Cook until golden brown. Serve with warm cooked rhubarb, whipped cream and a little maple syrup.

Rhubarb & Melon Salad

Cut 400 g rhubarb in 2 cm pieces. Put in a saucepan together with 2 tbsp sugar and 2 tbsp white wine. Let the rhubarb melt on a low heat. Chill. Make 500 g melons into balls with a melon baller, or cut into pieces. Put melon and 1 bunch of chopped mint leaves into saucepan and mix with rhubarb. Chill for a couple of hours. Put salad in small bowls and garnish with fresh mint leaves. Serve cold.

Rhubarb & Strawberry Sherbet

Wash 500 g strawberries, hull and mash. Press 2 cups cooked rhubarb through a sieve, add 2 tbsp lemon juice, 1/8 tsp salt, 1½ cups sugar and ¾ cup cream and mix. Pour into a plastic container and freeze without stirring until firm. When ready to serve, scrape up thin layers of the mixture with an inverted spoon, beat back and forth in the container until smooth and serve immediately.

Spicy Rhubarb

Cut 460 g rhubarb into large pieces. In a large bowl mix together 150 ml pink ginger cordial (available from major supermarkets) and 85 g brown sugar. Toss the rhubarb in liquid, put everything in a roasting tin and grill for 10–15 minutes until lightly charred and tender. Meanwhile, whisk 150 ml whipping cream with 3 tbsp icing sugar and a touch of vanilla extract. Remove rhubarb from tin using a slotted spoon, arrange on plates and pour a little syrup over the top. Garnish cream with orange zest.

Rhubarb & Ginger Jam

I adore this recipe. While some jams can be too sweet and kill the taste of the fruit, the tart and ginger twist of this jam works well. Perfect on scones, pikelets or your morning toast. I look forward to making this jam with the freshest of rhubarb from my small plot.

Makes 6 x 300-g jars.

- 1.5 kg fresh rhubarb, washed
- 1.5 kg white granulated sugar
- 2 lemons, juice of
- 80 g stem ginger in syrup, drained and finely chopped
- 25 g butter

Chop rhubarb into 2.5-cm lengths and place in a large preserving pan with sugar. Stir in lemon juice, then place pan over a low heat and cook, stirring, until sugar dissolves.

Bring to boil and continue boiling, stirring occasionally, until jam thickens. This will take about 1 hour. To test whether it's set, spoon a little onto a chilled saucer (see page 18). If the jam wrinkles when pushed with a finger, it's ready.

Stir in stem ginger and cook for a further 5 minutes. Scoop away any scum and stir in butter. Carefully spoon jam into clean, sterilised jars, seal and label. Store in a cool, dark place for up to six months.

Rhubarb & Tarragon Vinegar

This vinegar takes on a pretty pink colour from the rhubarb and an interesting flavour. Use it as you would tarragon vinegar – especially with fruity salads – to tenderise meats, or in marinades.

Makes 1 x 2-litre bottle.

- 3–4 stalks rhubarb, well washed and trimmed
- two sprigs fresh tarragon, few extra if liked
- 6 peppercorns
- 2–3 stalks lemongrass or strips lemon peel
- 3 tbsp granulated sugar
- 1.5 litres cider vinegar

Chop rhubarb into short lengths. Place all ingredients in a stainless steel saucepan. Heat gently until sugar dissolves, then bring just to boiling point and boil 30 seconds. Turn off heat and rest until cool.

Strain then pour into sterilised jars (see page 18) and cork when settled. If liked, sprigs of well-washed tarragon may be tucked into the bottles for a pretty effect and more potent tarragon flavour. The vinegar can be used immediately.

Rhubarb & Pineapple Chutney

Rhubarb has an obvious identity crisis – not quite a fruit and not quite a vegetable. Partnered with pineapple it can dispel some apprehension, as this is quite a delightful relationship. It is great with Indian or South East Asian food. This chutney will keep up to 12 months. **Makes 4 x 450-g jars.**

- 500 g rhubarb, chopped
- 3–4 red onions, peeled and chopped
- 350 g fresh pineapple, chopped
- 200 g sultanas
- 2 limes, halved and finely sliced
- 2 limes, juice of
- 2 stalks lemongrass, very finely sliced
- 2–3 red chillies, finely sliced
- 4 cloves garlic, peeled and chopped
- 3-cm piece fresh ginger, peeled and grated
- 600 ml cider vinegar
- 500 g demerara sugar
- 2 tsp mustard seeds
- 2 tsp coriander seeds, coarsely crushed
- 1 tsp salt

Put first 11 ingredients into a large non-aluminium saucepan, and bring to boil. Simmer uncovered for 15 minutes, stirring occasionally. Add remaining ingredients. Stir to dissolve sugar.

Cook over a gentle heat, uncovered, stirring frequently, until very thick. This will take about 1½ hours. When ready, a wooden spoon drawn across the bottom of the pan should leave a trail. Cool, then taste, adding salt as necessary. Pour into sterilised jars (see page 18). Seal with lids when cold. Store in a dark cool place for one month before using.

Rhubarb Zabaglione

A grown-up version of rhubarb and custard, where you spoon through the frothy, hot sweet sauce to a tart rhubarb mixture. The zabaglione mixture is best served immediately, although it will hold together for 10 minutes if left over the pan of warm water. Note: this recipe contains partly cooked egg yolks and should be avoided by pregnant women, the very young and the elderly. **Serves 6.**

- 125 g caster sugar
- 150 ml water
- 300 g rhubarb, cut into 2.5-cm chunks
- 5 tbsp Marsala (or other dessert wine)
- 6 medium egg yolks

Place 50 g of sugar in a large pan with the water and cook over a low heat, stirring occasionally, until sugar has dissolved. Add rhubarb and bring to boil. Remove pan from heat immediately, cover and leave to stand for 5 minutes, until softened.

Meanwhile, place remaining sugar, Marsala and egg yolks in a large bowl set over a pan of simmering water. Whisk continuously with an electric whisk until creamy and thick enough for a trail of mixture to remain on the whisk. This should take about 5–6 minutes.

Divide rhubarb mixture between six 120-ml serving glasses and spoon over the Marsala mixture. Serve immediately.

Rhubarb & Orange Cake (pictured)

This is good either warm, as a pudding with whipped cream, or cold, as a moist fruity cake. Keeps for 2–3 days in an airtight tin. **Serves 6–8.**

350 g rhubarb, cut into 4-cm lengths
200 g caster sugar
½ orange, finely grated zest and juice of
140 g butter, softened
2 eggs, beaten
½ tsp baking powder
85 g self-raising flour
100 g ground almonds

Topping
25 g butter
25 g light muscovado sugar
½ orange, finely grated zest of
70 g slivered almonds
icing sugar for dusting

Mix rhubarb with 50 g of caster sugar and orange zest. Set aside for 1 hour, stirring once or twice.

Preheat oven to 190 °C/375 °F. Butter and line the base of a 23-cm round loose-bottomed cake tin with baking paper. Cream butter and remaining caster sugar in a bowl until fluffy. Add eggs, one at a time, beating well after each addition. Add baking powder, flour and ground almonds. Beat gently until smooth, taking care not to over-mix. Stir in orange juice. Spoon into tin and level with a spoon. Drain rhubarb in a sieve over a bowl. Spoon chunks over cake mixture. Bake in oven for 25 minutes.

Reduce oven to 180 °C /350 °F. For topping, melt butter, then stir in sugar, orange zest and almonds. Sprinkle over cake and cook for another 15–20 minutes or until firm in the centre. Cool in tin for 20 minutes, then transfer to a rack. Peel off the paper and dust with sugar before serving.

Rhubarb Crumble

Fruit crumbles are always popular and this one is particularly so due to its nutty crumbly topping. Muscovado sugar has a more caramel, rich taste over normal brown sugar, but normal sugar can be used if desired. **Serves 6–8.**

60 g wholemeal flour
60 g oat bran
60 g soft butter
120 g muscovado sugar
60 g raisins
60 g ground almonds
75 g walnuts, coarsely chopped
500 g rhubarb

Preheat oven to 180 °C/350 °F. Mix flour and oat bran in a bowl then rub in butter until mixture is crumbly. It will seem heavier than a normal crumble topping. Add about two-thirds of the sugar, and the raisins, ground almonds and walnuts.

Wash rhubarb well, trim and cut into short lengths. Lay in an ovenproof dish approximately 21 cm x 4 cm deep. Sprinkle over remaining sugar, then crumble topping. Smooth down with a spoon and bake in an oven for 40 minutes. Serve hot or warm with cream or ice cream.

Rosmarinus officinalis

Rosemary is a good compact herb for any garden and kitchen. Upright rosemary shrubs not only act as zesty and aromatic hedges or space fillers, but there are many uses for the spiky leaves of the plant.

The ancient Greeks claimed that rosemary was 'good for the brain'. Infusions of rosemary leaves are said to help heighten concentration and improve memory, and in fact many wreathes of rosemary were worn when intense concentration was needed. It has been eaten or drunk to relieve anxiety and depression. During the Plague, rosemary leaves were often worn around the neck to keep away smells and prevent people breathing in the germs. Rosemary is described as 'dew of the sea', which refers to its pungent aroma and blue carpet of flowers. But beware, rosemary is a strong, piquant flavour and can overwhelm food.

It is easy to grow, with a little maintenance in the spring, in planters or in a space in the garden. The rosemary plant can creep and crawl over walls and down railings, or stand upright as a standard potted plant. The flowers have culinary benefits, used in purées or desserts, or summer fruit salads.

HOW TO GROW

A perennial woody shrub growing to 1.5 m or taller, rosemary can be grown from seed or cuttings. Plant in a sunny open position in limy sandy soil. Rosemary is usually grown on the Mediterranean coastline so is quite tolerant of prevailing salty winds and enjoys New Zealand gardens. Crushed eggshells are good manure. Prune tips every spring and summer for vigorous growth. If pruned well, rosemary plants should keep bringing on sweet and tender tips. Put the cuttings on the barbecue to create a heavenly smell and impart flavour to fish and meat.

Rosemary can be grown as a companion plant for cabbage, beans, carrots and sage. It helps to deter moths, bean beetles and carrot flies.

PICKING & STORING

Fresh — Pick the tips of the rosemary plant. The soft stem parts will have a better flavour than the wooden stems. Keep fresh sprigs in plastic bags for a few days or keep stems in a glass of water.

Dried — Hang fresh sprigs to dry in a warm, dry place. Strip leaves off the stems before storing. Dried leaves are often used in cooking as they will break down better in the cooking process. The hardy dried stems are good to keep and use as skewers for barbecue food or to be burned on a fire to emit a pungent aroma.

Preserves — Keep rosemary sprigs in olive oil or vinegar, or preserve with vegetables like beetroot. It is the piquant flavour that is desirable to preserve, rather than the woody stems.

CULINARY USES

Rosemary is an intensely aromatic herb, and its digestive benefits often see it being paired with more fatty cuts of meat. It is at its best when accompanying roast lamb dishes, pork, chicken, tomato-based sauces, breads and stuffed vegetables. Use it fairly sparingly or it could overpower other more delicate flavours in the dish. Add to scones and breads, and to crab apple jelly to serve with meat dishes. It is delicious cooked with preserves.

The spiky green leaves, which look almost like thick pine needles, can toughen when cooked and unless finely chopped are best removed from food before serving.

QUICK PICKINGS

Rosemary Butter

Place 125 g butter, 1 tbsp chopped fresh rosemary, ½ tsp freshly ground black pepper and 2 tsp grated orange rind in a small bowl. Beat together with a hand beater or wooden spoon. Spoon mixture onto a sheet of greaseproof paper, shape into a roll 4 cm in diameter, roll in paper, and twist ends of paper to secure. Refrigerate until firm. This can be used with roast lamb, beef or chicken.

Rosemary Oil

Clean and dry 5–6 rosemary sprigs, about 15 cm long. Place in a clean bottle or jar and top up with 250 ml extra virgin olive oil. Add 1 tsp white wine vinegar, screw on top or lid firmly and place on a windowsill. Every time you pass, give the bottle or jar a good shake. Leave for two weeks then strain oil into a clean bottle, pop in a fresh sprig of rosemary and screw on top. Keep in a cool place.

Rosemary Stuffing

Heat 2 tbsp butter in a saucepan. Add 1 finely chopped onion and cook until soft. Remove from heat and cool. Stir in 2½ cups cooked long-grain rice (approx 1 cup uncooked rice), zest of 1 orange, 1 egg, ¼ cup toasted pine nuts, ¼ cup chopped parsley, the leaves of 3 sprigs of rosemary, finely chopped, and 1 tsp chicken stock powder. Season with salt and freshly ground black pepper. Stir well to combine ingredients. Then cover and refrigerate until ready to stuff a whole chicken. Alternatively, fresh brown breadcrumbs can be used instead of rice, if desired.

Anchovy & Rosemary Sauce

Crush the leaves from 2 sprigs of rosemary with a mortar and pestle. Add 12 salted anchovy fillets and pound to a paste. Slowly add the juice of 2 lemons and stir to blend. Finally add 150 ml olive oil, a few drops at a time, and stir until well combined. You can use a food processor, but the mortar and pestle provide a thicker, more textural sauce. Keep refrigerated for up to one month.

Rosemary & Wine Marinade

Heat 2 tbsp oil in a saucepan over a medium heat. Cook leaves of 2 sprigs of rosemary and 1 clove garlic in the oil, stirring frequently. Remove from heat, stir in ½ cup dry red wine, 1 tsp sugar and season with salt and freshly ground black pepper. Use to marinate lamb chops, cutlets, pork steaks or any cut of beef.

Spiced Rosemary & Plum Chutney

Red plums deliver the best flavour in this chutney. Rosemary combined with the other spices balances out the tartness with a striking flavour. Bring this chutney out at Christmas time and serve with turkey or ham. **Makes about 2 litres.**

1 kg plums, pitted and chopped
500 g tomatoes, peeled and chopped
3 medium onions, peeled and chopped
3 medium carrots, peeled and chopped
1 large apple, peeled and chopped
150 g raisins
320 g brown sugar
2 tsp coarse cooking salt
875 ml malt vinegar
1 cinnamon stick
½ tsp cloves
3 small dried red chillies
1 star anise
5 sprigs rosemary
1 tsp black peppercorns

Combine plums, tomatoes, onions, carrots, apple, raisins, sugar, salt and vinegar in large saucepan. Stir over heat without boiling, until sugar is dissolved. Tie cinnamon, cloves, chillies, star anise, rosemary and peppercorns in a piece of muslin. Add muslin bag to pan, bring to the boil, simmer, uncovered, stirring occasionally, for about 2 hours or until mixture is thick. Discard muslin bag. Pour into hot sterilised jars (see page 18), seal when cold.

Roasted Potatoes with Garlic & Rosemary

If you need an excuse to grow fresh rosemary in your garden, choose this one. An easy dish to match with your roast dinner or weekend brunch. **Serves 4–6.**

1 kg roasting potatoes, peeled
125 ml olive oil
2 tsp onion stock powder
salt and freshly ground black pepper
2 sprigs fresh rosemary, finely chopped
6 large cloves garlic, peeled and very finely chopped

Preheat oven to 200 °C/400 °F. Cut potatoes into 1-cm cubes. Turn potato cubes onto a clean tea towel or absorbent paper towel and pat dry.

Put oil in a large roasting tin and heat in oven for 10 minutes. Add potatoes, sprinkle over the onion stock powder and plenty of salt and pepper. Bake potatoes for about 20 minutes, turning often, or until golden.

Remove dish from oven and sprinkle over rosemary and garlic. Return potatoes to oven and cook about 3–4 minutes more, until the garlic is just starting to change colour (be careful not to burn). Serve immediately.

Rosemary & Olive Bread (pictured)

The olives marry beautifully with fresh rosemary from your garden in this recipe. Making bread doesn't need to feel like it takes forever. It is a simple process with some therapeutic kneading. A good electric mixer helps. **Makes 1 large loaf.**

- 2 tsp dried yeast
- 600 ml tepid water
- 2 tsp sugar
- 6 tbsp olive oil, plus extra
- 2 sprigs fresh rosemary, finely chopped
- 1 kg plain flour, plus extra
- 2 tsp salt
- 150 g black olive paste
- coarse sea salt and fresh rosemary sprigs and whole olives, for sprinkling

In a small bowl mix yeast, 1/2 of the water and sugar. Allow to stand for 5 minutes, until frothy. Mix in oil, rosemary and remaining water. Place flour and salt in a large mixing bowl. Add the yeast mixture to the flour and mix quickly to form a soft dough. If using an electric mixer use the dough hook attachment to make life easier. Leave the dough to slowly turn for 5 minutes to allow the bread to stretch and become elastic.

Alternatively, turn onto a lightly floured surface and knead for 5–8 minutes until smooth and elastic. Oil a large baking tray or lasagne dish. Divide dough in half. Roll out one half to a 30-cm square, place on the baking sheet or in oiled dish. Spread over olive paste to within 1 cm of the edge.

Roll out remaining dough and use to cover the filling, pinch the edges to seal. Brush the top with olive oil and sprinkle with sea salt, rosemary sprigs and whole olives. Cover with oiled plastic wrap and leave to rise for about 1 hour until the dough has doubled in size and springs back when pressed. Preheat oven to 220 °C/425 °F. Bake bread for 15–18 minutes until risen and golden. Serve warm.

Grilled Leg of Lamb with Rosemary Salt

Rosemary and lamb go together like basil and tomatoes. They complement each other's flavour zone so well that sometimes it would seem strange to cook lamb without rosemary. Rosemary salt is a slightly different way to fully bring out the flavour in this wonderful and easy recipe. **Serves 6.**

300 ml plain yoghurt
7 cloves garlic, peeled and thinly sliced
4 sprigs rosemary, stems removed and coarsely chopped
½ tsp freshly ground black pepper
1 x 2.5-kg piece boneless, butterflied leg of lamb
1½ tbsp sea salt

Rosemary salt
1 tsp finely chopped fresh rosemary
1 tbsp sea salt

To marinate lamb, stir together yoghurt, garlic, rosemary and pepper in a baking dish or sealable plastic bag. Add lamb, turning to coat completely. Marinate in fridge, covered, turning over once or twice. Leave for about 5 hours.

Bring lamb to room temperature, this may take about 1 hour. Preheat oven grill to 200 °C/400 °F. Remove lamb from marinade, discarding marinade, and put on a work surface. Run skewers horizontally through meat, about 3 cm apart, first lengthwise then crosswise to form a grid. Skewering the meat makes it easier to move and turn over. Sprinkle with salt.

Place meat in an oiled roasting dish at the top of the oven. Cook for 25–30 minutes, turning half-way through cooking. Remove skewers. Transfer lamb to a cutting board and let stand 10 minutes before thinly slicing.
To make the rosemary salt, stir together rosemary and sea salt and serve in a small dish with lamb.

Mustard & Rosemary Chicken

Take care to cook chicken properly on grill plates – a brown and charred outside may not mean a well-cooked centre. Insert a small knife and if the juices run clear the chicken is cooked. Any sign of pink means it isn't. This simple chicken dish is teamed up with potatoes and spinach. Cook them how you like – the chicken speaks for itself. **Serves 4.**

4 chicken breast fillets
1 tbsp wholegrain mustard
½ lemon, juice of
1 tbsp olive oil
1 tbsp finely chopped rosemary leaves, plus extra sprigs, to serve
1 clove garlic, peeled and crushed
600 g potatoes, quartered
250 g baby spinach leaves
20 g butter
1 lemon, cut into wedges

Combine chicken, mustard, juice, oil, rosemary leaves and garlic in a bowl and toss well to coat. Heat a chargrill plate on high. Cook chicken in batches, for 15–18 minutes, until cooked through and browned.

Meanwhile, boil, steam or microwave potatoes until just tender. Drain and place hot potatoes in a large bowl with spinach and butter, and toss gently until spinach starts to wilt and butter melts.

Serve chicken fillets with potatoes and lemon wedges and top with extra rosemary sprigs.

Rosemary Shortbread

Rosemary has a very distinctive flavour and, paired up with a soft buttery biscuit like shortbread, makes quite a subtle treat. These biscuits are perfect served after dinner with cheese or as a great snack in the cookie jar. **Makes 20–24 biscuits.**

110 g caster sugar, plus extra for dusting
2 tsp chopped rosemary leaves
230 g softened butter
2 lemons, finely grated zest of
300 g plain flour
50 g cornflour

Preheat oven to 150 °C/300 °F and line a baking sheet with baking paper. Place sugar and rosemary leaves in a food processor. Blend until rosemary is very finely chopped, then add butter and lemon zest and process until pale and creamy. Transfer to a large bowl and beat in flour and cornflour until it forms a stiff dough.

Place on a sheet of baking paper and lay another sheet on top. Then gently press down with a rolling pin and roll out to 3–5 mm thick. Lift off the top sheet and stamp out the biscuits with a cookie cutter. Using a palette knife, lift them off the bottom sheet of paper and carefully transfer to baking sheet. Lightly press together remaining dough and repeat.

Prick biscuits with a fork and bake in centre of oven for 12 minutes or until a pale golden brown. Remove to a cooling rack (they will still be soft, so be careful moving) and liberally dust with extra caster sugar. Serve once cool and crisp.

Sage

Salvia officinalis

Sage is an aromatic, strongly flavoured herb with many uses. Traditionally green sage is used more for cooking and purple sage is more medicinal. It's often grown in herb gardens, pots or borders for its petite violet-blue flowers that bloom in spring.

Sage is the saviour in the herb garden. It is said to have a variety of useful medicinal properties, so it is easy to see why this plant made it into our food. Sage complements strong-flavoured foods and aids in the digestion of fats. Sage tea used to be in high demand for the treatment of nervous complaints, and recommended as a tonic for rheumatic pain and anaemia. Sage has antiseptic properties, too. Use it as a balm on cuts, sores and ulcers. Gargles of sage have been administered for coughs and sore throats. And sage plants were planted on graves because the smell of the plant is said to alleviate grief.

A word of warning; although small amounts are quite safe when cooking, pregnant and breastfeeding woman should not take therapeutic doses. Sage contains thujone, which can trigger fits in epileptics.

HOW TO GROW

Sage is a perennial plant, which grows into a half-metre-high shrub. It is an attractive plant and can be grown easily in pots or containers, either from cuttings or from seed for those varieties which flower. The plants can become woody after three or four years so it pays to re-plant or split up the existing plant to make fresh growth. Sage hates wet roots, so don't over-water. The plants will tolerate dry conditions really well. Other than that, it is a real no-care plant and will benefit from the constant picking of leaves and de-heading of flowers.

PICKING & STORING

Pick leaves from the edges of the plant. The outer leaves will be full of flavour and picking them allows the younger tips to grow outwards. The stems can be quite woody so take the leaves off the stem before use.

Fresh — Once picked, place bottom of stems into cold water to keep fresh. Fresh leaves are, surprisingly, milder in flavour than dried leaves. They can be stored in plastic bags in the fridge.

Dried — Cut the sprigs of sage in the spring when they are at their best and before the flower stalks grow. Hang to dry in a warm, well-ventilated place. Once the leaves are dried, they must be kept in containers in a cool dark place to keep the grey-green colour and powerful flavour. Dried sage leaves are often a key component of dried herb mixes.

Preserve — The flavour of sage is best preserved in jellies. To make sage jelly, use the apple jelly recipe (page 160) and substitute sage for the mint. This jelly can be used with strong-flavoured game meats to cut through the strong oily flavour.

CULINARY USES

The strong, distinctive flavour of sage can be used dried or fresh to counteract the richness of some foods like pork, duck and oily fish, as well as to assist digestion. As a flavour it is regularly used in stuffings, sauces and jellies. It works well with onions and garlic. In Italy sage is the classic ingredient in saltimbocca (see page 216), and is commonly used in barbecues to flavour meat. The leaves are hardy so don't break down as readily as finer herbs.

Make instant stuffing for chicken breasts by putting sprigs of sage under the skin with garlic and herb cheese. Good with pork and apples. Add a couple of chopped leaves to transform apple sauce. Sage can be added to lamb burger patties to make a gastronomic treat. Sage will dramatically change the flavour of whatever it is added to.

QUICK PICKINGS

Chorizo & Sage Risotto

In a frying pan heat 2 tbsp olive oil. Toss 1 red onion, finely sliced, in oil until tender. Add 400 g sliced chorizo and 6–8 fresh sage leaves. Cook until heated through and the red oil of the chorizo starts to seep out. Add 200 g arborio rice and cook for 2–3 minutes. Add 125 ml red wine and allow the liquid to be absorbed. Slowly add about 750 ml hot chicken stock a ladleful at a time until all has been absorbed. The rice should be all'onda (see page 18). When cooked remove from heat and stir in 50 g butter and serve sprinkled with plenty of pecorino cheese.

Sage & Onion Stuffing

Dice 1 onion finely and sauté in frying pan with 1 tbsp olive oil and 4–6 finely chopped sage leaves. Add this to 100 g fresh white breadcrumbs, 1 Granny Smith apple, peeled and grated, 25 g butter and season with salt and freshly ground black pepper. You may use an egg to bind the stuffing. This mixture can then be stuffed into a fresh free-range chicken or whole duck.

Roast Red Onions & Sage

Preheat oven to 220 °C/425 °F. Slice the tops off 4 large red onions, then peel. It is important to keep the root part intact, or the onion layers will separate. Cut into quarters. Place onions in a roasting tin. Pour over 4 tbsp olive oil and 2 tbsp balsamic vinegar then sprinkle over 1 tbsp finely chopped sage leaves. Season well with salt and pepper. Toss well, so they are all coated, and cover loosely with foil. Place in oven for about 45 minutes, then remove foil and cook for a further 10 minutes, until they are soft and caramelised. Serve immediately.

Sage & Orange Roast Potatoes

Preheat oven to 220 °C/425 °F. Place 3 tbsp olive oil, the zest of 1 orange and 4–6 roughly chopped sage leaves in a roasting tin. Place in oven for 5 minutes. Dry 3 large peeled and diced potatoes on a clean tea towel. Tip potatoes into the roasting tin. Toss around to coat with oil and season well with salt and pepper. Place in oven and roast for 40–45 minutes, basting often, until golden brown and cooked through.

Butter & Sage Pasta

Melt 4 tbsp butter in a sauté pan and continue cooking until a golden brown colour appears in the thinnest liquid of the butter. Add 8 sage leaves and remove from heat. Add juice from ½ lemon and set aside. Cook 500 g pasta according to instructions on the packet. Drain pasta, reserving about ½ cup of the cooking liquid. Gently pour cooking liquid into butter sage mixture and return to heat. Reduce slightly then add pasta to pan. Toss through well and season to taste with salt and freshly ground black pepper. Toss through ¼ cup grated Parmesan and serve immediately.

Sage Tea

Sage's medicinal properties have made sage tea a respected tonic worldwide for a very long time. It is very soothing and great to cure any digestive ailments. Beware, if you are pregnant or breastfeeding, don't drink this tea, it can have an effect on the young infant. **Makes 4 cups.**

- 4–6 sage leaves
- 2 lemon verbena leaves
- 1 large strip lemon rind
- 1 tsp sugar
- 2 tbsp white wine, optional
- 1 litre boiling water

Wash sage and lemon verbena leaves. Place in a non-metallic teapot. Add lemon rind, sugar and wine if wished. Pour over boiling water and allow to infuse for 4–5 minutes. Strain into cups. The tea will be stronger if left to infuse for a longer time. Strained tea can be poured over ice cubes or chilled to make a refreshing cold drink.

Sage & Garlic Stuffing

Every cook needs a good stuffing recipe in their repertoire. Fresh sage is the ultimate for poultry. Forget the dried packets of herbs and bland combinations, this stuffing has plenty of flavour and works well with a free-range, corn-fed bird. **Makes enough to stuff a chicken.**

- 8 pieces of stale bread
- 1 onion, peeled and finely chopped
- 4 cloves garlic, peeled and crushed
- 8 fresh sage leaves
- 2 celery stalks
- ¼ cup fresh parsley, chopped
- salt and freshly ground black pepper
- 1 lemon, finely grated zest of
- 60 ml olive oil
- 1 egg

Place bread in a food processor and pulse until fine breadcrumbs form. Remove and place in a bowl. In the same food processor add onion, garlic, sage leaves, celery and parsley. Pulse until well minced. Add to breadcrumbs. Season well with salt and pepper and add lemon zest. Mix in olive oil and egg. Use this stuffing for turkey, chicken or pork.

Chicken & Sage Saltimbocca (pictured)

Saltimbocca means 'jump into the mouth' in Italian and is traditionally made with veal. Here I have used chicken as a more accessible meat, but switch back to the traditional veal if you have it. **Serves 4.**

4 chicken breasts
salt and freshly ground black pepper
60 g prosciutto
8–12 fresh sage leaves
85 g mozzarella, thinly sliced
1 tbsp olive oil
1 tbsp butter
2 spring onions, finely chopped
125 ml dry white wine
250 ml chicken stock
½ lemon, juice of
2 tbsp butter, softened
to serve, 4–6 fresh sage leaves

Trim any fat and membranes from the chicken breasts. Remove extra tenderloin attached. Place each breast between sheets of plastic wrap. Pound with a cooking mallet or rolling pin until about 5 mm thick. Remove the wrap and season both sides of meat with salt and pepper.

Spread thin slices of prosciutto and sage leaves over top of flattened chicken breasts, leaving an edge around the outside of about 5 mm. Cover prosciutto with sliced or grated mozzarella. Fold breasts in half and secure with toothpicks.

Heat oil and butter in a large, heavy frying pan over medium–high heat until fragrant and golden. Add chicken packets and sauté, turning once, until lightly browned, about 3 minutes each side. Remove to a platter and cover with foil to keep warm. Add spring onions to pan. Cook stirring until wilted, about 1 minute, and then pour in white wine. Scrape bottom of pan with a wooden spoon to loosen the browned bits, boil until wine is almost evaporated. Add chicken stock and lemon juice.

Boil over high heat until reduced. Remove from heat and swirl in second measure of butter. Taste and adjust seasonings, adding a bit more lemon juice if you like. Pour sauce over the chicken. To serve, sprinkle with extra sage leaves.

Pork with Apple & Sage Butter

Best served with creamy mashed potatoes to mop up the outstanding sauce. Great comfort food. **Serves 4.**

750 g Granny Smith apples
300 ml apple juice
6–8 fresh sage leaves, finely chopped
50 g brown sugar
1 tsp ground cinnamon
½ lemon, grated rind and juice of
4 pork loin chops
50 g butter
1 onion, peeled and sliced
½ tsp fennel seeds, toasted
3 tbsp calvados or brandy
300 ml chicken stock

To make apple and sage butter, chop unpeeled apples and place, core, pips and all, in a pan. Add apple juice and sage, bring to boil and simmer gently for 30 minutes.

Press mixture through a sieve into a clean pan. Add brown sugar, cinnamon and lemon juice and zest, bring to boil and simmer gently for 30 minutes, stirring frequently to prevent sticking.

Preheat oven to 160 °C/325 °F. Trim pork of any excess fat, then wash and pat dry with paper towel. Melt 40 g of butter in a large frying pan. Add onion and fennel seeds and fry gently for 10 minutes until golden and soft. Remove with a slotted spoon and set aside.

Add remaining butter to pan and fry pork chops for 3–4 minutes on each side. Remove and cover with foil and place in oven to keep warm. Add calvados or brandy to pan and boil until almost evaporated, then pour in the chicken stock and continue boiling until reduced by half. Return onions to pan, whisk in three tablespoons of apple and sage butter and heat through.

Serve pork chops with sauce and extra apple and sage butter.

Sage & Bacon Scallops

For a great finger food or starter to a meal, I love these sage scallops. Some people remove the red coral of a scallop, thinking that it is bitter. I prefer not to waste any part of the delicious mollusc. These are great served with béarnaise sauce. **Makes 12.**

12 plump scallops
salt and freshly ground black pepper
6 rashers streaky bacon
12 sage leaves
toothpicks or bamboo skewers
1 tbsp olive oil
2 tbsp butter
2 tbsp lemon juice
to serve, béarnaise sauce (see page 257)

Rinse scallops and dry on a paper towel. Season well with salt and pepper. Cut bacon in half. Lay a sage leaf on each piece of bacon and then wrap the leaf and bacon around each scallop. Secure with a toothpick or bamboo skewer.

Heat a heavy-based frying pan or grill plate. Heat oil and butter until bubbling but not browning. Stir in lemon juice. Cook scallops for 3–4 minutes, turning regularly until bacon has browned. Serve as an entrée with fresh salad leaves or as a finger food with béarnaise sauce.

Salad Leaves & Lettuce

Butter, iceberg, rocket, endive, radicchio, mizuna, cos

I could write endlessly about the uses of salad leaves. There are many, many different types of leaves that we can use in a tossed green salad. With the advent of bags full of mesclun available now in our supermarkets, salads have been transformed from the days of a bowl of iceberg lettuce and a few tomatoes.

Mesclun mix simply means a certain mix of baby salad leaves. These can include rocket, baby beet leaves, endive, mizuna, and cresses like watercress or lamb's lettuce. A mesclun mix of salad greens can be grown easily, as it is the immature leaves of these plants that are picked and thrown in the salad bowl.

Most salad leaves and lettuces need to be treated the same way while growing. They like warm soil, so that's why we harvest so many salads in the summer. Many of these leaves started out as medicinal herbs, and have been brought to our plates by modern European cuisine, for garnishing.

HOW TO GROW

Any lettuce can be grown very easily from seed. All types are available, and simply need warm moist soil to germinate. The trick is not to grow too many of any one seed at once. Unlike other vegetables, lettuce and salad leaves don't have a long shelf life or the possibility of preservation, so are best picked fresh and eaten straight away.

Choose healthy organic soil with plenty of blood and bone mixed in. Lettuces suck up nutrients out of the soil, so need a good base. Many lettuces are grown hydroponically, because all they really need in life is a good nutrient mix to grow. It will only take about 6 weeks from seeds to edible seedlings for some of the mizuna, endive or rocket leaves. They can sprout to flower and turn to seed very quickly under extreme growing conditions, so pick leaves early. Single pots of different varieties will keep a family fed throughout the spring and summer months. Mix up the seeds and seedlings to make your own mesclun mix.

PICKING & STORING

Salad leaves are only good fresh. Forget trying to freeze, dry or store them for long periods of time. The fine leaves will begin to wilt as soon as they are picked. Pick the outer leaves off the plant. Leave the inner leaves to produce more and more leaves. Whole lettuces don't necessarily need to be harvested. Take the colander to the garden and pick only as much as you will need for your salad.

When choosing leaves, avoid any damp or brown-edged leaves and soft set cores. All lettuces should be stored in the vegetable crisper or in an airtight paper-towel-lined plastic bag in the fridge for up to five days.

TYPES OF SALAD LEAVES

Rocket

A bitter, pungent, tonic herb with a slightly hot, peppery flavour. The flowers, seeds and oil of rocket are edible. Rocket's botanical name is *Eruca vesicaria*, the subspecies being sativa, from the Latin 'eruca' meaning 'downy stem' (like a caterpillar). Classified more as a salad herb than lettuce, rocket is often called arugula in American cookbooks.

Rocket makes the ideal side salad to accompany strongly flavoured meat and fish dishes such as marinated chicken or well-seasoned fish or seafood.

Butter Crunch Lettuce

Butter lettuce's soft leaves have a milky, buttery flavour and are loosely packed from the core, forming an open-rose shape. These lettuces vary considerably in size, from very small to large. Its leaves are a strong green colour and are great in mixed salad.

Cos Lettuce

This lettuce has crisp, bright green leaves that wrap together tightly to form an elongated head. The leaves get smaller as you reach the core, which could be removed when washing. It is a robust lettuce, with a mild, almost nutty flavour. Sometimes called Romaine lettuce, cos leaves are great in salads. Its most traditional use is in Caesar salad.

Radicchio

Although radicchio is technically a chicory herb, it is still used in the same way as most lettuces. Its colour ranges from ruby to pink and even white. It has a pleasant bitter, pepper flavour and is mostly used in mixed salads and pastas, or grilled for hot dishes.

Iceberg Lettuce

Iceberg is a crisp, tightly packed lettuce. Regarded as the common garden-variety lettuce, it has dark green outer leaves and small white inner leaves. With its neutral flavour, iceberg can be used raw in salads, braised, or stuffed, and is often used in soups.

Lollo Biondi

Tight, curly, fairly coarse leaves spread out in rosette form in both the red and green varieties of coral lettuce, which make them easy to cut as needed. Shred the leaves for use in mixed salads or sandwiches.

Endive Or Frisée

These sprawling lacy leaves are part of the chicory family of lettuces.

SALAD DRESSINGS

Cook's Tips

Dressings & Vinaigrettes

- *Vinaigrette traditionally contains mustard, and French dressing is the same thing but made without mustard.*
- *Instead of whisking in a bowl, use a small jar with a lid and put in all the ingredients. Give it a good shake. Your aim is to dissolve the salt and powders and emulsify the oils with the vinegars.*
- *Salad leaves must be dry, otherwise the dressing slips off and stays at the bottom of the salad bowl. You want to coat the leaves.*
- *Toss the salad well. Use your hands! It is the best way to be delicate with the beautiful, fragile just-picked leaves.*
- *Salad dressings can easily be made well ahead of time. If using fresh herbs however, leave it until the last minute, so that herbs don't turn brown.*

Italian Vinaigrette

Whisk together 2 tbsp red wine vinegar, ½ tsp salt and ⅛ tsp black pepper in a bowl, then add 5 tbsp extra virgin olive oil in a slow stream, whisking until emulsified. **Makes about ½ cup.**

French Vinaigrette

Whisk together 3 tbsp white wine vinegar, 1 tsp Dijon mustard, ½ tsp salt, ⅛ tsp black pepper, 2 tsp finely chopped shallot in a bowl. Add 6 tbsp extra virgin olive oil in a slow stream, whisking until emulsified. Perfect for potato salads and French bean salads. **Makes about ½ cup.**

Balsamic Dressing

Mix a few grindings of salt and pepper, 1 clove crushed garlic and 2–3 tsp balsamic vinegar. Slowly whisk in 4 tbsp extra virgin olive oil until dressing thickens. Taste and adjust seasoning. Perfect for tomato salads, pasta salads. **Makes ½ cup.**

Sun-Dried Tomato Dressing

Mix 2 pieces sun-dried tomato in oil (shredded), 1 tbsp wine vinegar, pinch of sugar and a few grindings of salt and pepper. Slowly whisk in 6 tbsp extra virgin olive oil. Taste and adjust seasoning. Perfect for mozzarella and avocado salsa, pasta. Tastes sweet and sour. **Makes ¾ cup.**

Honey & Mustard Dressing

Mix 1 tsp clear honey, ½ tsp wholegrain mustard with 1 tbsp cider vinegar. Add 4 tbsp extra virgin olive oil, a spoonful at a time, and mix until dressing thickens. Season to taste with salt and freshly ground black pepper. Tastes sweet and sour, perfect for chicken. **Makes ½ cup.**

Poppy Seed Dressing

Mix 1 tsp poppy seeds, 2 tsp lemon juice, 1 tsp honey, 3 tbsp sunflower oil, salt and pinch mustard powder. Add more lemon juice and/or honey to taste. Tastes sharp and tangy. Perfect for fruit salads, leafy salads with croutons. **Makes ½ cup.**

Yoghurt Dressing

Mix 2–3 tsp cider vinegar with salt and freshly ground black pepper. Mix in 6 tbsp natural yoghurt and leave to stand for 10 minutes. Stir in 1 tbsp chopped fresh mint and season, adding more vinegar if needed. Perfect for potato salads, cucumber salads, lamb. **Makes ¾ cup.**

Salsa Verde Dressing

Pick over 1 bunch parsley and remove stalks. Place parsley, ½ cup olive oil, ⅛ cup capers, 2 cloves garlic, 1 hard-boiled egg yolk, 1 tbsp lemon juice, 1 tsp wholegrain mustard, freshly ground black pepper, ¼ medium onion, chopped, and 6–8 anchovies in a food processor and process until smooth. Add extra olive oil and lemon juice to make thinner consistency for salads. **Makes 1 cup.**

Avocado Dressing

Mix 2–3 tbsp sour cream, 2 tbsp extra virgin olive oil, few drops Tabasco sauce, 1 tbsp chives, finely chopped, and season with salt and freshly ground black pepper. Mash 1 small avocado with 4 tsp lime juice, then whisk into sour cream. Tastes creamy with a spicy kick. Perfect for Mexican food, baked potatoes, chicken. **Makes ¾ cup.**

Ranch Dressing

Combine ½ cup mayonnaise, ½ cup sour cream, ½ cup buttermilk, 1 tbsp crushed garlic, 1 tsp dried oregano, 1 tsp dried dill, 1 tbsp dried chives, 1 tbsp parsley, 2 tbsp grated Parmesan, 1 dash Tabasco sauce, 1 tbsp Worcestershire sauce, 1 tsp ground white pepper in a bowl or jar and stir or shake really well. Refrigerate for at least ½ hour before using. If the dressing is too thick, add a little extra buttermilk to thin.
Makes 1½ cups.

Garlic Dressing

Mix 1 tbsp white wine vinegar, ½ cup oil, 1 tbsp lemon juice, 2 cloves crushed garlic, 2-cm piece fresh grated ginger, 1 tsp soy sauce, 1 tsp sugar together in a bowl or glass jar. Shake and combine well.
Makes ½ cup.

Endive, Chickpea & Calamari Salad

Endive, or frisée, is a pretty lettuce to use in salads. It holds its frizzy shape and is a great flavour. Squid can be replaced by prawns or scallops in this easy salad.
Serves 4.

85 g endive leaves
200 g frozen squid rings
1 tbsp sesame oil
420-g can chickpeas, drained and rinsed
12 small black olives
10 cherry tomatoes, halved
2 small shallots, finely chopped

Dressing
1½ tsp whole coriander seeds
1 tsp clear honey
2 tbsp fresh lemon juice
6 tbsp olive oil
1 clove garlic, peeled and crushed

Rinse endive leaves thoroughly and dry. Store in a sealed plastic bag in fridge until needed. Run squid rings under warm water until softened. In a frying pan heat sesame oil until hot. Quickly toss squid rings in oil for 1–2 minutes until just tender. They won't take long. Too long in the heat and they will turn rubbery. Set aside.

To make dressing, fry coriander seeds (without any oil) over a medium heat until fragrant and a shade darker. Cool, then grind to a coarse powder using a pestle and mortar. Put in a screw-top jar with the remaining dressing ingredients and shake until evenly mixed. Taste and season, then set aside until needed.

Just before serving, put all salad ingredients in a large bowl and toss with just enough dressing to coat without drowning.

Crispy-Skin Smoked Chicken, Rocket & Orange Salad (pictured)

Duck breasts can be used instead of chicken in this dish. Any type of strong meat, such as chorizo or salami, complements the rocket leaves. **Serves 4.**

4 smoked chicken breasts, skin on
2 tbsp olive oil
1 tbsp sea salt
4 oranges, segmented
200 g rocket leaves
2 spring onions, sliced into thin strips

Dressing
160 ml balsamic vinegar
160 ml fresh orange juice
1 tbsp brown sugar
1 orange, finely grated rind of

Brush chicken breasts with olive oil, then rub with sea salt. Place a non-stick frying pan on medium heat, then place breasts skin-side down in pan and cook for 2–3 minutes. Turn and cook for another 2–3 minutes. Transfer chicken to a rack to drain excess fat, cover and rest for 5 minutes.

Combine orange segments and rocket in a bowl. Slice chicken breasts diagonally and place on a serving plate. Place salad on top, pour over dressing and garnish with spring onions.

To make dressing, place balsamic vinegar, orange juice and brown sugar in a small saucepan on medium heat. Simmer for 5 minutes until reduced slightly, then remove from heat and add orange rind.

Lettuce Stuffed with Chilli Beef

Iceberg lettuce leaves are superb. They crunch in a salad and can be easily cooked. If you take the time to grow two or three in a planter box you will discover a whole new taste in lettuce. **Serves 4.**

1 onion, peeled and chopped finely
50 g butter
1 kg minced beef
2 tbsp chilli paste (see page 79)
few drops of Tabasco sauce
100 g unsalted crushed peanuts, chopped
1 iceberg lettuce, separated into whole leaves
bamboo skewers

Sauté onion in butter until golden. Add mince, stirring constantly so meat separates. Cook for 5–10 minutes until browned. Add chilli paste and Tabasco, stir through and cook for a further 10 minutes. Sprinkle with nuts and gently stir into mixture.

Place 2 tablespoons of mince in each lettuce leaf and secure with a bamboo skewer. Eat immediately.

Spiced Prawn, Cos Lettuce & Pasta Salad

Cos lettuce is traditionally reserved for a Caesar salad. It holds dressing and vinaigrettes well. Orecchiette pasta is sometimes called 'little ears' pasta. This is a tasty meal or a great side to a barbecue. **Serves 4–6.**

- 300 g orecchiette pasta
- 1 small red onion, peeled and finely diced
- ½ red chilli, deseeded, finely diced
- 3 tbsp white wine vinegar
- 100 ml extra virgin olive oil
- salt and freshly ground black pepper
- 350 g prawns, cooked and peeled
- 130 g baby cos leaves

Cook pasta according to packet instructions. Be sure to add a spoonful of vegetable or olive oil to the water as this helps to prevent the pasta sticking. Stir regularly.

Meanwhile, put red onion and chilli in a large bowl. If you like your food hot, include the chilli seeds. Whisk in vinegar and olive oil and season to taste.

Drain pasta and run briefly under cold tap until it is warm, as opposed to hot. Shake well and tip into bowl with chilli and onion. Mix well until thoroughly coated in the dressing. Leave to cool then stir in prawns and cos leaves. Make sure everything is well-dressed. If serving much later, add prawns and greens just before you serve.

Endive & Radicchio Salad

Every year I plant just one or two of these lettuces. If you pick the outside leaves when needed you can make up your own mixed lettuce salad. Pick the leaves just before serving, rinse well. Flavour with a dressing and serve. **Serves 4–6.**

- 125 g radicchio
- 150 g endive leaves
- 1 tbsp Dijon mustard
- 1 tbsp sherry vinegar
- ½ tsp sugar
- ½ tsp salt
- ½ tsp freshly ground black pepper
- 3 tbsp grapeseed or canola oil
- 1 tsp sesame oil
- 3–4 radishes, thinly sliced
- 2 spring onions, finely chopped
- 1 tbsp sesame seeds, toasted
- 1 tsp black sesame seeds (optional)

Soak radicchio and endives in a large bowl of very cold water to crisp, 10 minutes, then drain and dry.

Whisk together mustard, vinegar, sugar, salt, pepper, grapeseed or canola oil and sesame oil in another large bowl until emulsified. Add endives, radicchio, radishes, spring onions and sesame seeds and toss until coated well. Serve immediately.

Silver Beet

Beta vulgaris

Silver beet can bring back memories of badly cooked, over-boiled, slimy green mush that quickly goes cold on the plate and is far from appetising. However, start with a few seeds, grow your own tender leaves, and silver beet takes on a whole new look. It is fast growing, will thrive all year round in most gardens, and if we learn to cook the green leaves properly, we will find that silver beet is indeed good to eat!

Silver beet is very easy to grow. A pot by the back door with a few plants can give a nutritious green-vegetable fix to any meal. Three or four plants can give enough leaves to feed a family for a week.

It is highly nutritious, being a good source of iron, vitamins and fibre, and we should eat silver beet every day. With simple treatment silver beet can take on its own flavours and evolve from dreary, slimy and 'steer-well-clear-of' to a tasty supplement to most meals.

Silver beet is just as good for adding colour to the garden as it is for cooking or adding raw to salads. Silver beet also goes by the name 'Swiss chard' or 'native spinach' and can even come in a red-stemmed or rainbow variety, which is a not-so-distant relation to beetroot. Cooking with flavours like bacon, garlic, smoked cheese or fresh herbs can put flavour back into a somewhat insipid vegetable. It's time to rejoice in the possibilities of silver beet.

HOW TO GROW

A simple plastic pot, wooden planter or a semi-shady patch of garden can become the silver beet section in your garden. Grown very easily from seed, or even more easily from pre-prepared seedlings, it can be transplanted into well-drained soil that has been enriched with compost and a little general-purpose fertiliser. It needs to be regularly watered though, and also favours slightly salty soils.

Silver beet plants can grow in the semi-shade and require a few hours of sunlight per day to thrive. In warm climates it is possible to sow seed year-round for a continuous supply. In spring the plants tend to 'bolt to seed' which means you don't tend to get the best out of your plants. For better results, plant your seeds in autumn for a good winter crop of greens.

PICKING & STORING

Pick leaves when the air is cool and the sun is not beating down and wilting the leaves – just before cooking dinner or first thing in the morning. Leaves of any age can be taken, but it pays to cut from the outer leaves in, to allow the centre leaves to thrive.

Fresh — Silver beet leaves are best kept in the fridge. A newspaper or plastic bag will keep in the moisture. But, like salad vegetables, the leaves will lose their moisture as soon as they are picked. It is far better to keep cultivating plants in your garden and pick fresh leaves when you need them.

Freeze — You don't see frozen silver beet often, which is probably because it grows all year round. However if there is an abundant supply, quickly blanch the chopped leaves, squeeze out most of the juice and pack into freezer bags. Remove as much air as possible from the bag and seal. Label and date bag and use within three months of freezing.

CULINARY USES

Silver beet leaves go well with cheese, eggs, bacon and cured meats or in any salad. Garlic, beans and fresh herbs bring out the earthy flavour of this perennial vegetable. The younger the leaves, the more succulent and sweet they are. Choose small new leaves for fresh coleslaw and larger deeper green leaves to be blanched like spinach and used in any dish.

To make older silver beet leaves more palatable, it is better to remove the centre white rib on each leaf. In younger leaves these are nice, textural and have a flavour all of their own, but in older leaves the white stems can be a bit tough and wooden. The best way to do this is to cut a V shape up the centre of the leaf, taking out as much of the centre stem as possible. The leaves can be chopped or finely shredded for cooking.

To cook green or red silver beet, soak thoroughly in cold water, including the stems (which are quite tasty when cooked). Remove any mud and grit and look for insects curled up in the leaves so there are no crunchy surprises later. Slice crosswise into strips and place in a large flat shallow saucepan with a lid. Add a cup of water, a few spoonfuls of butter and a pinch of salt.

Bring to a boil slowly, then immediately turn heat down to a simmer. Allow to simmer covered, stirring occasionally, until white stems have turned transparent. It usually takes about 4–5 minutes of cooking. Remove from heat, and drain. Serve with other green vegetables with the main meal.

QUICK PICKINGS

Silver Beet & Kumara Mash

Peel and quarter about 1 kg kumara. Barely cover with water and cook for 15–20 minutes until tender. Drain. Meanwhile, steam 250 g silver beet leaves until stems are tender. Mash kumara and silver beet together using a potato masher or stick blender. Add ½ cup milk, 2 tbsp olive oil and plenty of salt and freshly ground black pepper to taste. Serve hot with dinner.

Silver Beet Salad

Shred 1 bunch silver beet and put in a bowl with 3 rashers cooked chopped bacon, 3 cups bean sprouts, and ½ cup roasted cashew nuts. Toss salad ingredients together with garlic dressing (see page 223) and serve.

Silver Beet & Ricotta Cannelloni

Preheat oven to 180 °C/350 °F. Shred 1 bunch silver beet very finely, mix with 250 g ricotta cheese. Season with salt and freshly ground black pepper. Stuff mixture into tubes of dried cannelloni pasta. Lay stuffed cannelloni in a shallow dish. Cover with 400 g ready-made pasta sauce and 2 cups grated cheese. Bake for 40 minutes, until pasta has softened.

Balsamic Silver Beet

Wash 1 bunch of silver beet and chop or tear into pieces, discarding tough stems. Sauté 2 chopped tomatoes over a medium heat in a large heavy-based frying pan until cooked to desired consistency, 5–15 minutes. Add 2 tbsp balsamic vinegar, silver beet and some water if needed. Cover and steam vegetables until cooked, about 8 minutes. Check occasionally to see if there is enough water in the pan. Season well with salt and freshly ground black pepper and serve.

French Silver Beet

Sauté 1 bunch coarsely shredded silver beet with 2 cloves crushed garlic in 1 tbsp olive oil until wilted, about 5 minutes. Sprinkle with 4 tbsp grated Parmesan and serve immediately.

Baked Eggs with Silver Beet & Mushrooms

For brunch, we sometimes don't realise the importance of greens. This dish provides all the creamy splendour of soft cooked eggs and the fresh taste of crisp silver beet. Choose tender new leaves for this recipe. **Serves 4.**

250 g silver beet leaves
¼ cup finely chopped onion
1 clove garlic, peeled and finely chopped
2 tbsp butter
125 g mushrooms, thinly sliced
80 ml cream
¼ tsp salt
¼ tsp black pepper
⅛ tsp freshly grated nutmeg
4 large eggs
2 tbsp finely grated Parmesan
to serve, brown bread, toasted

Put oven rack in upper third of oven and preheat to 230 °C/450 °F. Bring 2 cm water to a boil in an ovenproof heavy-based frying pan (not cast-iron). Add half silver beet and cook, turning with tongs, until wilted, about 30 seconds. Add remaining silver beet and wilt in same manner, then cook, covered, over moderately high heat until silver beet is tender, about 2 minutes. Drain under cold running water. Gently squeeze handfuls of silver beet to remove as much liquid as possible, then coarsely chop.

Wipe frying pan dry, then cook onion and garlic in butter over moderately low heat, stirring, until softened, 2–3 minutes. Add mushrooms and increase heat slightly, then cook, stirring, until mushrooms have softened and have exuded liquid, about 3 minutes. Stir in cream, salt, pepper, nutmeg and chopped silver beet and bring to a simmer. Remove frying pan from heat and make 4 large indentations in silver beet mixture. Break an egg into each indentation. Cook until egg whites are set but yolks are still runny, about 7–10 minutes. Lightly season eggs with salt and pepper, then sprinkle with Parmesan. Serve immediately on toasted brown bread.

Silver Beet & Cannellini Bean Soup

This has the flavours of the famous Tuscan soup ribollita (which means 'reboiled'), to which you add bread slices before setting aside to allow the flavours to develop, then bring to the boil. **Serves 6.**

400-g can cannellini beans
2 tbsp extra virgin olive oil
2 red onions, peeled and sliced
6 cloves garlic, peeled and sliced
2 stalks celery, washed and sliced
18 silver beet leaves, washed and stems removed, leaves chopped into pieces
1 tbsp tomato paste
2 litres chicken stock
2 slices pancetta or bacon, chopped
4 sprigs flat-leaf parsley
salt and freshly ground black pepper
to serve, freshly grated Parmesan
12 slices ciabatta bread, brushed with olive oil and grilled

Drain and rinse beans. Heat a little olive oil in a large saucepan and fry onion and garlic over a low heat until fragrant but not browned. Add celery and silver beet and stir for a further 1–2 minutes. Stir in tomato paste, then pour in stock and add pancetta or bacon and parsley. Cook over a low heat for about 30 minutes. Add beans and cook for a further 10 minutes. Set aside for at least 2 hours, or overnight, to allow the flavours to develop.

Gently reheat soup and serve in warm bowls, making sure ingredients are distributed evenly. Season to taste and sprinkle with grated Parmesan and drizzle with extra virgin olive oil. The whole pieces of grilled bread can be dropped in soup before eating.

Silver Beet & Potato Gnocchi (pictured)

I find that these take time to prepare, but the small morsels are filling and flavoursome and a wonderful meal on a cold winter's night. **Serves 4.**

900 g baking potatoes
1 kg silver beet, leaves only
200 g plain flour
1 tsp salt
¼ tsp ground nutmeg
to serve, Parmesan, freshly grated

Sage butter
100 g butter, melted
8–10 fresh sage leaves

Preheat oven to 200 °C/400 °F. To make gnocchi, scrub potatoes well and prick outside with a fork. Bake directly on an oven rack until soft, for about 1 hour. While potatoes are still hot, split in half and scoop out soft flesh. Push pulp through a sieve using the back of a spoon.

Bring a large pan of water to boil. Remove centre white stalk from silver beet leaves and finely shred. Drop leaves into water and cook for 2–3 minutes, until tender. Pour into colander and drain well. Allow to cool slightly and then squeeze out any extra water by wrapping leaves in a tea towel and squeezing hard. Chop finely.

Place potato and silver beet in a large bowl and add flour, salt and nutmeg. Stir vigorously, then turn out onto a work surface and knead until smooth and blended. Bring a pot of well-salted water to a simmer in a large saucepan. Roll about 2 tbsp of dough into a cylinder 2 cm wide. Cut into pieces 2 cm long. Roll each piece against the tines of a fork while pressing a small dent on the opposite side with your finger.

Drop gnocchi into simmering water and cook until they float, about 2 minutes. They should hold a firm shape and be chewy to bite. If they turn out slimy and soft, knead more flour into dough then test again. Cook remaining gnocchi, and drain well. Serve immediately on warm plates or bowls drizzled with sage butter and garnished with some Parmesan.

To make sage butter, heat butter in a saucepan and when it is just about to boil, reduce heat. Add sage leaves. Cook for a few seconds, turning the sage leaves, until they are crisp.

Silver Beet, Ham & Smoked Cheese Gratin

This can be a meal in itself, accompanied by creamy mashed potato, or as a side dish to a pan-fried steak or schnitzel. The smoked cheese imparts a great flavour, but can be replaced by any tasty flavourful Cheddar. **Serves 4.**

800 g silver beet leaves
100 g butter
100 g plain flour
900 ml milk
250 g smoked cheese, grated
salt and freshly ground black pepper
¼ tsp ground nutmeg
350 g cooked ham, cut into strips
100 g fresh breadcrumbs

Preheat oven to 200 °C/400 °F. Remove white stalks from silver beet leaves with a sharp knife. Roughly chop leaves. Cut stems into 4-cm lengths. Cook stems in a pan of salted boiling water, for about 3 minutes, then add leaves and simmer for 2–3 minutes until both are just tender. Drain thoroughly, making sure that every possible last drop of cooking water is pressed out.

Melt butter in a saucepan. Tip in flour and stir over a low heat for 1 minute. Remove from heat and gradually stir in milk, increasing the quantity until it has relaxed to a creamy consistency. Bring to boil, stirring, then simmer gently for a good 5 minutes to cook out the taste of raw flour. Add two thirds of cheese to sauce and allow to melt. Season with salt, pepper and freshly ground nutmeg.

Mix cooked silver beet with ham and sauce. Spoon into a greased gratin dish and smooth the top. Mix remaining cheese with breadcrumbs. Sprinkle evenly over gratin, and bake for 25–30 minutes, until brown and sizzling. Serve immediately while hot.

Silver Beet & Pumpkin in Filo Pastry

This pie goes a long way for dinner or a picnic lunch. Use strong cheeses to complement the vegetables. **Serves 4–6.**

500 g silver beet leaves
800 g pumpkin, peeled and diced
100 ml olive oil
3 cloves garlic, peeled
150 g feta or blue cheese
250 g cottage cheese, drained through sieve
200 g Cheddar, grated
salt and freshly ground black pepper
12 sheets filo pastry
100 g butter, melted
1 tbsp poppy seeds

Remove white stalks from silver beet. Roughly chop leaves. Bring large pot of water to boil. Blanch silver beet leaves for 5 minutes, until softened. Remove from water and drain well in a sieve. When cooled slightly, wrap wilted silver beet leaves in a tea towel, and squeeze out any excess water. It needs to be quite dry with no moisture.

Preheat oven to 180 °C/350 °F. Place diced pumpkin in a roasting dish and drizzle over olive oil. Slice garlic cloves and sprinkle over pumpkin pieces. Bake in oven for 30 minutes, until tender. Allow to cool.

In a large bowl, combine silver beet, roasted pumpkin, feta or blue cheese, cottage cheese and Cheddar. Season to taste with salt and pepper. Grease a 26-cm square baking dish with butter. Lay a sheet of filo pastry across the bottom, brush with melted butter. Repeat with 3–4 layers of filo pastry, brushing melted butter over pastry each time. Spread silver beet and pumpkin mixture over pastry. Top with a flat piece of filo pastry. Then, scrunch each remaining piece of pastry into a rough ball and place on top, probably 5 or 6 pieces. Brush over carefully with melted butter and sprinkle with poppy seeds.

Bake in oven at 200°C/400°F for 35–40 minutes, until top is well golden and the mixture is set. Allow to cool slightly before slicing.

Silver Beet & Feta Flan

A well-made flan, with crisp pastry and a tasty filling, makes a good choice for a light meal. By using ready-made pastry, this flan becomes even simpler to whip together. **Serves 4.**

8 silver beet leaves, chopped
2–3 sheets pre-made short crust pastry
3 eggs
salt and freshly ground black pepper
good grating of nutmeg
few pinches dried oregano
60 ml milk
60 ml cream
¼ cup Cheddar
100 g feta, crumbled
50 g Parmesan, grated

Preheat oven to 180 °C/350 °F. Cook silver beet in a saucepan of boiling water uncovered for 8 minutes. Drain, refresh with cold water and leave to drain. When cool, wring out any excess water with your hands. Chop finely.

Grease a 23-cm flan tin with oil. Lay pastry sheets over base and press to line bottom. Prick pastry with a fork. Lay a piece of baking paper over top and fill with baking beans. Bake in oven for 8 minutes. Remove paper and beans and set aside.

Break eggs into a bowl, sprinkle over ¼ tsp of salt and add pepper, nutmeg and oregano. Beat lightly with a fork, then add milk, cream and Cheddar. Blend together, then mix in feta and silver beet.

Sit the pastry-lined flan ring on a lined baking tray. Turn the filling into the pastry case and sprinkle over Parmesan. Bake flan in oven for 30 minutes, or until top is golden and the pastry cooked. Cool on tray for 5 minutes, then slide onto a cooling rack. Serve warm.

Silver Beet Coleslaw (pictured)

Coleslaw doesn't have to be just an accompaniment to a barbecue – a yummy variation is to serve this salad in tall cocktail glasses with a sprinkling of blue cheese and toasted sesame seeds. **Serves 6.**

350 g red cabbage leaves
300 g savoy cabbage leaves
6 young silver beet leaves
¼ cup fresh parsley, chopped
2–3 spring onions, finely chopped

Dressing
150 g mayonnaise
150 g unsweetened yoghurt
50 ml milk
2 tsp Dijon mustard
salt and freshly ground black pepper

Wash all cabbage leaves very well in cold water and remove stalks and hard ridges. Using a sharp knife shred leaves very finely. Remove the white stalk from the silver beet leaves. Cut leaves very finely. In a large salad bowl or platter, combine salad ingredients and toss through the parsley and spring onions.

To make dressing, mix together all ingredients in a small bowl or jug. Spoon over salad and using two forks, mix in well until all dressing is incorporated into the leaves. Serve as an accompaniment to your main meal or as a lunch salad with cheese and bread.

Strawberries

Fragaria ananassa

Ever picked a ripe, rosy-red strawberry on a summer's day? Pure perfection! Fragaria, the classical name of strawberries, simply means fragrance. And when you pick a fresh strawberry straight from the garden you understand why. They are full of scent, sunshine and sweetness.

The original wild strawberries are indigenous to Britain, where they still grow, nestled among violets and other flowers in the undergrowth. Strawberries now grow all over the world in the warmer climates. Here in New Zealand we have a magnificent commercial crop of berry fruit every year.

They are exceptionally easy to grow in your own garden, and even easier to propagate more plants each year. In a small garden, strawberries thrive well in a contained pot or planter. Or, they can be easily planted as the border to some of your flowering plants or bay trees, for an annual crop of fragrant berries.

HOW TO GROW

As long as the birds can be kept away there is no reason why strawberries can't become a favourite in your urban garden or balcony. Plant your strawberry plants in winter or early spring – it is better to have the plants settled into a pot while the weather is still cold. Choose pots that are wide and can allow runners to be put down into a rich composted soil with excellent drainage. You will need a warm, sheltered site, with protection from birds, and keep the strawberry plants well-watered. As with all plants, regular feeding will boost growth.

Surround the plants with pine needles, straw or black plastic to keep the fruit clean. Plant strawberry plants amongst your flower pots, to keep the birds away from the developing fruit, or place netting over all the plants. The birds will try for the fruit as soon as they start to colour and the scent comes on.

For excellent fruit production, cut off any runners that appear before flowers form. After the fruit season, let the runners spread. Each runner has a series of little plants attached and these can be pegged into the soil until they are growing strongly or, if they have already formed roots, cut free and planted. This will propagate a whole new set of plants for next year.

PICKING & STORING

Pick small amounts of fruit at a time. Small berries can easily get crushed. It is important to pick them as they become ripe, otherwise your crop will be lost to birds and insects very quickly.

Fresh — If you can resist eating the berries there and then, the fruit is best to be refrigerated. Place in a bowl or thin plastic container in the not-so-cold part of the fridge. Eat or use within 2–3 days at the most.

Freeze — Whole strawberries don't freeze well. The flesh tends to break down and once thawed the fruit becomes very pulpy. This is ok if you are going to make jam or cook with them in the near future. A way of helping the fruit stay whole when freezing is to dip them in water and roll them in sugar. Freeze them on a tray individually, then place in freezer bags and use within 3–4 months. Strawberry pulp can be frozen for use in winter desserts.

Preserve — Strawberry jam is by far the favourite way of storing strawberries. Strawberry sauces, coulis or strawberry pulp are all good ways of keeping the integrity of the fruit flavour.

CULINARY USES

Common sense tells us that strawberries are ideal for any sweet dessert. Traditionally the berries can be used for cakes, muffins, gateaux, meringues, fruit salads, summer puddings or smoothies.

Cook's Tip

How to hull a strawberry.
To remove the top leaf and core of the strawberry, hold the strawberry by the base of the fruit. Using a sharp paring knife or fruit knife dig a little way into the top of the strawberry, under the leaf. Circle around, holding the leaf down with your thumb. You should be able to remove the leaf and the centre white core.

QUICK PICKINGS

Strawberry Coulis

Hull 200 g ripe strawberries. Using a potato masher or fork, mash until pulpy. Gently simmer strawberries with 4 tbsp sugar for 5 minutes. Allow to cool slightly. Stir in 50 ml crème de cassis (optional). Purée sauce in a blender or with hand blender. Pass through a fine sieve to remove seeds. Use sauce fresh or freeze in plastic, freezer-proof container.

Balsamic Strawberries

Choose really good, aged balsamic vinegar. Hull some fresh, room-temperature strawberries, not over-ripe and squishy. Serve strawberries with a dipping bowl of balsamic vinegar, and accompany with a ripe Brie and sesame crackers.

Antipasto Strawberries

Serve small fresh strawberries with caper berries, goat's-milk cheese, slices of ham or Parma ham, and dipping bowls of Dukkah and freshly ground black pepper.

Strawberry Salad

Sprinkle passion-fruit pulp and icing sugar over strawberries for a dessert served with elderflower whipped cream. Put 60 ml elderflower cordial and 1 tbsp icing sugar into a bowl. Gradually whisk in 300 ml cream until it holds its shape.

Strawberry Mille Feuille

Bake two sheets of pre-made puff pastry until well cooked and sandwich together with good strawberry jam, whipped cream, egg custard and plenty of fresh strawberries. Dust the top with an extravagant layer of icing sugar then score a grid pattern in the icing sugar by laying a red hot metal skewer across it several times.

Summer Compote

Simmer some dried figs and prunes, a cinnamon stick, star anise, a clove or two, some sugar, orange zest and a little water until the fruit is plumped and the liquid spicy and syrupy. Cool and mix in plenty of halved strawberries. Serve in small bowls over mascarpone or ricotta.

Strawberry Fool

Mix some hulled, sliced strawberries with whipped cream. Fold in some Greek yoghurt or sour cream and add icing sugar to sweeten to taste. Add a strawberry liqueur as an option. Serve in cocktail glasses with fresh sliced strawberries and sweet waffle crackers.

Eton Mess

Hull and slice some strawberries. Stir strawberries through a light egg custard. Fold in whipped cream. Crush some pre-made meringues and mix through the strawberry custard mix. Pile into glasses and serve topped with extra strawberries and crumbled meringue.

Strawberry Dip

Mix 100 g hulled strawberries with 200 g softened mascarpone in a food processor or blender. Add ¼ tsp cinnamon and ¼ tsp allspice. Serve in chilled bowl with oat crackers and fresh slices fruit. Great accompanied by a strong blue cheese.

Frozen Strawberry Daiquiri

Perfect on a hot day and a great way to enjoy the spoils of your own garden.
Serves 1.

- 60 ml white rum
- 2 limes, juice of
- 1 tbsp strawberry liqueur
- 1 tsp sugar
- 4 large strawberries
- a scoop of very small ice cubes or crushed ice

Put all ingredients into a blender and process until smooth and thick. Pour into a glass and serve immediately.

Strawberry Jam

Choose slightly under ripe fruit, which contains more pectin than ripe or over-ripe fruit, so the jam sets better. Any jam will benefit from using a sugar thermometer. You will get the right temperature for the sugar and then it will set properly. **Makes 8–10 x 200-g jars.**

1.8 kg small whole strawberries
3 lemons, juice of
1.8 kg white sugar
50 g sachet pectin sugar
1 tbsp butter

Wash, drain and hull strawberries and put in a large glass bowl. Sprinkle over lemon juice and sugar, then mix gently. Tip mixture into a large wide pan or preserving pan (about 4.5 litre heavy-based pan). Heat gently, stirring constantly, until sugar has dissolved. Do not allow jam to boil at this stage.

Stir in butter (this stops the jam becoming scummy) then bring to a rolling boil. Once jam reaches this stage you need to start timing. Boil hard for 4 minutes (be sure to time this exactly) until jam reaches setting point (see page 18). The jam is ready when it reaches 105 °C/220 °F on a sugar thermometer.

Remove jam from heat and skim off any scum with a large metal slotted spoon. Leave to cool for 10–15 minutes. If you pot jam when it's too hot all the fruit rises to the top. Stir gently to distribute fruit, then pour from a heatproof jug or ladle into warm sterilised jars (see page 18). Fill jars right to the top, because as jam cools, it contracts. Waxed discs must fit the jars exactly to form an airtight seal and prevent mould forming. Seal, label and wipe with a clean damp cloth. Keeps for six months to a year if stored in a cool dry cupboard.

Cook's Tip

Stir some of your favourite liqueur into the jam before pouring it into jars. Brandy, rum, kirsch and liqueur de fraises (strawberry liqueur) are particularly good.

Strawberry Canapés

Delicious starter or finisher. Serve at a cocktail function or as a complement to a cheese platter. **Makes about 48.**

Walnut Oatcakes

1 cup oat bran
½ cup walnuts
125 g butter, chopped
160 g plain flour
1 tsp baking powder
1 tbsp brown sugar
¼ cup milk
¼ tsp salt

Cheese Spread

250 g goat's feta
125 g cream cheese
125 g sour cream
2–3 tbsp mixed herbs like chervil, mint, chives and parsley
250 g strawberries, hulled and sliced

To make oatcakes, place the bran and walnuts in a food processor and blend until finely chopped. Add butter and process until combined and resembles breadcrumbs. Add flour, baking powder, brown sugar, milk and salt and process until stiff dough forms. Wrap in plastic wrap and place in fridge for 30 minutes.

Preheat oven to 160 °C/325 °F. Roll out dough on a lightly floured surface until about 6 mm thick. Cut into 5-cm rounds and place on baking-paper lined trays. Bake for 20 minutes or until golden. Cool on wire racks.

To make cheese spread, in a bowl or food processor mix feta with cream cheese and sour cream. Add chopped herbs. Pipe or spread onto oat biscuits and garnish with strawberries. Top with freshly ground black pepper.

Strawberry & Cinnamon Shortcake

This dessert is equally good made with raspberries, but it is a perfect way to use up an abundance of strawberries. **Serves 6–8.**

200 g ground almonds
200 g butter, softened
200 g caster sugar
200 g self-raising flour
1 tsp cinnamon
1 egg, plus 1 egg yolk
500 g strawberries, hulled and sliced
icing sugar, for dusting
to serve, whipped double cream mixed with Greek yoghurt

Preheat oven to 180 °C/350 °F. Line base of a 23-cm springform cake tin with baking paper and grease sides.

In a food processor, mix ground almonds, butter, sugar, flour, cinnamon, egg and egg yolk until evenly mixed and forming a soft dough.

Spread half mixture over base of tin in a smooth layer with no gaps (it is easiest to do this with two forks). Put strawberries on top. Top with remaining cake mixture and spread carefully using two forks to press mixture down.

Bake in centre of oven for 1 hour. Check after 40 minutes, if the top is getting too brown, cover loosely with foil. When cooked, the shortcake should be slightly risen and dark golden brown.

Cool in tin slightly, then loosen the edges with a knife and remove. Slide onto a plate and dust with icing sugar. Serve warm, in wedges, with spoonfuls of cream and Greek yoghurt.

Strawberry & White Chocolate Muffins (pictured)

Muffin recipes make it easy to get baking with strawberries. Kids can get involved with all stages, just give them a hand putting the tray in and out of the oven. **Makes 12.**

500 g plain flour
4 tsp baking powder
¼ cup sugar
100 g white chocolate buttons
50 g butter
3 eggs
300 ml milk
250 g strawberries, hulled
icing sugar, for dusting

Preheat oven to 200 °C/400 °F. Grease 12-hole muffin tin. Sift flour and baking powder into a bowl. Mix in sugar and chocolate buttons. Melt butter. Lightly beat eggs and milk together. Make a well in the centre of the dry ingredients. Add butter, milk mixture and sliced strawberries.

Mix quickly until just combined. Three-quarters fill the greased muffin tins with mixture. Bake in oven for 15 minutes or until muffins spring back when lightly touched. Serve warm, dusted with icing sugar.

Mascarpone & Strawberry Semifreddo

This is a great way to use up over-ripe strawberries. Semifreddo simply means semi-frozen and this one is the simplest semifreddo ever. It's rich and creamy without being too sweet. Add a dash of liqueur if you are feeling naughty. This will keep for up to two months in the freezer. **Serves 6.**

500 g strawberries, hulled
175 g icing sugar
1 lemon, juice of
500 g mascarpone

Mash strawberries well with a fork. Stir icing sugar and lemon juice into mascarpone until smooth. Mix in mashed strawberries, leaving some of the mixture unstirred to create a ripple effect.

Transfer to a rigid, plastic container and freeze for 2–3 hours until semi-frozen. Serve in scoops. If the semifreddo has been frozen for a few weeks, transfer to the fridge for 2–3 hours before serving to get that semi-frozen taste and texture.

Strawberry & Ricotta Cheesecake (pictured)

This delicious version of a cheesecake can be made a day ahead and glazed just before serving. It is a light dessert with all the sweetness of fresh strawberries.
Serves 8–10.

25 g amaretti or malt biscuits, crushed
500 g ricotta cheese
4 eggs, separated
3 tbsp plain flour
250 g caster sugar
2 oranges, finely grated rind of
5 tbsp Cointreau or Grand Marnier
250 g strawberries
3 tsp gelatine
1 cup hot water
½ cup strawberry jam
to decorate, icing sugar and a few extra strawberries

Preheat oven to 180 °C/350 °F. Grease a 23-cm round springform cake tin with butter. Dust with crushed amaretti or malt biscuits.

Put ricotta, egg yolks, flour, sugar, orange rind and liqueur in a food processor and process until well blended. In a clean, dry bowl, whisk egg whites until stiff. Gently fold ricotta mixture into egg whites. Pour mixture into cake tin and bake in centre of oven for 40–45 minutes until just golden and springy to touch. Remove from oven and cool on a wire rack. Once cool, chill in tin – don't worry if it sinks.

Hull strawberries and cut in half. Arrange the strawberries on the top of the cake. Sprinkle gelatine into the hot water and add jam. Stir well until gelatine has dissolved. Pour jam mix over strawberries. Chill again for at least 30 minutes or until ready to serve. Carefully remove cake from tin and serve each slice dusted with icing sugar, with extra strawberries.

Sweetcorn

Zea mays

When Christopher Columbus went to Cuba, he was given two gifts. One was tobacco and the other was something the natives called 'mais'. Mais, or corn as we now call it, was and still is the staple food of South America. It was used in every way including eaten fresh. The Aztecs had corn-planting ceremonies, and the plant plays an integral part in their history and way of life.

Today only about one-fifth of the corn grown in the world gets eaten by people. Domesticated animals eat their share and the rest goes into manufacturing many non-food products. The versatility of corn has led to some countries in the world growing just corn and no other crops. Your home garden doesn't need to be so regimented. We grow corn for eating pleasure.

The fresher the sweetcorn the juicier and sweeter it will be. As soon as it is picked the sugar starts to turn to starch. The sweetcorn season is short, as the husks ripen quickly at the hot end of summer. Grow your own and there is a good supply of sweetcorn straight from garden to table. Four to five plants will give a family 2–3 decent feeds.

Corn is rich in good carbohydrates and natural sugars and starches. It is also rich in vitamins A, B and C and can provide much magnesium, potassium and iron to our diet. It is best lightly boiled and seasoned with salt and doused with butter.

HOW TO GROW

Growing corn is easy. Make sure your soil is rich and fertile and has plenty of organic fertiliser ploughed into it. Sow sweetcorn seeds 3 cm deep and about 15–20 cm apart. In the ground is best but a sturdy deep polythene pot is also good. It is important that the plot is large enough to support 2–3 rows of corn, as they mutually support each other as they grow. The rows of corn also help pollination, especially as sweetcorn uses wind pollination to fertilise the crop.

Use generous amounts of blood and bone and general fertiliser when planting the seeds as sweetcorn plants are very hungry. Make sure you plant the seed after frosts have finished, they need warm soil so plant towards the end of November. Mound the soil around the base of the sweetcorn stalks to give extra support, or use stakes and twine. When the cobs appear they tend to get quite top-heavy.

Remember to shake the male flower heads at the top onto the female parts, which eventually become the corn cobs. This will ensure all the corn ears are fully established, and guarantee a bigger crop.

PICKING & STORING

Sweetcorn is ready to be picked when the tassels of the cobs begin to dry off and go brown. Pick one and shed the husk to see if the kernels are ready. If you stick your finger into the centre of a kernel and the juice pops out at you then they are ready. Twist the cobs away from the stem and get the pot on to cook.

Fresh — Fresh corn can be eaten off the cob, or the kernels sliced off. Keep the cobs in the fridge in the salad cooler. They won't last forever, and as the husks start to brown that means the kernels are probably going mouldy. Eat as fresh as possible.

Freeze — Corn can be frozen, either by slicing off all the kernels (see cook's tip below) or by cutting the cobs into smaller pieces, or freezing the whole cobs. It is best to remove the husks before freezing, and quickly blanching the pieces will help preserve the flavour.

Dried — Dried corn is usually ground up and goes into such foods as tortillas, and corn chips. Corn is equally successful dried and ground as the wheat that goes to make flour.

CULINARY USES

Whole corn cobs are best cooked in large pots of boiling water. Do not add any salt to the water though – it will only toughen the kernels. Instead, add a little sugar to sweeten it. Cook for about 10–15 minutes or until the kernels are tender. Don't over-cook. The flavour and tenderness will disappear quickly.

Sweetcorn is obviously best eaten straight off the cob. Many diners have different techniques for eating a cob – there is the 'typewriter' pattern from left to right, or around and around, or just plain random, with butter dripping down their cheeks. Alternatively, take a sharp knife and slice all the kernels off.

Sweetcorn can accompany many flavours. Sweet, sour, salt and hot will all go well with corn. Chillies or strong-flavoured herbs, other summer vegetables like courgettes, potatoes, peas and beans, as well as salty sauces, like soy and anchovy, or lemon and lime juice all go well with sweetcorn.

Cook's Tip

Slicing off corn kernels.
Before removing kernels from a corn cob, strip away the husk (leaves) and the silk (the hair-like strands encasing the corn). Holding blunt end of cob in one hand and a sharp knife in the other, cut downwards to slice off the kernels. Work your way round the cob in 8–10 slices.

QUICK PICKINGS

Sweetcorn Cakes

In a bowl mix together 300 g raw sweetcorn kernels, 1 tbsp curry powder, 2 tbsp rice flour, 3 tbsp plain flour, ½ tsp salt and 2 tbsp light soy sauce. Stir well to make a thick dough. Heat some oil in a shallow frying pan. Drop small spoonfuls of dough into the hot oil. Shallow-fry, turning once, until golden brown. Drain and allow to cool. Serve with sweet chilli sauce (see page 79).

Endive, Corn & Capsicum Salad

Cook 2 corn cobs in boiling water for 10 minutes or until tender, then drain and set aside to cool. Heat 2 tbsp olive oil in a frying pan over medium heat. Fry 1 yellow capsicum, seeds removed and sliced, until softened, then season with salt and freshly ground black pepper. Pour in 1 tbsp sherry vinegar and cook for a few more minutes. Remove from heat. Slice kernels off corn. Place 1 bunch endive lettuce leaves, corn and capsicum onto a serving platter. Season again and drizzle the remaining sauce from the frying pan over the salad.

Sweetcorn Muffins

Preheat oven to 220 °C/425 °F. Beat 2 eggs in a small bowl and add 150 g sweetcorn kernels, 1 tbsp chopped chives, 2 cups self-raising flour and 2 tbsp milk and season with salt and freshly ground black pepper. Mix to a thick, smooth batter. Put a drop of oil in each hole of a 12-hole muffin tin.

Three-quarters fill each hole with batter. Bake in oven for 8–10 minutes until risen and golden. Serve topped with crispy bacon, home-made tomato sauce (see page 274) and a sprig of dill.

Sweetcorn Purée

To make your own creamed corn, cook 3 corn cobs in boiling water for 10–15 minutes. Cut away kernels using a sharp knife (see facing page). Purée corn in a blender and then place in a saucepan. Add ½ cup cream and ½ cup liquid chicken stock. Heat to boiling and season to taste with salt and freshly ground black pepper. Best served with grilled or roasted chicken.

Fried Corn

Cook 3 corn cobs in boiling water for 10–15 minutes. Cut away kernels using a sharp knife, scraping the milk from the cob as well (see facing page). In a frying pan cook 2–3 rashers of streaky bacon until crispy. Remove bacon, and using fat that is left in pan, toss in corn kernels and fry. Add diced crispy bacon, 1 tsp salt and 1 tsp sugar to pan and heat through. Serve topped with finely snipped chives and chopped fresh parsley. **Serves 4.**

Sweet & Sour Sweetcorn Relish

If you can resist cooking corn and smothering it with butter, this tangy relish is a great way to use up cobs of corn. **Makes about 4 cups.**

1 kg pineapple, chopped
2 tsp coarse salt
2 sweetcorn cobs, peeled
1 litre malt vinegar
2.5-cm piece fresh ginger root, peeled and grated
3 cloves garlic, peeled and crushed
2 large onions, peeled and finely chopped
2 medium red capsicums, finely chopped
1 tbsp tomato paste
500 g white sugar

Place pineapple in large bowl, sprinkle with salt, cover and stand overnight. Rinse pineapple, discard liquid. Use a sharp knife to cut the kernels away from corn cobs (see facing page).

Combine pineapple, sweetcorn, vinegar, ginger, garlic, onions, capsicums, tomato paste and 2 cups water in large heavy-based saucepan. Bring to boil, simmer, uncovered, for 30 minutes. Add sugar, stir over heat, without boiling, until sugar is dissolved. Bring to boil, simmer, uncovered, stirring occasionally, for another 30 minutes or until mixture is thick. Pour into hot sterilised jars (see page 18). Seal when cold.

Barbecued Sweetcorn

A different method of cooking corn is to marinate the cobs. The freshness of the cobs is usually flavour enough, but this recipe is delicious and another way to serve up summer cobs.

4 sweetcorn cobs, husks removed
1 red chilli, deseeded and finely sliced
1 tbsp sesame oil
2 tbsp soy sauce
2-cm piece fresh ginger root, peeled and grated
2 tbsp honey or palm sugar
50 g butter, melted
1 tbsp sesame seeds
salt and freshly ground black pepper

In a large pot, bring to the boil some cold water. Cut corn cobs in half. Plunge cobs into the water for 10–15 minutes until just tender. Remove and place in cold water. Allow to drain.

In a glass jug or bowl mix together remaining ingredients. Pour marinade over corn cobs and leave to stand for 1–2 hours. Oil a barbecue grill or grill pan. Heat until hot and smoking. Grill for 2–3 minutes, basting with leftover marinade and turning to avoid burning. Serve immediately.

Spicy Sausage & Sweetcorn Hash

You can use smoked sausage, chorizo or salami. The more flavour in the meat the better. This is a great brunch treat to share with friends along with a good strong coffee. **Serves 4.**

1 tbsp olive oil
400 g sausages
700 g new potatoes, cut into chunks
2 corn cobs, husks removed
2 tbsp chopped fresh coriander or parsley
to serve, 300-g jar spicy tomato salsa

Heat oil in a large frying pan. Cut sausages into bite-sized chunks and fry until just cooked, about 10 minutes. Meanwhile, bring a large pan of salted water to the boil, add potatoes and cook for 8–10 minutes. Drain well.

Cook corn cobs in a pot of boiling water for 10–15 minutes. Tip potatoes into frying pan, season and fry until they take on a bit of colour. Remove kernels from cobs (see page 250). Stir in sweetcorn and heat through. Season. Sprinkle with coriander or parsley, then drizzle some salsa over.

Bacon Corn Chowder

This is a hearty winter soup. If you have an abundance of corn cobs, strip the kernels from the cobs and freeze, to make this and many other winter dishes. **Serves 4.**

25 g butter
2 bacon rashers, chopped
1 large potato, peeled and chopped
2 sticks celery, chopped
1 large onion, peeled and chopped
1 green capsicum, chopped
1 bay leaf
3 corn cobs
2 tbsp plain flour
600 ml milk
2 chicken stock cubes
2 cups water
to garnish, chopped fresh herbs

Heat butter in a large saucepan. Add bacon and cook, stirring, until bacon is crisp. Drain on absorbent paper towel. Add vegetables and bay leaf to same pan, cook, stirring occasionally, for about 5 minutes, or until onion is soft. Cut the corn kernels from the cobs (see page 250).

Stir in flour, cook for 1 minute. Gradually stir in milk. Bring to the boil. Simmer until mixture thickens. Add bacon, corn, crumbled stock cubes and water to pan. Bring to boil, simmer, uncovered, for about 5 minutes, stirring occasionally, or until heated through. Remove bay leaf. Serve soup garnished with chopped fresh herbs.

Sweetcorn Pilaf

A vegetarian accompaniment, or a side to any meal. Canned corn kernels can work in this dish, but the fresh taste of corn straight from the cobs is best with fresh onions and herbs. **Serves 4–6 as a side dish.**

200 g long-grain or basmati rice
25 g butter
4 fresh corn cobs, kernels cut off with a sharp knife
1 bunch spring onions, sliced
salt and freshly ground black pepper
good handful of fresh mint leaves

Cook rice in a pan of boiling salted water for 10–12 minutes until tender. Remove from the heat, drain well and fluff with a fork.

Meanwhile, melt butter in a frying pan. Stir in corn kernels and spring onions and season well. Fry gently for 5 minutes until tender, then remove from heat. Coarsely chop mint. Stir mint and rice into sweetcorn, mixing well. Check seasoning and serve.

Tarragon

Artemisia dracunculus

When I think of tarragon I think of poaching chickens and béarnaise sauce. The beauty of this herb is that it enhances so many more foods. It has an aniseed flavour without being fennel, it has a spicy piquancy without being pepper and it is a full-flavoured herbal essence that inspires many a cook.

Dracunculus is Latin for 'little dragon', referring to the medicinal use of tarragon in years gone by. It was a handy plant to have around to help cure stings from serpents and snakes. It also used to be made into a tea to help cure flatulence, and in fact this is still considered a good reason to add tarragon to your daily cooking.

French tarragon is a sophisticated, full-flavoured herb, native to southern Europe and parts of Asia. Russian tarragon has much less flavour, and is often described as an impostor. Tarragon grows well in colder climates and temperate areas. It enjoys New Zealand soil, and just when you think the plant has died off and gone from your garden, spring brings another season of lengthy stems of that special flavour.

HOW TO GROW

French tarragon is a perennial plant, which dies down in late autumn. It grows from root propagation, simply meaning that separating the root clumps in early spring will give you more plants to spread in your herb garden. Plants should be divided about every three years, otherwise roots become overcrowded.

Grow pots of tarragon in a sunny sheltered position with well-drained sandy soil and compost added to allow for good root development. Roots will rot if over-watered. Place your pots in a sheltered spot in the winter months, and cut back unnecessary stems and leaves.

PICKING & STORING

The growing tips have the most flavour. It is good to trim the long stems back regularly to encourage growth of the tender leaves. Picking the leaves as you need them is the perfect way to harvest tarragon.

Tarragon won't grow all year round, so if you need the hefty flavour in the winter, drying or freezing the leaves works well. Dried herbs don't tend to have as much flavour and the general rule is to use twice as much as fresh.

Fresh — Keep tarragon leaves in a plastic bag in the fridge. The leaves will go black pretty quickly once picked, so pick sparingly and use quickly.

Dried — Dry the leaves by placing stems with leaves on paper towels or brown paper and leaving in a warm dry place.

Freeze — Freezing the leaves in freezer bags will give you at least the flavour to work with when leaves are thawed. The colour of the leaf won't be true. Alternatively, purée in a food processor and place in ice cube trays.

Preserve — Tarragon vinegar or oil is the best way to preserve the flavour (see below).

CULINARY USES

Tarragon has a mild aniseed flavour and accompanies most fish, chicken and egg dishes. Artichokes, mushrooms, courgettes and tomatoes all work well with tarragon. Best of all, tarragon has a natural affinity with butter and a simple tarragon butter works well on top of seared steak, toasted bread or fried poultry.

Tarragon vinegar is best used in sauces, soups and stored for fresh vinaigrettes on crisp salad leaves. For simplicity, mix finely chopped tarragon with mayonnaise and mix in shredded chicken or crab meat. Frozen tarragon can be added to stews and casseroles. The flavour will strengthen a red wine gravy. But watch the leaves aren't too black or woody, or the only flavour you'll get is a rotten one.

QUICK PICKINGS

Tarragon Vinegar

Slightly bruise fresh tarragon leaves, place in a sterilised bottle and add good quality white wine vinegar. Use about 6 sprigs of tarragon to 2 cups white wine vinegar. It is best to leave tarragon vinegar for at least 10 days before using to allow flavours to develop. Store in a cool, dark place such as a cupboard.

Tarragon Butter

Mix 150 g softened butter with 2 tbsp fresh chopped tarragon leaves and the juice of ½ lemon until well combined. Roll up in a piece of plastic wrap or greaseproof paper, secure ends and place in fridge. When hard, slice off pieces with a warmed knife and serve on top of grilled steaks.

Light Tarragon Cream Dressing

Perfect for potato salads. Mix together 200 g fromage frais, 2 tsp tarragon vinegar, 2 tbsp chopped fresh tarragon, salt and black pepper. Sprinkle 1 tbsp of chopped tarragon over the salad after you've dressed it.

Tarragon Chicken Breasts

Preheat oven to 190 °C/375 °F. Stuff four chicken breasts with a mixture of 1 tbsp fresh chopped tarragon, 50 g breadcrumbs, 2 tsp lemon juice and 1 tbsp olive oil. Bake in oven for 20–30 minutes.

Tarragon Oil

Put a few sprigs in a bottle of extra virgin olive oil. Leave to marinate for about a month and you'll have a delicious flavoured oil, perfect for sautéing fish and chicken.

Tarragon & Garlic Sauce

To make a quick sauce for grilled salmon, melt 50 g butter in a pan and fry 1 clove crushed garlic and a chopped shallot until softened. Stir in 1 tbsp chopped fresh tarragon.

Béarnaise Sauce (pictured over)

A delicate flavoured sauce, perfect for grilled steak, poached fish, chicken or steamed vegetables. This sauce will keep for about 1 week in the fridge. **Makes about 1½ cups.**

2 tbsp tarragon vinegar
2 tbsp white wine vinegar
1 shallot, very finely chopped
175 g butter, cut into pieces
3 egg yolks
1 tbsp cold water
½ tsp salt
salt and freshly ground pepper
8 tarragon leaves, finely chopped

Combine tarragon vinegar, white wine vinegar and shallot in a small heavy-based saucepan, set over high heat and boil until liquid has almost evaporated. Remove from heat and leave to cool slightly.

Clarify butter by melting it in a small saucepan over a low heat: do not boil or brown. Skim off any foam. In a small heavy saucepan or in the top of a double boiler, combine egg yolks, water, shallot mixture and salt, and whisk for 1 minute. Place saucepan over a very low heat or place the double boiler over barely simmering water and whisk constantly until egg yolk mixture begins to thicken and whisk begins to leave tracks on base of pan. Remove from heat.

Whisk in clarified butter, drop by drop until sauce begins to thicken, then pour in butter a little more quickly, making sure it is absorbed before adding more. When you reach milky solids at bottom, stop pouring. Season to taste with salt and pepper and add fresh tarragon leaves.

Steamed Vegetables with Lemon Tarragon Butter

Perfect with light fish and chicken dishes. It can easily be adapted for other seasonal vegetables – green or runner beans, leeks and broccoli are all good. **Serves 6.**

900 g mixed vegetables, such as baby carrots, baby courgettes and sugar snap peas
175 g butter, cubed
2 shallots, finely chopped
5 tbsp tarragon vinegar
½ lemon, juice of
2–3 tbsp fresh tarragon, chopped
salt and freshly ground black pepper

Lightly steam or boil mixed vegetables, starting with baby carrots, then adding sliced courgettes and finally sugar snap peas.

Melt a cube of butter in a small pan. Add shallots and cook for 3 minutes until softened. Pour in vinegar and cook until reduced by half. Remove from heat and carefully whisk in remaining butter cubes.

Stir in lemon juice and chopped tarragon. Season with salt and pepper. Pour warm sauce over hot steamed vegetables.

Tarragon-poached Chicken with Autumn Vegetables

A versatile dish with tasty chicken and vegetables. The remaining poaching liquid can be refrigerated for up to 3 days or frozen for up to 1 month and used as a base for soups. **Serves 4.**

4 litres chicken stock or water
500 ml dry white wine or verjuice
4 fresh bay leaves
15 black peppercorns
2 tbsp sea salt
4 cloves garlic, peeled
1.5-kg free-range chicken, excess fat removed
2 bunches tarragon, plus extra sprigs to serve
salt and freshly ground black pepper
1 bunch baby carrots
4 small parsnips
8 small leeks, trimmed
2 spring onions, trimmed
to serve, crusty bread and avocado dressing

Place chicken stock or water, white wine, bay leaves, peppercorns, sea salt and garlic cloves in a 5-litre stockpot and bring to boil.

Rinse chicken and pat dry with absorbent paper towel. Place three-quarters of the tarragon sprigs in chicken cavity, then stuff remainder under breast skin and season chicken inside and out with sea salt and pepper.

Place chicken, breast-side down, into simmering poaching liquid, ensuring it is fully submerged. Cook chicken over low to medium heat for 15 minutes; it is important to ensure poaching liquid doesn't exceed a slow simmer. Remove pot from heat, cover with a tight-fitting lid and leave chicken to steep for 3 hours at room temperature to complete cooking process.

Using tongs, carefully remove chicken from poaching liquid and place on a tray to drain. Strain poaching liquid through a fine sieve, then return to a clean saucepan and bring to boil. Cook carrots and parsnips for 3–4 minutes, leeks and spring onions for 2–3 minutes, one at a time in the simmering liquid. Remove with a slotted spoon and keep warm while cooking other vegetables. Season to taste.

To serve, place chicken and vegetables on a deep platter and spoon a little warm poaching liquid over. Serve with avocado dressing (see page 223) and crusty bread.

Mushroom & Tarragon Lasagne

Use interesting mushrooms for this dish – big brown flat ones or button mushrooms will do. Dried porcini or cep mushrooms are great as well. **Serves 4.**

500 g fresh mushrooms, cleaned
75 g butter
1 tbsp olive oil
65 g plain flour
600 ml milk
2 tbsp tarragon, freshly chopped
salt and freshly ground black pepper
6 sheets fresh lasagne
50 g Parmesan, freshly grated

Slice mushrooms. Heat 50 g butter in a pan, and gently fry mushrooms for about 4–5 minutes, then remove with a slotted spoon.

Put remaining butter and oil in pan, then add flour and stir for about 1 minute. Gradually add milk, whisking all the time, then simmer for about 5 minutes, until thick and smooth. Add tarragon and mushrooms and season with salt and pepper to taste.

Preheat oven to 180 °C/350 °F. Grease a 25 x 20-cm lasagne dish. Place 2 sheets of lasagne on base, then a third of the mushroom sauce, then 2 more lasagne sheets, then more sauce, then final lasagne sheets. Spoon over remaining sauce and top with Parmesan.

Bake in oven for 45–50 minutes, until golden brown. Leave to stand for at least 10 minutes before cutting.

Tarragon & Lime Meringues with Strawberries

The sophisticated aniseed of tarragon and the tang of lime are a good balance for the summer sweetness of fresh strawberries. **Serves 6.**

6 large egg whites, at room temperature
350 g caster sugar
2 tsp cornflour
1 lime, finely grated zest of
1 tsp lime juice
1 tsp tarragon vinegar
1 tsp finely chopped fresh tarragon
to serve, 200 g strawberries, hulled, whipped cream and strawberry coulis

Preheat oven to 180 °C/350 °F. Line a large square baking sheet with baking paper.

Using an electric mixer or whisk, and a very clean and dry bowl, beat egg whites to stiff peaks. Slowly add sugar 1 tablespoon at a time. Continue whisking until all sugar is incorporated and appears to be dissolved, about 10 minutes. Fold in cornflour, lime zest and juice, tarragon vinegar and tarragon.

Spoon tablespoonfuls of meringue mixture onto baking paper with enough room between each for spreading. Put in oven and immediately reduce temperature to 140 °C/275 °F. Bake for 1 hour, then turn off oven and leave in oven for several hours or even overnight until thoroughly cold. Serve with fresh strawberries, whipped cream and strawberry coulis (see page 240).

Thyme

Thymus vulgaris

A small leaf with such huge flavour. The scent of thyme brings on thoughts of winter comfort foods, stews, hearty casseroles, braised game meats and deep-dish pastry pies. There are hundreds of thyme varieties, all with different flavour notes. Wild thyme, broad-leaved thyme and silver 'posie' are the best varieties for cooking. But there is also lemon thyme or pizza thyme and even purely ornamental thyme plants with not much flavour at all.

Thyme is like parsley, it can be transposed across so many flavours that small amounts appear in many dishes. The stems are woody, so a cook is only interested in the small circular leaves. A small amount gives a lot of flavour. A selection of different potted thyme plants in your ever expanding herb garden helps to keep this spreading herb in check. Thyme can be used as a ground cover in a garden, and often you'll find a lazy cat sprawled over it in the sunshine. They too are attracted to the distinctive scent of this delicate herb.

HOW TO GROW

Endless varieties of thyme are available but probably common thyme and lemon thyme are the most useful for the beginner. Common thyme is a perennial plant. Care for it well and it will keep coming back year after year. Give thyme plants room and they will go for it – most thyme plants can grow to a height of 50 cm.

Lemon thyme forms a mat of short stalks 15–20 cm in height. Plant in a sheltered yet sunny position with a well drained compost soil. The plants can grow well from seeds or propagate from cuttings or root division. Water regularly in the hot summer months. It will look after itself in winter.

PICKING & STORING

A fantastic herb to have in the garden, this perennial provides flavour all year round. Prune regularly and use the cuttings to dry some leaves if needed. I keep a pot of thyme by my back door; it looks great and adds flavour instantly to many a dish.

Fresh — Thyme leaves can be stored in plastic bags. The wooden stalks need to be stripped off the leaves before use.

Freeze — Not much need for freezing as this herb is available all year round.

Dried — Dry stalks of thyme on brown paper. Remove leaves from stalks and store leaves in a plastic bag. Thyme is one of those dried herbs that is a component of so many mixed herbs. In a Tuscan blend, Moroccan blend or even in Dukkah, thyme complements the flavour of other herbs extremely well. When dried it holds its flavour very well.

CULINARY USES

Thyme is an expectorant. Make an inhalation by pouring boiling water over a handful of leaves and breathing in the vapour. Hot thyme tea is good for aches and pains.

Add to red meat casseroles to aid digestion, or mix with onion, breadcrumbs and sage for pork stuffing. Thyme is often made into bouquets garnis, where the flavour is drawn out of the leaves, but then taken out to remove unnecessary wooden bits in the dish.

Try this eighteenth-century seasoning to add interest to dishes: Mix 1 part each of sweet basil, sweet marjoram, and summer savoury with 1½ parts thyme and grated rind of 1 lemon and a sprinkling of grated nutmeg. This can be used to flavour many of your favourite meat and vegetable dishes.

Thyme complements winter root vegetables like carrots, parsnips and turnips. It will blend well with other herbs such as rosemary and basil. Acid tomatoes, lemons, limes and other citrus work well with thyme. Salty cheese, like feta or goat's-milk cheese, likes to be marinated with thyme and olive oil.

QUICK PICKINGS

Thyme Biscuits

Preheat oven to 200 °C/425 °F. Sift together 320 g plain flour with 1 tbsp baking powder and 1 tsp salt. Add 1 tbsp sugar and cut 8 tbsp butter into mixture, but do not overwork. Stir in ¾ cup buttermilk, 1 egg and 2 tbsp fresh chopped thyme. Turn dough onto floured bread board. Knead a dozen times. Roll dough into golf-ball-size balls. Bake on an ungreased cookie sheet for 12–14 minutes, until done. Serve hot. **Makes 15 biscuits.**

Thyme & Tomatoes

Slice 4 ripe tomatoes. Sprinkle over 2 tbsp fresh chopped thyme, 2 cloves garlic, and sea salt and freshly ground black pepper. Drizzle with a good quality extra virgin olive oil. Leave at room temperature for an hour or two. Serve with cold meats, breads and fresh cheeses.

Thyme Rolls

Blend 200 g cream cheese, 1 tbsp freshly chopped thyme, 1 tbsp chopped parsley, and 1 clove finely minced garlic together in a bowl or food processor. Spoon onto a piece of waxed paper and roll up into a 2–3-cm diameter log. Refrigerate overnight. Slice into 1-cm wheels and serve on crackers.

Thyme Pita Pizzas

Cut 6 flat pita breads into 6 triangles each. Brush top of each triangle with a little olive oil. Sprinkle lightly with some fresh thyme leaves and finely chopped oregano leaves. Toast in hot oven until golden brown. Serve hot as an appetiser or use for dinner bread.

Lemon Thyme Tea

Bring 2 cups water to a boil and remove from heat. Add 3–4 sprigs thyme leaves and steep for 5 minutes. Strain into cups and add ½ tsp honey. Relax and enjoy.

Spring Onion & Thyme Soup

Peel and chop 400 g potatoes. In a heavy saucepan, melt 100 g butter, then toss potatoes and ¾ cup chopped spring onions in the butter. Sweat, covered, over moderately low heat for 10 minutes. Add 2½ cups chicken stock and 2 thyme sprigs and simmer until potatoes are very soft, about 15 minutes. Discard sprig and purée to a soup. Transfer to a saucepan, stir in

$2\frac{1}{2}$ cups milk and 1 tsp fresh chopped thyme leaves. Season with salt and freshly ground black pepper, and simmer until heated through, about 5 minutes. **Serves 6.**

Thyme Beans

Rinse 250 g green beans in cold water, snap off ends and cut into 5-cm lengths. Cut half an onion into small slices and place with beans, in a rice steamer. Cook until tender, about 15 minutes. Drain and set aside. Melt 60 g butter in a saucepan and add other half onion, thinly sliced, 1 tsp lemon juice, 1 tsp fresh chopped parsley, 1 tsp fresh chopped thyme leaves, $\frac{1}{4}$ tsp paprika and season with salt and freshly ground black pepper. Simmer for 5 minutes. Add beans and toss well, completely coating beans. **Serves 6–8.**

Raspberry Thyme Vinegar

The vinegar will keep for a year or longer. Mix with a little balsamic vinegar and a good olive oil and you have a great vinaigrette to serve with new potatoes. **Makes 1.5 litres.**

1 litre champagne or white wine vinegar
60 g sugar
150 g fresh raspberries
4 sprigs fresh thyme, rinsed and patted dry

In a non-reactive saucepan combine vinegar and sugar and bring almost to a boil, stirring to dissolve sugar. Place berries and thyme in a 1.5-litre heat-proof, non-reactive container and pour vinegar over them.

Cool to room temperature, cover, and let stand at room temperature for at least 48 hours and up to 2 weeks.

Strain vinegar, discarding softened berries and discoloured thyme. Transfer vinegar to a storage bottle (or to a decorative decanter), add a few fresh raspberries and a sprig of thyme as garnish, and store in a cool place, out of direct sunlight.

Garlic Thyme Chicken

A quick meal idea all the family will like. It doesn't take long and makes use of the valuable thyme plant growing in the pot next to your back door. **Serves 4.**

2 tbsp olive oil
6 chicken thigh fillets, quartered
1 medium onion, peeled and sliced
4 cloves garlic, peeled and crushed
$\frac{1}{2}$ lemon, juice of
125 ml cream
125 ml chicken stock
6 sprigs fresh thyme, finely chopped
500 g spinach, washed
2 tsp cornflour
2 tsp water

Heat oil in non-stick frying pan, add chicken in batches, cook, stirring, until browned and just tender, remove from pan.

Add onion, garlic and lemon juice to pan, cook, stirring, until onion is soft. Add cream, stock, thyme, spinach and blended cornflour and water, cook, stirring, until sauce thickens slightly. Return chicken to pan with any juices, stir until heated through. Serve chicken mixture with pasta or creamy mashed potatoes.

Asparagus Soup with Thyme

If you have a massive plot of land, then grow asparagus, but if not, wait for spring asparagus with anticipation. This is a fresh-tasting soup, with plenty of spring thyme sprigs for an injection of herbal flavour. **Makes about 6 cups.**

100 g shallots, peeled
1 clove garlic, peeled
700 g asparagus, tips cut off and reserved
200 g potato
2 tbsp butter
4 sprigs fresh thyme
750 ml vegetable or chicken stock
½ lemon, juice of
salt and freshly ground black pepper
to serve, sour cream and fresh thyme sprigs

Finely dice shallots and garlic. Chop asparagus and potato. Melt butter in a heavy-based pan over a medium to low heat. Add shallots and garlic to the pan and coat well with butter. Then stir in thyme. Reduce heat to low, cover and cook until shallots are softened, about 5 minutes.

Add asparagus, potatoes and stock and bring to boil. Reduce heat, cover loosely and simmer until vegetables are tender, about 15 minutes. Steam asparagus tips over boiling water until crisp tender, about 90 seconds. Tip into ice water to stop cooking. Drain and dry, and put to one side.

Strain solids, reserving cooking liquid. Add cooked vegetables to food processor or blender and pulse. With machine running add cooking liquid. Process until smooth. Return purée to a clean saucepan and stir in remaining cooking liquid. Season with lemon juice, salt and pepper, and heat. Garnish with reserved asparagus tips, a dollop of sour cream and fresh thyme.

Lamb Filo Parcels with Thyme

These delicate packages of pastry are another way to serve lamb. Incredibly simple to prepare, they can be made ahead of meal-time for your guests or family. If you don't have raisins use apricots or dried figs instead. **Serves 4.**

8 lamb cutlets, bones removed
8 fresh thyme sprigs, washed and chopped
75 g raisins
salt and freshly ground black pepper
8 sheets filo pastry
125 g butter, melted

Preheat oven to 190 °C/375 °F. Shape cutlets into neat rounds, removing any visible fat if preferred. Mix thyme, raisins and seasoning together in a bowl. Brush each sheet of filo pastry with some butter and fold in half to form eight squares. Brush with a little more butter then place a lamb noisette in the centre of each square.

Top with thyme and raisin mixture. Fold pastry over lamb and overlap in several places to make a parcel, brushing with a little more butter to help keep pastry in position. Place on a baking sheet and cook for 25 minutes. Serve with sugar snap peas and new potatoes.

Elderflower Thyme Poached Pears

Elderflower cordial is very old-fashioned, but is making a comeback in delicatessens and supermarkets across the country. Elderflowers grow wild in the UK and are harvested for juice and jellies every year. Here in New Zealand a cottage industry has sprung up to supply the juice. In this recipe the juice works well with pears and fresh thyme from your garden. **Serves 4.**

4 large ripe firm pears, Bosc or Bartlett
¼ cup elderflower cordial concentrate
250 ml water
180 ml maple syrup
2 cinnamon sticks, slightly crushed
2–3 sprigs fresh thyme
4 strips lemon peel
to serve, mascarpone

Peel pears. Use a melon baller to core pears by pushing smaller end of baller into bottom of pear, and turn it to bore a hole and scoop out seeds and fibrous core. This will leave stem intact. Cut a thin slice off the bottom of each pear to provide a flat, even bottom. Set aside.

In a medium saucepan, add remaining ingredients. Bring mixture to a boil. Add pears and arrange standing with stems pointing up. Reduce heat and simmer, covered, 20–30 minutes or until pears are tender. Baste pears with liquids.

Remove from saucepan. Continue to cook liquid until reduced to about ¾ cup, about 15 minutes. Serve pears drizzled with sauce and a dollop of mascarpone on the side.

Iced Lemon Thyme Fairy Cakes (pictured)

Thyme leaves give a wonderful essence to these fairy cakes. They are fairly quick to make, and best eaten fresh. **Makes 12 cakes.**

165 g caster sugar
12–15 fresh lemon thyme sprigs
165 g butter, softened
½ lemon, juice of and zest, finely grated
3 large eggs, lightly beaten
260 g self-raising flour, sifted
pinch of salt

Lemon Icing
200 g icing sugar
1 lemon, juice of
to garnish, sprigs of thyme flowers or silver balls

Preheat oven to 200 °C/400 °F. Place 12 paper cake cups in a muffin tray. Put sugar and lemon thyme in a food processor and process until finely chopped. Add butter and lemon zest and process until fluffy. Add eggs while machine is still running. Stop processor and gently mix in lemon juice, flour and salt.

Divide mixture between cake cups. Bake at top of oven for 12–15 minutes or until well risen and golden. Test by lightly pressing cakes with your fingers (the sponge should bounce back).

A few minutes before cakes are ready, stir enough lemon juice into icing sugar to form a thick icing. When cakes are baked, transfer to a wire rack and put a blob of icing in centre of each. This will spread across the cake. Decorate with thyme sprigs or silver balls and eat as soon as cakes are cool.

Tomatoes

Lycopersicon lycopersicum

A tomato plant in the garden is one of life's simple pleasures. You soon realise that a tomato picked from its vine when ripe is very different and far superior to the greenhouse tomatoes we can buy readily all year round. The difference is akin to eating a piece of chocolate compared to eating a piece of cardboard! Of course, it is a luxury that tomatoes are available in all seasons. The Italians would harvest their pomodoros in the summer and spend days, drying, peeling, and storing their 'love apples' for use all year.

Tomatoes are easy to grow. Much literature is produced supplying tips and hints for the best in plant production. But like anything it is trial and error. Choose a patch of your garden that is your favourite tomato spot and cultivate that spot. I use a couple of old concrete laundry tubs that were left behind in a renovation and cultivate the soil all year, ready to transplant three or four grafted seedlings. That can give more than enough tomatoes for fresh summer eating and preserving for winter months. A little bit of love and attention and the abundance of red fruit is a pure delight.

HOW TO GROW

Choose a sunny spot, sheltered from prevailing winds and with plenty of room for a vine to grow. Some allow their tomatoes to grow free along the ground, however, other than needing ample room in your garden you also have to be very diligent with rotting tomatoes and unruly vines. Using large load-bearing stakes, like bamboo or wooden rods, helps train the vines towards the sky. Tie the long and prolific stems to the stakes. Any tomato plant is going to need plenty of manure and organic compost to improve the soil. They need a good food base to help growth. Fertilise well while growing as well, with liquid blood and bone or specialised tomato feed.

Growing tomatoes from seed isn't at all difficult as long as the soil is warm. In fact, the seeds germinate readily in the most unlikely places – and soils. Seedlings available from good plant shops offer a good way to have a more instantaneous start to your pomodoro crop. Tomatoes need at least three months of warm weather to produce reliable crops. Plant from October onwards. As the fruit develops, ensure your plants get a steady supply of water.

Pinching laterals encourages more robust growth. It simply means removing the side shoots from the main stems. Plant basil beside tomatoes to improve their health and flavour. Basil also helps repel flies, thrips and mosquitoes. But watch for pesky birds and insects, which can get your crop first. Try draping a mosquito net or

some kind of netting over the whole plant after the fruit has set.

Tomatoes like growing in the same area year after year and prefer compost made with their own stalks and leaves.

PICKING & STORING

Allow the fruit to ripen on the vine for the sweetest crop of tomatoes ever. Be careful when touching the fruit before it has ripened as they can easily come away from the trusses upon which they grow.

Fresh — Fresh fruit is best stored at room temperature, to continue developing its natural sweetness, but keeping tomatoes in the fridge is the easiest way to prolong their fragile life.

Dried — Tomatoes can be dried in the sun or slow dried in the oven (see facing page).

Freeze — Frozen tomatoes are good but the flesh tends to go pulpy and watery. It is better to transform the flesh before freezing. Pulp in a blender or make into a soup or sauce. Remove skin and seeds and the remaining flesh is easily stored in plastic bags or ice cube trays.

Preserve — There are countless ways to preserve tomatoes – paste, purée, chutney, relish. This chapter outlines a few good ways to make use of your summer harvest.

CULINARY USES

In our everyday cooking tomatoes go with just about anything. Best partnered with strong-flavoured herbs and cheeses, they can also be paired with soft melting cheese, seafood, chicken, and in fact any type of meat. Basil of course is a natural accompaniment to any tomato dish, but then so too are oregano, onions, eggplant, courgettes and garlic.

In a casserole tomatoes provide a natural tenderising property. In Mexican or Italian food they often hold the chilli taste and give moisture to the base sauce. In salads, they provide colour as well as soft texture and, of course, what would we do without fresh, sweet, vine-ripened tomatoes on toasted bread simply seasoned with salt and freshly ground black pepper.

Cook's Tip

To peel a tomato, cut a small cross in the non-stalk end of the tomato. Bring a pot of water to the boil. Drop each tomato, one by one, into the water and count to 20–30 seconds (no longer or they will become too soft and the flesh pulpy), then lift them out with a slotted spoon. Plunge into ice-cold water. Remove the cores and skin with a small sharp knife.

Cook's Tip

To remove the seeds from a tomato, use your fingers under running water, or use a teaspoon to pull away the inner watery sacks of seeds. Deseeding tomatoes is often a good idea because their watery centres can dilute the richer flavour of the flesh. It is especially good to deseed if making dishes with a chunky texture, such as salsas, or if you want a richly flavoured sauce. If a recipe doesn't specify this though, leave the seeds in as they do provide liquid.

QUICK PICKINGS

Semi-Dried Tomatoes

Cut tomatoes in half and lay facing up on a baking tray. Sprinkle equal amounts of sugar and salt over tomato halves. Put cut-side up on a baking sheet; cook at 140 °C/275 °F for 2–2½ hours until most of the liquid is dry.

Tomato & Avocado Salsa

Peel and remove seeds from 2–3 tomatoes. Finely chop flesh and place in a bowl. Add to this a finely diced red onion, finely diced avocado, finely diced cucumber and snipped fresh chives. Season well with salt and freshly ground black pepper and stir in a small amount of good quality olive oil and a squeeze of fresh lemon juice. Serve with steak, fish or as an accompaniment to any barbecue or brunch feast.

Fresh Tomato Pasta Sauce

In a large bowl combine 3 large peeled tomatoes with 3 cloves garlic, ½ cup fresh basil leaves, 120 g cream cheese, ½ cup extra virgin olive oil, 2 tbsp red wine vinegar and salt and freshly ground black pepper to taste. Let the sauce stand, covered at room temperature, for at least 1 hour. Just before serving, in a saucepan of boiling salted water cook your choice of pasta until al dente, drain it well, and add it piping hot to the sauce. Toss pasta well with sauce.

Chilled Tomato Soup

Put 1 small red chilli, deseeded, 1 peeled onion and 2 cloves garlic in a food processor and blend to a paste. Add 1 red capsicum, deseeded, 450 g peeled and deseeded tomatoes, 50 ml olive oil and 100 g fresh white breadcrumbs and continue processing until vegetables are very smooth. Tip mixture into a large bowl and stir in 600 ml iced water. Cover and chill for at least 4 hours before serving. To serve, ladle soup into bowls and garnish centre with chopped pepper, cucumber and tomatoes.

Bloody Mary

Peel and deseed 4–6 large ripe tomatoes. Process until juicy in food processor. Run through a sieve. For every 150 ml of tomato juice add 50 ml vodka (use chilli vodka from page 79 for extra spice), 2 dashes Worcestershire sauce, a squeeze of lemon juice, a pinch of celery salt, 2–3 dashes Tabasco, and black pepper. Serve in tall glasses with a swizzle stick or stalk of celery.

Mediterranean Salad

Cut 6 tomatoes into chunks, removing cores as you go. Cut 1 telegraph cucumber into chunks. Slice 1 red onion, 2–3 spring onions and roughly chop 1 bunch of fresh flat-leaf parsley. Toss all ingredients in a large bowl with ½ cup of Italian vinaigrette (see page 222). Put on a platter or shallow bowl. Crumble over 200 g feta, 150 g black Kalamata olives, 2–3 tbsp drained capers and top with 4–5 anchovies, roughly chopped. Season with salt and freshly ground black pepper, and serve.

Smoky Tomato Relish

A good-quality smoked paprika imparts the flavour to the tomatoes in this preserve. Alternatively, a smoked salt can be used. **Makes about 1 cup.**

1 tbsp olive oil
1 onion, peeled and diced
1 clove garlic, peeled and crushed
500 g tomatoes, peeled and diced
2 tbsp brown sugar
2 tbsp sherry vinegar
1 tsp smoked paprika
salt and freshly ground black pepper

Heat olive oil in a saucepan over a medium heat. Add onion and garlic and cook for 3–4 minutes until soft. Add tomatoes and any juice. Cook for 3 minutes until reduced slightly. Add sugar, sherry vinegar, smoked paprika, and season with salt and pepper. Cook for 4–5 minutes until thick and reduced. Serve warm or cold.

Whole Tomatoes in Jars (pictured)

This is a great way to store tomatoes. They look fantastic in large jars on the shelf, and when brined for long enough can be used in all sort of tasty dishes for a spicy tomato taste. I prefer to use mine for winter curries and stews, and proudly remember my summer tomato-growing skills with fondness. **Makes 1 x 4-litre jar.**

2 kg firm tomatoes
1 litre white wine vinegar
625 g granulated sugar
3 tsp curry powder
2 tsp black mustard seeds
2 tsp white mustard seeds
2 tsp turmeric
2 tsp salt

Bring a pot of water to boil. Make a cross incision on top of each tomato. One by one, drop tomatoes into water and leave for 20–30 seconds. Remove using a slotted spoon and plunge into ice-cold water. The skins should begin to come away from the tomatoes, and can be then peeled easily with a knife.

Combine vinegar, sugar, curry powder, black and white mustard seeds, turmeric and salt in a pan. Stir over medium heat until sugar is dissolved. Bring to boil, remove from heat. Pack tomatoes into hot sterilised jars (see page 18), cover with hot vinegar mixture, seal. Keep refrigerated.

Tomato, Lemon & Chilli Jam

(pictured on previous page)

This jam makes a perfect dip on an antipasto platter filled with cold meats and creamy cheeses. I serve it with barbecued lamb or as a side to Asian dumplings and wontons. I use home-grown cherry tomatoes for this recipe, but larger tomatoes can be substituted. However, you may want to remove the skins first. **Makes 4 x 330-g jars.**

4 fresh red chillies
1 kg cherry tomatoes
1 kg sugar
2 lemons, finely grated zest and juice of
1 tsp sweet paprika
1 tsp balsamic vinegar

Deseed chillies using a sharp paring knife, preferably wearing plastic gloves, and remember to wash your chopping board and knife thoroughly.

Put tomatoes in a 10-litre preserving pan or heavy-based saucepan with sugar, lemon zest and juice. Bring slowly to boil, stirring as sugar dissolves, then simmer for 5 minutes. Skim any foam, add chilli, paprika and balsamic vinegar.

Return mixture to boil, stirring frequently, and boil for 30 minutes until setting point is reached (see page 18). Remove from heat and leave fruit to settle for a few minutes. Ladle jam into hot sterilised jars (see page 18), then seal.

Tomato Sauce

(pictured on previous page)

Everyone should have a go at making tomato sauce at some time in their life. You appreciate where the complex flavours come from. If the tomatoes are from your garden, then the next time you team tomato sauce with fish and chips you'll be so satisfied with your own sauce you'll never go back to the bought stuff. **Makes about 6 cups.**

3 kg firm ripe tomatoes
2 onions, peeled
5 medium apples
1½ cups white vinegar
2 tbsp salt
750 g brown sugar
½ tsp pepper
pinch cayenne
2 lemons, juice of
1 tsp whole cloves
1 tsp whole allspice
2.5-cm piece fresh ginger root

Roughly chop tomatoes, onions and apples and place in a large heavy-based pot. Cover and bring to boil, simmer gently for 30 minutes, or until tomatoes and apples are soft and pulpy.

Cool slightly and push mixture through a sieve. Return sieved mixture to saucepan. Add vinegar, salt, sugar, pepper, cayenne and lemon juice. Tie whole cloves, whole allspice and ginger in a piece of muslin and add to tomato mixture.

Bring to boil, stirring, until sugar is dissolved. Boil gently, uncovered for 1¼ hours. Remove muslin bag, pour mixture into hot, sterilised jars or bottles (see page 18) and seal.

Fried Green Tomatoes

A Southern States of America-inspired recipe. Polenta is ground-up corn and gives the tomatoes a crunchy coating. The tart taste of green tomatoes is just so refreshing in this dish. **Serves 4.**

100 g Parmesan, freshly grated
½ cup polenta
salt and freshly ground black pepper
4 green tomatoes, sliced
50 ml olive oil
to serve, streaky bacon rashers

Combine Parmesan and polenta, and season with salt and pepper. Cover both sides of tomato slices with mixture. Heat olive oil in a heavy-based frying pan. Fry tomato slices until golden brown. Drain on absorbent paper towels and serve with grilled bacon.

Tomato Bean Bake

This is what I call a store cupboard dish. When there isn't time to get to the shops, this is a recipe that can be achieved quickly with great results. Meals can always magically appear when you have vegetables growing in your own garden. **Serves 6.**

1 tbsp oil
3 bacon rashers, chopped
1 onion, peeled and sliced
2 cloves garlic, peeled and crushed
800 g tomatoes, roughly chopped
1 tsp ground cumin
1 green capsicum, chopped
1 courgette, chopped
310-g can red kidney beans, rinsed and drained
310-g can butter beans, rinsed and drained
2 tbsp fresh parsley, chopped
50 g fresh Parmesan, grated
to garnish, chopped fresh chives

Topping
250 g self-raising flour
50 g butter
2 tbsp fresh chives, chopped
125 ml milk

Preheat oven to 190 °C/375 °F. Heat oil in a pan, add bacon, onion and garlic, cook stirring, until onion is soft. Add tomatoes and cumin, simmer, uncovered, for 10 minutes. Add capsicum and courgette, simmer, covered, for 10 minutes. Stir in beans and parsley. Spoon mixture into a 2-litre ovenproof dish.

To make topping, sift flour into a bowl and rub in butter to resemble breadcrumbs. Stir in chives and enough milk to make soft dough. Knead dough lightly on a floured surface until smooth. Roll out to 1½ cm in thickness. Cut rounds from dough using a 5-cm cutter.

Arrange topping over bean mixture, and sprinkle with Parmesan. Cook in oven for 15 minutes. Reduce heat to 180 °C/350 °F, cook for 5 minutes, or until lightly browned and cooked through. Serve garnished with chives.

Tuscan Tomato Soup

The sweeter and riper the tomatoes, the better the flavour of this soup. Choose vine-ripened tomatoes, and fresh summer basil leaves. This is a great soup to freeze to bring out the summer flavour in the cooler days. **Serves 6–8.**

10 large ripe tomatoes
50 g butter
60 ml olive oil
2 carrots, peeled and diced finely
2 stalks celery, chopped finely
2 onions, peeled and chopped finely
1 tsp brown sugar
2 tbsp tomato purée
400-g can cannellini beans, drained
½ cup fresh basil leaves, chopped
salt and freshly ground black pepper
to serve, freshly grated Parmesan and fresh basil leaves

Bring a pot of water to boil. Make a cross incision on top of each tomato. One by one, drop tomatoes into water and leave for 20–30 seconds. Remove using a slotted spoon and plunge into ice-cold water. The skins should begin to come away from the tomatoes, and can then be peeled easily with a knife. Finely chop tomatoes, removing any hard centre cores and put aside.

Heat butter and oil in a large heavy pot. Cook carrot, celery and onion over low heat until soft but not brown. Add tomatoes, sugar, tomato purée, beans, half the basil and cook for 20 minutes over medium heat. Stir in remaining basil, season with salt and pepper. Sprinkle with Parmesan and fresh basil leaves. Serve immediately.

Warm Stuffed Tomatoes with Couscous

Make your home-grown tomatoes more interesting. A stuffing like couscous gives texture without taking away from the delicious summer flavour of the tomato. **Serves 4.**

1 small red onion, peeled and thinly sliced
50 ml balsamic dressing (see page 222)
4 large vine-ripened tomatoes
salt and freshly ground black pepper
200 g feta
1 tbsp olive oil
125 ml chicken stock or water
250 g instant couscous
1 tbsp flat-leaf parsley, chopped
100 g baby rocket leaves

Preheat oven to 180 °C/350 °F. Pour boiling water over onion, and leave for five minutes. Drain and toss with a tbsp of balsamic dressing. Set half the onion aside.

Quarter tomatoes crosswise and season well with salt and pepper. Reassemble each tomato, placing a slice of feta and some of remaining onion between each slice. Drizzle with oil. Bring stock to boil, pour over couscous and set aside for five minutes. Run a fork through couscous to break up grains, toss with parsley and reserved onions.

Bake tomatoes for 10 minutes or just until they wilt and feta is just golden in colour. To serve, toss rocket in remaining dressing, place a mound of couscous on four plates and top with rocket and a warm tomato.

Index